THE STORY OF THE
British AND
THEIR Weather

This book is dedicated to Jaqueline Ann Eliot, Shine On!

THE STORY OF THE
British AND THEIR *Weather*

PATRICK NOBBS

AMBERLEY

First published 2015

Amberley Publishing
The Hill, Stroud
Gloucestershire, GL5 4EP

www.amberley-books.com

British Library Cataloguing in Publication Data.
A catalogue record for this book is available from the British Library.

ISBN 978 1 4456 4452 3 (hardback)
ISBN 978 1 4456 4461 5 (ebook)

Typesetting and Origination by Amberley Publishing.
Printed in the UK.

Contents

Introduction   7
Part I Snow, Cold and Great Freezes   13
  1 The Great Victorian Blizzard and Easterly Gale,
      January 1881   14
  2 The Great Spring Snowstorm, March 1891   20
  3 The Last Thames Freeze in London, February 1895 26
  4 The Severe and Snowy Winter of 1947   34
  5 The Record-Breaking Winter of 1962/63   40
  6 The Kent Miners' Blizzard, March 1970   53
  7 White Christmas 1970   55
  8 The Highland and South-West Blizzards, 1978   57
  9 The Winter of Discontent, 1978/79   65
 10 Heavy Snowfalls and Record Cold, 1981/82   72
 11 The Great European Cold Wave, January 1985   78
 12 The Great Easterly Outbreak, January 1987   83
 13 The Wrong Kind of Snow, February 1991   89
 14 The Record-Breaking Cold and Snowy December of 2010 94
 15 Spring on Hold: The Snowbound Spring of 2013   99
 16 The Little Ice Age   103
 17 White Christmases   108
Part II Heat and Drought   115
 18 A History of Heat and Drought   116
 19 The Great Coronation Summer, 1911   125
 20 The Great Drought and Record-Breaking Summer of 1976 129
 21 The Long Drought and Record Heat, 1989–90   135
 22 The Hot, Arid Summer of 1995: A Rival to 1976?   140
 23 The Record-Breaking Heat and Drought of 2003   144
 24 Summer Month Comparisons, London   149
Part III Great Gales   153
 25 The Great Tempest, November 1703   154
 26 The Great Modern Catastrophe: The North Sea Storm
      Surge and Flood Disaster, January–February 1953 161

27 The Sheffield Gale, February 1962   169
28 The Deadly Glasgow Storm, January 1968   172
29 The Great October Storm of 1987   176
30 The Burns' Day Storm, January 1990   183
Part IV Tornadoes   189
31 The Great London Tornado, 1091   190
32 Britain's Most Deadly Tornado, South Wales,
    October 1913   191
33 The Record-Breaking Leighton Buzzard Tornado,
    May 1950   194
34 The Kensal Rise Tornado, December 2006   197
Part V Thunderstorms and Hail   201
35 The Derby Day Storm, May 1911   202
36 London's Deadly Sunday Thunderstorm, 14 June 1914   205
37 The Louth Disaster, 29 May 1920   208
38 All-Night Havoc in London, 9 July 1923   212
39 The Great Lynmouth Flood Disaster, August 1952   215
40 The South-East Supercell Storm, September 1958   221
41 The Hampstead Supercell Storm, August 1975   224
42 The Boscastle Flash Flood, 2004   228
Part VI Floods and Deluges   233
43 The Bristol Channel Flood, January 1607   234
44 The Deluge Summer of 1912   241
45 The March Thaw Floods, 1947   244
46 The Devastating Floods of September 1968   248
47 Severe Flooding in Wettest Autumn Ever, 2000   253
48 Record Rainfall: Two Disasters, One Record   256
49 The Winter Storms Crisis, 2013/14: An Unparalleled
    Natural Event?   260
Part VII Mild Winters   277
50 A History of Mild Winters   278
51 A Seasonal Reversal, 1974/75   282
Part VIII Mist, Fog and Smog   287
52 Mist, Fog and Deadly London Smog   288
Part IX Unusual Natural Events   293
53 The Laki Eruption and Sulphur Cloud, 1783   294
54 The Lewes Avalanche, December 1836   296
55 The Folkestone Earthquake, April 2007   300
56 The Great Fire of London, September 1666   304
Notes   309
Bibliography   313
Acknowledgements   315

Introduction

The weather in Britain, although often benign, has thrown some extraordinary events at us across the ages. Of those documented, a number have impacted substantially on the British Isles and our neighbours. In fact, the weather has occasionally changed the course of history, society and even human evolution.

Think of the gale-force easterly wind that drew flames from a small domestic fire into an uncontrollable firestorm, burning London to a cinder in September 1666. Although a great catastrophe, it put an end to both the plague and the cramped and dirty streets, which were soon reimagined and rebuilt to form a world-class city. A devastating tidal surge arrived unannounced one night in 1953, decimating our weak coastal defences and killing thousands; the bitter winter of 1962/63 was so severe that scientists became convinced a new Ice Age had arrived; the drought and fierce heat of summer 1976 was so intense and prolonged that it pushed Britain to the point of desperation, with domestic and industrial water supplies failing; the incredible gale of 1703 was so powerful it almost destroyed our domestic navy during a time of international crisis, blowing one ship and its terrified crew from Kent all the way to Norway; devastating floods; clouds of sulphur dioxide that poisoned the atmosphere and turned leaves and crops black; tornadoes, blizzards, violent storms and earthquakes; even a volcanically induced global winter lasting a thousand years and reducing humanity to just a few thousand individuals. All this and a great deal more makes up the material in this book, following the often surprising and extraordinary history of Britain's weather and its effect on a people that instinctively expect the unexpected and take nothing for granted.

As a nation, our experiences have taught all of us lessons of some kind. Does not experience make us wary of the weather when planning a barbeque, a weekend away or a holiday at the coast? This book provides a personal and historical narrative of Britain's weather. It encompasses the effects, both extraordinary and mundane, of the weather on our nation, our government, our military and our emergency services. Many of the more recent events will revive individual memories, and may challenge contemporary perceptions. Using scientific fact, and meteorological and statistical data, a numerical backdrop helps illustrate each story.

Britain has always been a leading nation in using science to fulfil its desire to predict and understand its weather. This stems greatly from a maritime heritage and commercial reliance on the sea. The sea plays a strong role in our national psyche, as does our relationship with the unpredictable weather that governs it. Our need to navigate our waters safely and, indeed, become their master, pushed us into establishing the world's first government-run meteorological office, which still exists today in the Met Office. From its initial aim – to protect both trade and human life from our erratic and unpredictable weather at sea – the Met Office has become a vast commercial and governmental enterprise that has put Britain at the forefront of meteorology since the science began.

In addition to the weather's perennial popularity as a subject of conversation in this country, in recent years the dramatic increase in meteorological data on the internet has created a new generation of weather fanatics. Amateurs can now watch the weather's every twist and turn online. These often passionate communities contain a range of enthusiasts, from those who simply favour certain weather scenarios to professional or semi-professional meteorologists. I would class myself as a keen amateur with a passion for all things weather-related.

Over the years, however, this passion has also become intertwined with a fascination for history. Most of the big weather events that have taken place in Britain have been recorded to a greater or lesser degree; and the impact they have had, both on day-to-day life and society at large, is sometimes more profound than many might imagine.

Outcomes of great battles, such as Waterloo in June 1815, were largely determined by the weather. Waterloo was compromised for Napoleon by incessant rain that left French guns stuck in deep mud, rendering them useless. The terrible summers of 1815 and 1816 were directly attributable to the vast eruption of Mt Tambora in Indonesia in April 1815. Incredible amounts of ash were thrust into the atmosphere in what was certainly one of the most powerful eruptions in recorded history, significantly cooling much of the planet as a veil of dust circulated through the atmosphere many times over. By 1816, this led to what became known as 'the year without a summer'. July 1816 was the coldest ever recorded in Britain, at 13.4 °C, and June and August were also remarkably cold. While the loss by the French at the Battle of Waterloo shifted the balance of power in Europe, over the following months much of the northern hemisphere saw food shortages and famine become widespread. In the north-east of the United States, Massachusetts saw winter-like conditions, with frost and snow throughout May and even into June 1816. Yet more startling were the widespread lowland snowfalls that blanketed the state, as well as others further south, on 7–8 June that year. This was unprecedented, and has not occurred since. The terrible weather hampered transport links, preventing proper distribution of produce from the south, and prices skyrocketed.

While this relatively recent event is well attested, two perhaps less well-known examples illustrate the huge impact on society and even humanity weather can have. The most recent occurred in AD 535; the other, vastly more ancient, around 73,000 Before Present (BP). You may now be wondering how we know what the weather was doing in 73,000 BP, let alone the impact it had on humanity; the answer is that we know quite a lot about it because it almost wiped humanity out.[1]

A vast lake in Indonesia holds a clue. This is Lake Toba, which was once the site of a 'super volcano' eruption. Rather than being a single mountain, super volcanoes are areas that sit above gigantic bubbles of magma pushing out from the earth's crust. They erupt over a colossal area. Another such site exists at Yellowstone Park in the western USA. Geological evidence clearly shows that the Toba eruption was felt dramatically right across the world. It also suggests that a long-lasting and global winter quickly ensued. This eruption coincides with an 'evolutionary bottleneck' found in our anthropological record that had long mystified scientists. On the volcanic explosivity index scale, which extends to 8.0, Toba scores 8.0, quite literally at the top of the scale, and is described as 'mega colossal'.

The volcanic winter that followed it by just a few months brought dramatic cooling – as much as 15 °C globally within three years. There would have been an almost instant Ice Age and this would have been fatal, or at least debilitating, to many species. Research into ice cores taken from Greenland shows the ash from the eruption as a thick, dark band that clearly illustrates the length and impact of the cooling. This could have lasted as long as a thousand years. A dramatic reduction in human evolution, as well as a huge decrease in population, shows up in our genetic record. In short, there weren't enough of us to breed in evolutionary changes. The total numbers of humans left could have dropped to as low as a thousand breeding pairs.[2] This rapid slowdown in our development is also apparent at the same time in other species such as chimpanzees, tigers, cheetahs and various types of monkey.

Despite some records, what is known about the events of AD 535 in Britain is limited. However, we do know that the climate changed suddenly for the worse, and appalling weather followed. Contemporary tree rings from close by in Ireland show very little growth at all in the period of 535–36. This indicates that a serious climatic downturn occurred. Historical records describe a great famine in 536, and reports from Rome described the sun's power as that of 'an eclipse which gave no warmth'. Huge hoards of gold were found in the largest contemporary Scandinavian settlements, perhaps acting as an appeasement to angry gods in harsh times, and in Peru the Moche culture seems to have come under fatal pressure through drought as a 'dense, dry fog' was reported across the known world.

The cause looks increasingly like another eruption. Among the initial suspects was a volcano in Papua New Guinea; however, spectrometric analysis has since shown the origin of the ejecta (the material forced out by the eruption) most likely to be from the Llopango caldera in El Salvador;[3] the eruption has been measured at a massive 6.9 on the scale.

This event set the human race on the move. It drove the Huns in the east to move west and south, pushed the Vandals to attack Rome, led to the sharp decline of Teotihuacan city in Mexico and the fall of the once great Persian Empire. This climatic cooling also coincided with the first great pandemic of bubonic plague, the so-called 'plague of Justinian', which spread from Asia and the Middle East as far north as Denmark and Ireland. The relationship between the two was not immediately apparent but it has since been speculated[4] that a major downturn in climate in China in 1347 saw a mass migration of rats from the east, leading to the Black Death pandemic that decimated the population of most European countries in 1348.

Cyclical climatic shifts occur quite regularly throughout history, although unusual weather has become more frequent as the twenty-first century has progressed. The decade of the 1940s is a good example of a cyclical event. No really cold winter took place between 1895 and 1939. However, a bitter winter suddenly began in early 1940 and the decade saw a succession of harsh winters thereafter. However, the 1940s also saw a notable rise in drought and hot summer weather, peaking in 1947. This year contained one of the coldest winters, some of the worst flooding and one of the hottest summers of the last century. This 'continental' style of weather could possibly also be linked to a natural, cyclical slowdown in the Gulf Stream.

A more dramatic disruption took place more gradually from about 1540, the culmination of a series of very hot years. A significant, long-term downturn in our climate then began, with frequent bitter winters and erratic periods of great summer heat and drought alternating with damagingly cold and wet summer seasons. Winter temperatures were significantly lower than in the present day. This long-term shift has been named the Little Ice Age.

Nevertheless, since the last Ice Age ended, man has flourished. Agriculture has become our staple in the warmer, more reliable climate of the present; yet we do remain vulnerable. The earth has begun to warm, and already there are signs that patterns of increasingly extreme weather could be linked to changes in climate that are proving hard to predict. Some of the decades of the twentieth century saw changes that can be attributed to natural cycles; however, a startling and undeniable rise in global temperatures has taken place since 1900 – and it is a rise that broadly continues today. Its causes remain the subject of massive debate among our scientific and meteorological communities, but evidence is mounting that human activity *is* driving it.[5]

As you will see, during the course of the history of British weather, science often seems influenced by current events. Cold winters have brought theories of new Ice Ages and rapid cooling, while heat and drought have almost always driven new evidence of both warming and drying trends. Man cannot afford to take too many risks with the climate, and, if science proves we need to act to ensure the survival of both ourselves and that of the flora and fauna that sustain us, we must act. Our vulnerability to weather and natural disaster is all too clear.

My fascination with the weather began when I was about four years old, with the movie *The Wizard of Oz* and the tornado that swept Dorothy's house into the air and off to Oz. An interest in all things meteorological grew from there, and when the summer of 1976 arrived its major impact on day-to-day life fascinated me. As the long, hot summer of 1976 drew to a close, my understanding and respect for the weather had grown substantially, as had my interest in all aspects of it.

This book is targeted at anyone who has an interest in history, weather and its social impacts alongside those with nostalgic interests or just the plain curious. After all, this is everybody's story. In some cases, the stories reflect my own experiences and those of the people I know. Sometimes, where the impact of events is wider than just the UK, I have included the experiences of our near neighbours. Nevertheless, the focus is very much on Britain. With space at a premium, I can also only provide a snapshot of the some of the greatest weather events and certain natural phenomena through the ages; a more comprehensive account would most likely comprise many volumes. Many of the more detailed accounts are from events of the last 300 years; this is largely because these occur during the period when scientific measures and detailed national and international accounts exist. Details and verifiable facts get harder to pin down with the passage of time, but nevertheless the distant past still plays a vibrant role in the story where space allows. Most of all, however, I hope this will be an enjoyable and informative journey to everyone who embarks on it.

PART I
SNOW, COLD AND GREAT FREEZES

The Great Victorian Blizzard and Easterly Gale, January 1881

The most severe snowstorm to strike the British Isles since reliable records began remains unequalled today. It struck the country in January 1881. In addition to the exceptional snowfall, the storm was accompanied by a violent easterly gale that caused chaos and destruction on a terrifying scale on land, the waterways and the seas around Britain.

January 1881 saw a cold spell begin early in the second week of the month. As the ponds and lakes became deep-frozen, skating became widespread. Winds that week were often light and skies clear, but frosts were severe, even in the city centres. This situation continued from 9 January into the weekend of 15–16 January, with temperatures falling remarkably low. The lowest values included -26.7 °C at Kelso and -24 °C at Blackadder, both in Scotland, and in England -23 °C was recorded at Hayden Bridge, and -21.7 °C as far south as Bury St Edmunds. Even the coastal site of Blackpool saw -18 °C, while at the normally clement town of Cheltenham the thermometer plunged to -17 °C. Kew Gardens, close to central London, saw night-time lows of -15 °C, a quite extraordinary reading.

On the evening of Monday 17 January, a stiff wind began to blow from the east and cloud gradually increased. By Tuesday morning, the wind was approaching gale force in the south, heralding a change in the weather and the onset of the greatest instrumentally recorded snowstorm in British history.

Although forecasts were very basic, by 1881 live telegraph reports from land and shipping positions allowed meteorologists to create an accurate analysis of the general synoptic situation. The Meteorological Office produced detailed daily reports, and on Monday 17 January they stated that pressure was dropping from the west and south, and a deep depression was approaching the channel. Detailed weather reports appeared daily in most newspapers, and warnings to shipping were also issued by telegraph. Concerns of the change in the overall pattern were thus communicated to shipping and the public with the inference that a strong easterly wind flow would develop. The wind duly picked up and on Tuesday the wind was reported to be 'blowing a perfect hurricane', even in central London. Nevertheless, the morning commute proceeded as normal, and trains and carriages brought thousands into the smoky metropolis as they did every day. The wind chill was immense, and shortly after 9 a.m. a light snow began to fall. It settled immediately and became progressively heavier as the morning wore on. With the fierce gale blowing, visibility dropped to almost nil. By early afternoon London was at a standstill, rail transport had been paralysed and telegraph communications soon failed as power lines were torn down by the high winds. Snow moved across the north as well. Manchester, Bolton and the mill towns became isolated as train travel slowed to a stop, and Wales was also reported to be experiencing significant snowfall. However, the further south you were, the closer you were to the depression and the more severe the snow became.

Over a twenty-four-hour period, the Isle of Wight had over 40 inches of level snow, with drifts 10 to 30 feet high. Portsmouth had 36 inches, as did Barnstaple, Havant, Okehampton and many other southern and western towns. Brighton received 24 inches, and central London around 10 inches by Tuesday afternoon. Snow fell right across South Wales up to Lincolnshire, with Manchester receiving a more modest 4 inches. Nevertheless, drifting was severe everywhere. Even in central London there was drifting snow 3 to 5 feet deep, but it was the high ground in the south that saw the most extraordinary drifts. These were well over 20 feet deep in places on the North Downs, and the snow continued to fall all night. In fact, the next morning, Wednesday 18 January, it was still snowing over much of southern England and the huge depths of lying and drifted snow now took on unprecedented proportions. Later analysis showed that the exceptional depths experienced on the south coast were attributable to a secondary low-pressure system that tracked just slightly south of the main storm. The storm pounded all of England and Wales, and even extended its effects to the normally clement city of Dublin, where tramcars were blocked in the streets for the first time since their introduction.

It was, however, more often the wind that caused most damage and provoked chaotic scenes such as those at Wolverhampton, where a trial at the county court was interrupted when the wind began to shake the building with such force that it was feared the roof might come in. No immediate damage was found, so the trial continued. The wind, however, increased during the afternoon and suddenly at 3 p.m. a violent gust brought part of the roof crashing down. It collapsed onto the public gallery, seriously injuring three people who had to be dragged from the rubble. Others in the court panicked and tried to clamber down from the balcony outside, which was at a considerable height; they had to be restrained by the bailiffs from doing so.

Reports from around the country told of the severity of the gale, and confirmed that the south coast was by far the area worst affected by snow. Nevertheless, it was the east coast that bore the brunt of the easterly gale. At its most fierce in Ipswich, the wind blew in the east-facing side of the town's clock tower, crushing it inwards and destroying the mechanism. On the Isle of Wight, at Ryde, several large vessels were torn from their moorings and ploughed into the pier, badly damaging it. Trains in and out of Portsmouth were suspended, and one reporter described the snow as so intense that objects a few yards away were rendered invisible. Most train traffic out of the city was suspended early on, and by the end of the day there were no trains running at all. Brighton was similarly cut off, and drifts came up to the eaves of sea-fronted buildings. In the West Country, places such as Taunton and Ilfracombe saw drifts 20 feet deep, and any habitation at altitude was hopelessly cut off from the outside world. Wales, too, saw terrific gales, and found links to many of its towns and cities dislocated, with numerous towns in need of liberation from the huge drifts.

London was impacted particularly badly by this storm. Over the preceding days, large blocks of ice had begun to build in the Thames. As the gale force winds began to blow, several barges in Woolwich found themselves in trouble, and were pounded at their moorings by both the fast-running water and great blocks of ice. As the blinding snow blew in, so did a rising tide and, driven on storm force winds, the combination of ice boulders and water began a destructive run upriver. By midday, the new pier at Woolwich had been completely destroyed by barges and other vessels becoming dislodged from their moorings and smashing into it. These vessels were then drawn out into the icy melee, crashing into each other, and at least ten were sunk. Two men were blown into the river and drowned at the Albert Docks in London, and by 1 p.m. the water was now over four feet above normal, crashing over the banks at Woolwich and Greenwich and up into Deptford. The freezing water did huge damage in the low-lying roads while cellars were flooded with icy cold filthy water, and some buildings were irreparably damaged. The water at Blackfriars soon began to reach unprecedented heights, and fears that it would break over the banks proved correct. In a very deprived area, the ice and water pounded the poorly built local tenements, drowning many vulnerable people in basement flats. The water got into the sewers and the flood spread up to Waterloo, creating chaos and leaving a dreadful trail of destruction. It was reported at the time that £2 million (over £200 million in today's money) worth of damage was caused in the areas affected.

At Dover, many of the mail ships and ferries that had been able to dock in the early morning soon pulled out of the harbour after a lugger was smashed to pieces there. They made their way out into the open sea for greater safety, but it was an unpleasant and long wait for the storm to die down. The wrought-iron Admiralty Pier gates were wrenched off their hinges by the howling gale,[1] and the pier was badly damaged, with great chunks of masonry torn off by the wild sea.

Out at sea, one dreadful event followed another. Fleets of east coast fishermen who had set out before first light were in great distress. Many were brought ashore by the storm on the Suffolk and Norfolk coasts, and at Woodford Haven a ship was sunk, with only her masts visible. The coastguard spotted a number of crew desperately clinging to the masts and the lifeboat was called out. It could not be launched from its usual place at Harwich because of the rough seas and had to be launched from the Great Eastern Railway pier. From there it set out into a spray-laden icy sea. Soon after its launch, a large wave tipped the lifeboat to one side and it capsized. The crew then had to be rescued using a 'rocket' device. In the freezing temperatures, one of the men died from exposure.

Further calamity soon followed. A schooner was driven ashore at Yarmouth, and one of her crew was killed while the rest were rescued. Thereafter, another vessel, the *Guiding Star*, was seen to be sinking, and the Yarmouth lifeboat, *Abraham Thomas*, set out to rescue the crew. The lifeboat was unable to manage the tremendous winds and sank, killing five of her crew. Two further crewmen made it ashore alive and survived, while two others later died of exposure at the local seaman's mission.

On the Continent, much of northern France and parts of Belgium were covered in deep snow. Towns across the region were cut off by vast drifts. The prolonged severe winter spell also had a big impact on wildlife. For the first time in many years, starving wolves were reported to be heading into populated areas in the vicinity of Nimes.[2] Hunting parties set out to eliminate the wolf pack, no doubt made desperate by the deep snow and lack of food.

The jet stream was pushed far further south than normal by a vast anticyclone over Scandinavia. This had a major impact as far south as the Mediterranean. The region found itself under the conveyor belt of low-pressure systems, normally located between Britain and Iceland. This brought torrential rain to the north and south of the region, impacting Spain in particular. The cities of Burgos and Salamanca suffered calamitous flooding, as did much of the Ebro valley that flows out into the Mediterranean at Tortosa. Agriculture was badly affected by the severe flooding, and damage to fruit trees and crops was widespread and was felt throughout the year. Madrid, high up on the central plain, found itself cut off from the entire outside world for three days as the heavy rain there fell in the form of a blizzard, which brought the country's capital city to a grinding halt.[3]

In the following days, Britain remained in the deep freeze and the temperatures stayed below zero nationwide. Kew, close to the centre of London, saw daytime maxima of -5 °C and exceptional night-time readings well below -10 °C for a sustained period. The papers at the time stated that the lowest recorded figure at Kew was actually taken some fourteen years before, on 4 January 1867, with a bone-chilling -18 °C. This reading seems almost unthinkable for Kew today, where some nearby gardens sport date palms. Wind speeds reached a sustained 60 mph on 18 January, and even several hours later were still pounding the capital at 50 mph. One can only imagine the wind chill, which must have been perishing. The lighter snow that continued to fall across much of the country the next day made any form of travel difficult, if not impossible, and transport paralysis was almost universal. January 1881 was also one of the coldest ever in the UK; the mean average of -1.5 °C makes it the fifth coldest January since 1659.

Our nineteenth-century counterparts were more accustomed to cold and snow than we are today, and heavy falls occurred more often. The experience of many thaws therefore meant people were likely to have experienced thaw floods. Those of 1814, for example, followed on from over a month of freezing weather during which a Thames frost fair was held. However, the thaw was rapid and the ice melted surprisingly fast, killing several people as it unexpectedly cracked, split and then flowed downriver. Heavy rain soon followed and the ice-laden waters reached record levels in places like the Medway in Maidstone, Kent. Among the media and the general public in 1881, there was therefore deep concern as to where all the snow would go when milder weather did finally arrive and which areas might be affected by flooding.

Deep worry was also expressed about the plight of the poor that had been made homeless by the flooding in London during the storm. Some funds were made available by public collection, which went some way to paying for repairs and replacing clothing, but one can be in little doubt that life in the Victorian age was a living hell for the poor in general, and in particular anyone not able to work or look after themselves. Cold winters picked large numbers of them off through starvation and hypothermia, while mild winters could prove equally deadly, with diseases such as cholera remaining active where frost could not kill off the bacteria in the water supply.

The cold lasted until 27 January, when a depression from the Atlantic moved slowly eastwards towards the anticyclone, which gradually began to weaken. Soon, cloud, mild air and rain spread right across Britain and the rain was heavy. The fears of flooding proved justified, and the millions of tons of snow that had built up caused numerous rivers to burst their banks, flooding town and country alike.

Taking a number of measures, including the strength of the wind, the depth of the drifts, the scale and breadth of the snowfall and the level and length of disruption caused, this blizzard definitely outclasses its nearest rival, the March 1891 blizzard. Even though the snow depths were incredible on that occasion, the spring sunshine quickly got to work on the snow, and the effects were comparatively short-lived for majority of the populace away from the hills and moorland. In contrast, the bitter temperatures and further snow that followed the 1881 storm, and the staggering strength of the wind, were the most defining, as well as the most unusual, features of this exceptional event. Other great blizzards that have rivalled, but never beaten, this monster storm occurred in 1947 in the south of England, in 1963 in many regions and in 1978 in both the West Country and separately in the highlands of Scotland. Nevertheless, it was the extraordinary gale that made the 1881 event so unique and so very destructive.

2

The Great Spring Snowstorm, March 1891

The last week of November 1890 saw the start of a cold spell that lasted many weeks, and December 1890 was the coldest December on record, with only 2010 coming close to beating it. This spell of bitter winter weather continued well into January 1891, with frost and snow persistent in most areas. February, however, saw a vast improvement from the outset, and the month was mild and clement across almost the entire kingdom. This mild spell, however, was not the end of winter, and an unexpected swing back to cold, wintry weather took place in the first week of March followed by a remarkable blizzard that swept across South Wales and the south and west of England. This proved to be one of the most severe snowstorms ever measured in southern Britain, despite its relative lateness in the season.

At the start of March 1891 temperatures were normal, and the first week of the meteorological spring was seasonally mild and clement. Gardens saw daffodils begin to flower early after a mild February and sunshine was more dominant than cloud and rain. It is easy, even for hardy observers, to forget that winter is never far away at that time of year and winter shocks are something many of us will have experienced when it seemed only days before spring had come to stay. Towards the end of the week pressure began to build strongly to the north-west of Britain, spreading down rapidly from Greenland over Iceland and towards Scotland. Shipping was iced badly to the north of Scotland for the first time in weeks and snow, hail and thunder showers occurred widely. By the weekend of 7–8 March, temperatures had become unseasonably cold right across the British Isles. The north wind veered into a fresh easterly, and a cold continental airstream brought bitter air from Scandinavia and eastern

Europe. As the cold set in, viciously strong winds began to exacerbate the sensation of cold and it was soon apparent that this was no ordinary spring cold snap. The cold intensified further to almost unbearable levels in the dry, bitter winds and people were crammed indoors next to fires and stoves, keeping as warm as they could.

In the Bay of Biscay, a depression began to form and deepen rapidly. On Sunday 8 March, this deepening feature pushed steadily northwards towards southern England, announced by a sheet of cloud that spread westwards across southern Britain. The night sky over London had a deep orange hue and the freezing, buffeting winds cleared almost every street of pedestrians by early evening. In the south-western counties, pressure fell overnight but the onset of the storm was extremely fast; sunny skies early on gave no inkling of the ravages to come.

In the days before satellite imagery and plentiful automated weather stations in the open sea, it was not easy to predict the path and intensity of depressions from the scattered existing reports from shipping. Nevertheless, from the meteorological office's synoptic evaluation that night, forecasters were aware that pressure was dropping to the south-west and, as the easterly winds were strengthening and cloud had increased across the south, a deep depression was approaching. Bulletins were issued to shipping warning of possible easterly gales early that week but there was uncertainty as to the extent of any oncoming snowfall.

On the morning of Monday 9 March, the first snowfall spread into south-west England, commencing at around ten past eleven that morning. It then began to sweep eastwards. Soon the coasts and headlands of Cornwall, Devon, Dorset and then Bristol were enveloped in a swirling blast of dust-like powdery snow that quickly piled up, leaving the entire south-western peninsula under deep snow, with a howling gale putting an end to the week's trading and shipping before it had even begun. The snow tore across land and sea, driven on the gale-force easterly and north-easterly winds, hissing through bare trees, over moorland rocks and through normally lush valleys, piling up into drifts against windward walls, while the bitter winds stripped nearby open land completely bare of almost anything.

The gale toppled trees in their thousands; it was reported at the Kitley estate in Yeovilton that a full 1,500 trees were felled; other estates suffered even greater losses right across Devon, Cornwall and Somerset. Fruit trees, great elms and firs were all decimated. Plymouth was almost immediately cut off, and any traffic was trapped in gigantic drifts driven by the ferocious gale; this fate befell the Penzance omnibus. The horses had to be set free after a nearby farmhouse refused them and the driver shelter (they were later found). The passengers were trapped in the carriage until Tuesday night. Windows left slightly ajar in these areas saw the fine snow blow in and cling in huge quantities to the insides of houses; it crept under doors, leaving great drifts, and caused severe structural damage in many areas, ripping off tiles, slates and even parts of roofs. The severe cold was made far worse by the gale. The driver of a trapped train at Torridge near Plympton was found on Tuesday suffering from severe hypothermia and was rescued just in time. He survived despite receiving terrible frostbite to his hands, legs and feet. The gale blew even 'hardy, muscular men' about like dolls, and many people were dashed against walls and other objects, causing several serious injuries.

By midday the snow had reached London, where it began to settle almost immediately. Once it began, it continued all night. The streets were quickly blanketed as great swirls of snow snaked across the lanes and parks with impunity, sneaking under doorways and through cracks in windows and piling into great drifts. On Monday night, the snow was deep enough to cover the wheels and axels of carriages in London, making it impossible for the horses to pull their weight in the slippery conditions. People were forced out of cabs into the swirling, blowing snow, and faced freezing walks to their destinations. The fine snow stuck like a sugary crust as it built up on any surface facing the brutal wind. It was reported that in Dulwich, just a few miles from central London, the wind had whipped up drifts 11 feet deep and Oxford Circus had 9 feet of drifted snow.[4] It is hard to even picture 9 feet of snow blocking central London today.

The 'channel low' that caused the snow to fall so widely moved east early on Tuesday. Many ships saw the pressure rise and believed the worst was over. However, no sooner had the frenzied disturbance cleared to the east than a fresh depression followed its predecessor along the English Channel. The snow was therefore continuous for nearly 48 hours, lasting throughout Tuesday in some places, and the gale force winds increased in ferocity, drawing out the chaos both on land and at sea. The fact that the snow was powdery and dry shows clearly that the temperatures were unusually low for March. Monday in Manchester failed to exceed 2 °C, and Tuesday could only muster 1 °C. In London and the south, temperatures were even lower. London failed to exceed 0 °C on Tuesday afternoon, and despite the length of the spring day the capital was again a deserted city, covered in a thick blanket of snow that lay across every street, and on each lake and pond, where ice stayed fast.

In Kent the blizzard managed to completely fill a 30-foot-deep railway cutting near Rochester, and on Monday night, a train on its way to Faversham was stuck in 6–7 foot drifts in a cutting near the town. Passengers waited all night in freezing conditions before they could be rescued, and the train had to be left in the cutting for days, as it could not be physically dug out of its snowy tomb. In fact, three locomotives were unsuccessful in pulling the train out because of the sheer depth and weight of snow. The train was not liberated for some considerable time.

Trains running into Portsmouth, Eastbourne and Newhaven all got stuck in deep drifts on Monday night, and did not make their destinations until well into the following day. At that time, there was a branch line that ran into Sandgate, between Hythe and Folkestone, and the London train became stuck in deep drifts. Passengers were stuck for twelve hours before the train could limp into the station.

The Isle of Wight was badly hit, as it was in the 1881 blizzard. Huge snowdrifts paralysed the island, and no traffic or mail was able to move around for much of that week. Further west, Devon and Somerset were completely buried by huge drifts, with sheep on the moors and hills lost in great numbers when tragically close to lambing. At Exeter, the telegraph lines were down so news from further east was unable to get through, except for the rare appearance of a train. The blizzard was so prolonged in the south-west it was reported that one railway cutting nearly 80 feet deep was buried, and remnants of the snow were still visible in June. The strong winds also brought flooding to the low-lying areas around Topsham, and many boats on the River Exe were sunk by the gale.

On the seas, it was a day of misery and death. The press reported that it was 'one of the worst days known' in the Channel at Dover, with the afternoon being plunged into darkness as the blizzard and gale descended on the coast. The sea was said to be 'boiling in rage' at the easterly gale. A steamship, the *Western Belle* of Exmouth, ran aground at Bognor, and the lifeboat was launched. As soon as the ship was reached, however, it smashed into a groyne on the beach and fell apart. The lifeboat managed to winch the crew ashore, but the effort left one of their number in a critical condition; he was thought unlikely to survive the exposure to the extreme wet and cold and later perished. Off Lydd in Kent, three vessels were observed in distress, one of them running out of control and on fire. The Lydd lifeboat was duly despatched, but the gale in the open sea proved too much for the lifeboat, and it capsized. Three of her crew drowned, as did two of those from the distressed ship.

One of the Folkestone fishing fleet ran aground in the same area, but its crew were saved. In fact, eight boats from the fleet had set out that day; by evening three were lost. At Hastings on the Monday evening, a great panic set in when the fourteen-strong fishing fleet was sighted returning to port at about 6.30 p.m. As the gale and snow were so fierce, it was assumed the boats would stay out to anchor and ride out the storm but three of their number came into to shore and all three were immediately damaged, with the masts and rigging blown down. A panicked crowd assembled on the beach facing the roaring sea and watching in horror as two of the boats smashed together and disintegrated. However, using cables, it was possible for the crews to be saved and the third boat to finally be winched in.

The Sandgate lifeboat was also despatched that Monday night, and three of its crew were lost trying to save a number of distressed vessels. Off the same coastline, a schooner named *Zingari* was lost with all hands drowned; so severe was the storm that a member of the coastguard, leaving duty at Beachy Head, froze to death walking home. The driver of the Sheerness to Sittingbourne mail coach was also said to be in a critical condition due to exposure, and only just survived the ordeal.

Watching the howling gale and blinding snow on Monday evening were the passengers of the steam ferry *Victoria*. The crossing from Dover to Calais was to leave on time despite the terrible conditions. Looking at the horrendous weather outside, only twenty of the fifty passengers scheduled to travel opted to do so. The Duchess of Edinburgh was one of those that stayed; at the same time, her husband, the Duke of Edinburgh, was stuck in Devon with all transport suspended. With only the grace of God on her side, the

Victoria set out at 7 p.m. and pressed on out into the open sea. The crosswinds were terrible, and immediately the steamer pitched and rolled; this battering lasted for several hours until one in the morning when the winds became even worse, described by one passenger as a 'hurricane'. Unable to continue in the dark because they were too near the shore and sandbanks off the coast of Calais, the captain weighed anchor. The ferry journey from Dover to Calais in 1891 normally took an hour, somewhat faster than today. Now, in the early hours of Tuesday 10 March, the ferry company had had no news since its departure, and began to fear the worst. Back on the ship, a slight easing of the winds meant that the ship's captain, Shirley, took up the anchor and moved to proceed to Calais, arriving finally at 5 a.m., and setting off back to Dover at 8 a.m. The passengers were full of praise for the captain, who was reported to have done an admirable job even though it could not have been a pleasant crossing. It wasn't until 11.45 a.m. on Tuesday that the ferry company had confirmation the *Victoria* was safely back at Dover.[5]

In Wales, as in Nottinghamshire and other mining counties, the fierce weather and strong winds meant mining activity was put on hold. The weather forecast in many papers on Wednesday included warnings from the Met Office that mining should be suspended or undertaken with caution because the very low pressure and severe gales heightened the risk of trapping gas in mines. In the Rhondda alone, this meant forty collieries were shut and 20,000 men sat idle while the snowstorm powered through. The winds were so strong in Mid Wales that two children were killed by a collapsing chimney in their home at Cwmavon and the town of Tredegar was said to be typical, isolated by vast drifts 18–20 feet deep and in 'a state of siege with access blocked in every direction'.

The Press Association made a statement that this was the worst storm since the great January blizzard of 1881, measured by the fact that at Windsor it was the first time since then that the elderly queen's hounds had to be kept indoors, and all hunting activities cancelled. Scotland had rather less snow in comparison with the south of England but temperatures were reported to be exceptionally low for March, conditions were 'icy and hazardous' and there was much disruption to rail travel. The cold air maintained its position over Scotland and the north of England for some days, but the strong March sun ensured that temperatures in the south rose enough to deliver a partial thaw and slush as early as Tuesday night, with a more general thaw beginning on Wednesday.

Spring is, without doubt, a capricious time of the year. High pressure can also bring warmth and sunshine as it did in 1968. Late March saw a tremendous spell of warm, even hot weather over southern England and much of northern Europe. Cromer and Santon Downham in Norfolk both recorded the UK's highest March temperature of 25 °C on the 29th. Yet only four days later, on 1 April, London struggled to reach 0 °C and snow was falling. More recently, while 17 °C was recorded on 5 March 2013 the south then witnessed a dramatic turnaround; one week later the region was visited by freezing temperatures, a snowy Channel low and afternoon temperatures of -2 °C in a gale-force easterly wind.

In summary, no March blizzard has ever come close to the extreme conditions delivered by the 1891 storm, and the fact that it was reported that drifts remained into June in some valleys in Dartmoor and Exmoor proves this point beyond any doubt. This event comes second only to the extraordinary 1881 blizzard and is likewise unparalleled in the modern era. Perhaps only January 1963 can serve as a modern comparison in terms of paralysis on such a vast scale. Nevertheless, there is nothing to say it could not happen again; I feel sorry for any future government that has to deal with such an eventuality.

3

The Last Thames Freeze in London, February 1895

The bitter winter of 1895 was the last of the great Victorian winters, and is viewed by some climatologists as a focal point after which the Little Ice Age concluded and the major warming of the current era began. It was forty-five years before a comparable winter occurred, and the rapid climatic warming trend across the globe that began after the turn of the century still continues apace today. Nevertheless, this winter brought incredible hardship to many in Britain, and was felt across much Europe and the northern hemisphere, especially in the US and Canada. This was the last time the Thames froze over in central London, and most of February was bitterly cold, with the UK's record lowest temperature of -27.2 °C measured at Braemar in Scotland.[6]

November and early December 1894 were wet and largely mild. Heavy rain drawn across the country on an aggressive jet stream meant repeated downpours, much of it focused on the south of Britain. So wet was the outset of November that the Thames burst its banks in many places, including Kingston-upon-Thames which was badly flooded, as were other similarly low-lying locations in the south of the country. After so many spells of soaking rain, the ground was saturated, swelling several major rivers. It wasn't until New Year's Eve that any sign of harsh winter weather became evident.

High pressure built strongly just to the west of Ireland during 30 December, while a large depression became established over Scandinavia. This created a northerly airstream which, the next day, brought a severe northerly blast rapidly southwards. This was accompanied by heavy snow, thunder, lightning and hail. In parts of the south-east, day turned to night as the marked front brought sweeping snow, gusty winds and hail down with such force that local structural damage occurred. After this point, the New Year brought with it bitterly cold winter weather. Although there was sometimes bright sunshine, low pressure became anchored progressively closer to the south-east of the UK, bringing increasingly frequent snow showers. Heavy snow then blanketed much of the country during the second week of January.

However, the Atlantic broke through from around 14 January, and milder air became established, bringing a brief thaw on the weekend of 19–20 January. Although this thaw was fairly widespread, it was mildest to the south and west. To the north of Manchester, it was only a temporary affair; here snow and ice remained at many higher locations throughout January.

On Monday 21 January, yet another severe cold front pushed down rapidly, north to south, to the great surprise of forecasters. Snow blanketed highland and lowland locations from Scotland right down to the south coast. Most of the snow fell to the east of Britain, with paralysing blizzards affecting eastern Scotland and East Anglia and the south-east with deep drifts, accompanied by extremely low temperatures. This weather pattern became deeply entrenched and would last without a break for a further six weeks.

Now a vast anticyclone grew right across Scandinavia and western Russia and some of the coldest weather ever recorded in Britain struck. As the high pressure dug in over the Nordic countries and the Baltic Sea, so isobars tightened to the south, pushing a pool of deeply cooled upper air westwards over the far south-east of England with readings as low as -18 °C at 850 mb (the lowest part of the Earth's atmosphere). This led to -10 °C being widely recorded across much of the UK during the day; in several areas – north to south – temperatures as low as -20 °C were being measured on standard equipment as the long nights allowed any warmth on the ground to filter away. Even London saw a reading close to -18 °C at Greenwich. Soon the Thames saw great lumps of ice flow in with the tide and begin to halt crucial river traffic in the city centre as the river then gradually froze over completely.

The first week of February was the harshest of the winter, especially to the north, where deep drifts and paralysis in the previous two weeks had been most severe. Regular heavy snowfalls began to pile up yet further, driven on relentless east winds. The snow soon took a toll on agriculture, general labour and also on shipping. Mines became unworkable, becoming too dangerous to work because of an elevated threat of gas poisoning and explosion. Unrest on the labour front soon began. As men sat idle, in the absence of any welfare, their money ran out. It was also at this juncture that the worst snow struck. In the first few days of February, much of the south had remained freezing but dry. Wednesday 7 February saw blizzards, driven on an easterly gale, strike both ends of the country. The effect of this deep, widespread snow was enormous.

In Lancashire, with most mills, mines and outdoor work at a standstill, there was panic because families in the towns were at risk of both starvation and hypothermia. In Blackburn, one of the principal mill towns, a great delegation of workers marched on the corporation (the then title of the local council) and demanded that work be found, or some means of relief given, to deal with times of forced lay-offs. It took large numbers of police to stop the workers from breaking into the council offices to be heard. Instead, the corporation allowed a representative delegation to address them and discuss ways in which labour could be found to keep thousands of working-class families from freezing to death.

In Cumbria an express train from London was trapped by vast drifts, as were many other trains across the country that day. From North Yorkshire to Cheshire, the papers were describing this as the 'sixth week of the storm' and the most severe winter since 1836 (see chapter 54). At Northallerton in Yorkshire, 'twenty-seven degrees of frost', -15 °C, was measured on 7 February. The strong winds kept the snow constantly drifting and deep drifts were reported down into Manchester; this despite there being only 6 inches of lying snow.

Countrywide coal was beginning to freeze together in the yards, making it hard to transport, and ships were icing up in a way most people had never witnessed before. A ship pulling into Liverpool on 8 February had every square inch covered in a vast case of ice, and its decks deep in snow. The *Peveril*, a ship travelling up the Humber from Copenhagen, was likewise coated in ice and snow. It drew a great crowd of fascinated observers, who marvelled at this bewitching sight as the vessel pulled into port. The cold across lowland Britain was reaching severe levels both day and night, and on 8 February Rutland in Northamptonshire recorded '35 degrees of frost', or -20 °C.

Meanwhile, in London, by 8 February the Thames was no longer navigable, being frozen right across at Blackfriars and the brand-new Tower Bridge. All canal traffic had now been at a standstill for some time, and numerous ships had fallen victim to the gales and blizzards that seemed to rage endlessly from the east. The Medway was completely frozen over at Rochester and, for the first time in living memory, icebergs were floating down from the North Sea and on to the east coast. Extraordinary sights became commonplace. In London, the frozen River Thames saw thousands of gulls touch down on pack ice that flowed not only upriver with the tide but also out to sea. As the flocks of gulls nested on the ice, they were taken on a leisurely journey down towards Dartford where they would feast on the fish that could not be caught by the iced-up fleets; all this without so much as the flap of a wing.

Scotland, like much of England, found itself almost cut off from the outside world during the storms of 7 February and most rail lines were either impassable or required significant work to unblock them. The Isle of Man was also badly hit, and many ships had to shelter there from the storms and blizzards ravaging the Irish Sea. Snow was so deep in Douglas that many householders had to be dug out of their homes. Bread and supplies were taken to those trapped but supplies of coal in particular soon became sparse. At the port of Ramsey, a schooner, *Margaret and Elizabeth*, was grounded by the great blizzard. It was some time before it was even seen due to the blinding snow and darkness. The lifeboat was brought out for launch at 8 p.m. but it proved impossible to get into the sea until, at 3 a.m., a further attempt was made. Once again, this proved impossible, just as flares, illuminated out to sea, clearly showed the vessel had not yet broken up and its crew were alive.

By Thursday morning, it was assumed the crew would be dead from exposure, and the schooner destroyed. Miraculously, however, dawn showed that both had prevailed. A huge crowd gathered on the beach and pier, as the cries of the crew could now be heard from the shore. In desperation volunteers helped carry the boat over snowdrifts to be launched off a low part of the pier from where it was dropped. Part of the front cladding of the boat was torn off as it hit the still raging waves below, and the lifeboat was thrown about mercilessly but the fearless crew were soon upon the listing vessel, now on its last legs. Much to the huge relief and great applause of the crowd, all were brought ashore alive and taken to safety.

Where once news from across the Atlantic would have taken nearly a month (the assassination of Lincoln took that long to reach London in 1865), telegraph communications soon brought news that Britain was not alone in the freeze. Across the northern hemisphere, the cold spell was of an unusually extreme nature. The north-east of the USA, the Midwest and all of Canada were gripped by unprecedented and widespread severe cold. Reports were also coming in from across Europe of a worsening situation.

In the Netherlands, all vessels going in and out of the Rhine estuary were trapped in a thick layer of ice. In Antwerp, and with no known precedent, the River Schelde was deeply frozen. With daytime temperatures as low as -15 °C, there was little hope of any improvement in the foreseeable future. The Rhine was also frozen throughout much of Germany and the freeze spread right down to the Mediterranean coasts of France and Spain and as far south as central Italy. The coastal town of Ancona, for example, was reportedly cut off numerous times from the outside world in February by deep snow in an area where sleet is rare. Many Adriatic towns experienced blizzards, freezing rain and gales for days on end. In Vienna the deep snow may not have been unusual, but the temperatures were brutal.

On the morning of 7 February, the Viennese awoke to -32.8 °C, and in other parts of the country even lower temperatures were recorded on the same day. On 8 February the maximum temperature in London failed to rise above -6 °C, and at Manchester the temperature did not rise above -5 °C after a low of -7 °C.

Despite much of the industrialised world being hit by this extraordinary freeze, the paralysis of Britain's ports and manufacturing sites had a far greater impact on the UK than on its two great industrial rivals, the USA and Germany. Industry was in decline in Britain and had been since about 1890. Although the first to industrialise, manufacturing output was hampered by a failure to modernise factories and technologies in most production methods; as its rivals sailed past Britain economically, the message concerning the need for new investment failed to hit home and the decline hastened. The challenging winter of 1895 provided a unique window on the country's economic vulnerability. German steel output was double that of the UK by 1890, and threats to Britain's colonies abroad were leading us towards war in South Africa. A long period of isolation also meant the country had few close political or industrial allies, making it even more vulnerable. However, Britain was not only weakening economically; its workers were in fact growing weaker and less productive as poor social conditions, poor wages and disease, along with successive governments' reluctance to tackle malnutrition, took their toll. As our competitors' wages and standard of living improved, so those of Britain's workers stagnated or even dropped. It took a shocking discovery in 1899, when the Boer War broke out, to begin to change attitudes. The majority of ordinary soldiers applying for service proved unfit. Poor diet, lack of basic sanitation and lack of any education meant that Britain could not raise the armies it needed to protect the Empire, and for the first time, significant social investigation uncovered the scale of these issues. Social deprivation began to be viewed as a cost and an economic weakness rather than an inevitable side-effect of rapid urbanisation.

Nevertheless, it was primarily the chronic lack of technological innovation that really held back growth. In 1880, Britain had a 22 per cent share of global industrial production. By 1890, this had fallen to 18 per cent, and by 1913 it was 12 per cent. German production grew from 10 to 12 per cent over the first decade and overtook Britain's share in 1913, reaching 14 per cent. The USA, however, provided the economic miracle of the age. In 1880, its output was only 14 per cent, but by 1890 this had grown to 23 per cent and by 1913 to 33 per cent. The winter of 1895 damaged the UK economy more than it did those of Germany and the US, and certainly contributed to the realisation that we needed to modernise to keep up.

On Friday 8 February, a record -27.2 °C was recorded at Braemar; that same night, -22 °C was recorded in Glasgow, -20 °C in York, -18 °C in Gloucester and -19 °C in Maidstone, where the Medway was frozen over completely. The weekend of 9–10 February saw the low temperatures continue, as did the gales. A number of ships went down, most notably the *Nelson Rice* off the Isle of Man, killing twelve.

The following week saw little material change, and in the south-east temperatures widely remained below zero by day and -10 °C at night. In London, reports from the main harbour, the London pool, were grim. The ice, 6–7 feet thick in places, wrecked many barges, some of which were torn from their moorings and followed the tidal ice flows out to sea. The river remained unnavigable. At Kingston, the ice was reported to be a foot thick. Here, people skated all week and an ox was roasted outside a booth on the river while an ice fair was set up, recalling the great Dickensian central London frost fairs of the Little Ice Age. Loch Lomond was reportedly frozen right across, with night temperatures in the Highlands widely below -20 °C. A number of skaters ventured out to the centre – some considerable distance – but the ice was not thick enough here and quickly cracked, plunging several of the skaters into the freezing water. Three were saved, but one young man drowned in the ice-cold Loch.

On 14 February the docks at Dover were entirely frozen over, and along the south coast fish began to wash up frozen to death, a sight that apparently had never been seen before. The docks at Chatham were also frozen, and all work ceased there, with the sea off Whitstable and Herne Bay frozen out as far as the eye could see. The garrison at Chatham even had to change its sentry rules because the temperatures were so low. Sentries were changed each hour instead of at dawn, to save any of the soldiers suffering frostbite. Despite the best efforts of local charities and poor houses, many elderly people were freezing to death in their homes, as evidenced by the death of a widow found completely frozen at home in the centre of Chatham.

By this time the Kattegat in Denmark, the nation's main approach by sea, was navigable only by the largest steamers and the North Sea remained deadly for shipping. One large German vessel that went down off Lowestoft had taken many lives and, such was the shock over the loss, an enquiry was undertaken in the German parliament to try to avoid a similar disaster in future. That week fresh blizzards swept through North Wales and much of the north-west, the region hit hardest by this winter overall, and thousands were left trapped without food and fuel for days.

Finally, on the weekend of 16 February the first break in the freeze began. It was not on a blast of Atlantic warmth, however. The vast anticyclone now sitting over the Nordic countries began to sink southwards, pushing the very cold air towards the Mediterranean. Sunny skies and milder weather came, but there was no end to night-time frosts. Nevertheless, 3 °C at Kew in London was reached on 16 February and readings crept up for a few days thereafter. By 20 February 8 °C or 9 °C was experienced across the south, and it was felt the worst was over. Scotland by then actually sat in even warmer air, and here the snow began to thaw everywhere except in the Highlands.

Of course, this was not the end of the cold. Next the high pressure moved westwards, sitting in the position it had taken at New Year, and the bitter air sitting to the north plunged back down the eastern side of Britain, bringing fresh snow and gales. Soon much of the country was back to square one, and 26 February saw yet another very cold pool push west from Scandinavia, covering most of the south in deep, drifting snow. This familiar pattern lasted for several days, and after nearly two months of bitter cold it must have felt like winter would never end.

It was not until the second week in March that milder weather finally spread across all of Britain, and winter was truly over. Luckily, with dry weather and clear skies continuing, no great floods were experienced and the vast drifts eventually declined in the increasing warmth of the daytime. Despite the snow, February was in fact a very dry month. The long-term rainfall record puts the total figure at only 11 millimetres, although this would have varied enormously from place to place.

Most notable is the period from 4–17 of February, which was one of the most intense spells of cold measured in Britain. Oxford, for example, recorded its lowest average minimum temperature of -5.6 °C, far colder than that of January 1963.

In the Central England Temperature (CET) averages, February 1895 ranks overall as the second-coldest February after 1947, and is the eighth-coldest month since 1659. However, in overall winter terms this extreme cold becomes less obvious. January 1895, averaging 0.2 °C, ranks as only the twenty-sixth-coldest month because of the mild period in the middle. The mild December of 1894 further obscures the severe nature of the winter overall, which ranks as only the sixteenth-coldest winter in the CET at 1.18 °C. January and February combined, however, give an average of -0.8 °C and this is among the top five coldest two-month periods the country has experienced since 1659.

4

The Severe and Snowy Winter of 1947

Apart from a couple of cold snaps in December and early January, there was no foretaste of the severe weather to come in the early winter of 1946/47. January opened wet and mild, and after a couple of days of cold with a little sleet and snow, some exceptionally mild weather pushed temperatures as high as 14 °C in southern England. There was no sign at that stage of any cold weather or even frost to come, and perhaps most people felt confident that, after so many mild weeks, the weather would stay benign and in the bounds of a normal winter.

As it turned out, 1947 was anything but normal weather-wise. It was a year of extremes; first came the cold and snow, then countrywide floods and then a strikingly hot and dry summer. Blocking anticyclones were not uncommon during the 1940s, and research has indicated that shifting tropical winds and other, cyclical phenomena may have disrupted the Gulf Stream, causing it to slow down during the 1940s, resulting in a somewhat 'continental' decade of weather. Whatever the cause, snow fell every day at some location in the UK for eight weeks, and long spells of sub-zero temperatures, severe snowstorms, transport dislocation, glaze and food and fuel deprivation all characterised one of the most severe winter events of the last 300 years.

As high pressure across the east and north of Europe merged and moved north, by 23 January cloud and strong winds from the east, as well as progressively lower temperatures, moved across the country. Snow showers began to feed in from the coastal strip late on the 22nd, and by the end of the 23rd there was a covering of snow in many eastern counties, from Kent to Northumberland. Temperatures fell quite sharply but persistent cloud cover meant record low temperatures were not experienced at that stage. The papers on 24 January noted that the Air Ministry was concerned that the severe spell, already affecting the Continent for some days, would become quite entrenched. They were right. Temperatures continued to fall, and by the 29th snow had reached the Scilly Isles, and almost the entire UK was seeing drifts deep enough to stop up most roads and railways. Under grey skies, it was commented that Britain felt and looked very much like the arctic.

In the cold winters of 1979 and 1963, there had been one particular blizzard that became synonymous with the beginning of an exceptional spell, particularly in the minds of those that lived through it. In 1947, for many this was the two-day blizzard that swept the south and the Midlands on 28–29 January. While from 23 to 26 January the east and south-east of England had been most affected by snow, this new storm buried much of the nation and left huge drifts that in places did not vanish until March. Eighteen hours of continuous snow battered the south, the Midlands and parts of the north, affecting cities such as London, Bristol, Leeds, Manchester and Sheffield. Scotland and the northernmost English counties were spared on this occasion. London saw maxima no higher than -5 °C on 28 January, and Lympne and Maidstone in Kent reported -12 °C during the late afternoon – exceptional cold under clear skies but unheard of under cloud. The run of sub-zero temperatures continued unbroken in much of England from 23 January until 1 February.

Unusual weather from across Europe was widely reported as the disrupted weather pattern played out further east and south. Belgrade reported yellow snow from sand brought up on southerly winds from Africa, floods killed an unknown number in eastern Turkey and the

German government reported that thirty-seven people had been frozen to death in Hamburg alone since the cold weather began. In Belgium, the sea was frozen solid at Knokke and right along the coastline out to sea for miles, and port traffic there was paralysed for the first time since 1895, as were canal and maritime traffic in most of Europe.

On 30 January the snow moved west, and for the first time seriously affected daily life in the south-west and Wales. The Scilly Isles endured 'seven degrees of frost' (-4 °C) and their worst snowfall for forty-five years. The freeze also took hold in the normally mild counties of Devon and Cornwall, with the low temperatures proving exceptional. At -5 °C Newquay had its coldest night in fifty-four years, and at -4 °C it was seventy-seven years since Falmouth had been so cold. The River Exe froze over at Exmouth, and Exeter and the higher areas inland were deep in snow, with drifts isolating communities across the region. Demand for electricity rose to record levels, and a shortage of coal was becoming more serious by the day as the railway system was now totally disrupted.

On the same day as the snow reached the west, the Electricity Board stated that the demand for power was too great. They gravely announced that power cuts across key cities would take place between 7 a.m. and 7 p.m. 'unless there is the strictest economy by consumers'. Up to 25 per cent of the country's supply would be cut. Blackouts had begun the previous night in south-east England, where it was reported 'many homes were without heat, light or the means to cook a meal, and in whole districts streets were in darkness'. Cuts of 15 per cent were expected in the south-west, and this was to spread across much of the country.

The London rush hour that Wednesday, 30 January, was described as chaotic; hundreds of trains were cancelled, many trapped by frozen points, and buses were getting stuck on even modest inclines across the city. And yet, people I have spoken to about that winter say the 'wartime' spirit returned to the country in those bleak days, along with a certain sense of pride. 'If Hitler could not defeat us,' one of my relations told me, 'we certainly weren't going to let the weather get the better of us.' Just as well, really, because worse was yet to come.

In fact, on 1 February the temperature in London actually rose above freezing for the first time in many days; pipes began to burst – the usual sign of a thaw up until recent times – and roads in Kent from London to Sevenoaks and Maidstone had 'single-lane traffic, passing through adequately'. Rail too began to get back to normal; coal supplies got through, and rain fell at a number of locations. Nevertheless, the Air Ministry warned the country that it was temporary. They were right again.

Snow returned with a vengeance on 2 February and from then fell daily somewhere in the UK for the rest of the month. At Croydon, 15 centimetres lay that morning, with Waddington in the east measuring 30 centimetres. Manchester had 8 centimetres, while to the west Bristol had 10 centimetres. Much of Scotland was badly affected for the first time, with up to 20 centimetres in places. On 4 February, a period of 100 hours of sub-zero temperatures began in England, and the strong easterly winds piled snow up to 'the eaves above the upper windows' of many houses. The worst snowfall so far was seen on 4 February to the north of Britain. This delivered 14-foot drifts in Derbyshire and widely across the north-west, where drifting snow ensured all forms of transport halted.

Another brief thaw on the 8 February saw 4 °C reported in London, and the forecast was for a slight thaw to continue across much of the UK. While this helped clear roads and railways, it again did nothing to shift the huge drifts outside of the big cities, and the RAF was still liberating people on a daily basis trapped in isolated areas, sometimes in desperate circumstances. The thaw lasted forty-eight hours. From 11 to 23 February, the most severe part of the winter began and a twelve-day period of sub-zero temperatures and regular snowfalls buried most parts of Britain in a deep blanket of snow. Even more trying for ordinary people was the lack of sun. Up until 23 February, some places saw no sun all month. Kew saw twenty-one consecutive days during which only one solitary minute of sunshine was measured. With fresh food in short supply, and given that rationing and limited access to basic ingredients already made for pitiful supplies, housewives were 'forced to be ever-more imaginative when trying to feed their cold and hungry broods'.

As the paralysis now became national, the coal crisis shot to the top of the political agenda. Not surprisingly, a debate was now raging on the need for development of nuclear power. At the time, many politicians and scientists doubted it could be initiated quickly or easily, particularly since the international community was unclear on how to proceed with the technology itself and how it should be shared, especially with Russia. What was very apparent, however, was that nuclear fuel would reduce the dependence on coal for power, a fact that was seriously impacting industrial production at a critical time. A total of 1.9 million people were laid off because the coal crisis was limiting industrial activity in every sector. On 24 February, gas supplies failed just as fresh blizzards struck the north and east, renewing the pattern of paralysis, slow recovery, then paralysis again.

People from all backgrounds were generally in a position now where they could only heat one room as it was; bedrooms were often below freezing, and water jugs and liquids would freeze solid overnight. People soldiered through, but such conditions were hazardous for young children. Many babies, as well as elderly people, were lost.

On the lighter side, just as in 1963, the length of the cold spell now offered a wide range of winter sports every weekend. Skating on natural ice is a great pleasure, and skiing, though not as fashionable then as it is now, was being widely practiced by those near enough, or with transport, to the right terrain. The Lake District offered magical scenes for those in the north-west that could get there, and the landscapes across the country presented fantastic beauty. The sun had shone brightly on 23 February for the first time all month, and, although cold, the lack of driving snow coaxed people out and about to enjoy the snow. The clear skies brought low temperatures, with -22 °C recorded in Scotland that night; traffic and transport were still in a severe state of dislocation, and no end was in sight after exactly four weeks of the freeze.

Winds turned westerly on 26 and 27 February as an Atlantic front crossed the country. It primarily affected the north and Scotland with heavy snow, but it also brought the highest temperatures of the month; 4 °C was quite widely reached across southern England and the Midlands, causing a gradual thaw. In Manchester the deep snow also began to thaw, but within twenty-four hours it was below freezing again and the thaw had ended, having had no material impact on the overall transport and coal crises. Scotland and England from Yorkshire northwards continued to be affected by snowfall in the last five days of the month, but there were slight improvements in the south of England and Wales.

Although 1 March was still bitterly cold, the day dawned under stunning blue skies and brilliant sunshine; the first day of meteorological spring seemed to at least bode well for calmer weather. However, the clear skies brought low minima. A bitter -18 °C was measured in Sussex, and -10 °C was reported over a wide area of the UK. Freezing fog began to affect many areas, and it became clear that winter was not going to give in easily to spring.

On 4 March, there were signs of a change. Temperatures lifted in the south as a low-pressure system nudged up from the Continent and rain and sleet fell in some areas, hinting at a mild Atlantic assault. This was reinforced when a second low looked as if it would follow a more northerly track and bring about a general thaw. What followed was another blizzard, this one so severe it 'cut the country in two', with England inaccessible from Scotland and vice versa. From Yorkshire down to London and across to Devon, the entire country ground to a halt. Wales, too, saw many trains buried, communities isolated for days and all roads impassable. Drifts reached 30 feet on high ground from the West Country to Yorkshire. In the Cotswolds, entire trees, farm buildings and houses almost vanished completely; the Midlands was equally bad, and no road north to south or vice versa could be passed. Collieries again ground to a halt, stopping production of coal in many key pits, and no trains could transport what there was. The effect on livestock was terrible; the lambing season had begun, and there was no way to help the ewes, or indeed the millions of cattle stranded or already dead throughout the countryside. It is estimated that more than 4.1 million sheep died, and 30,000 cattle were lost. Interestingly, lots of animals did manage to survive because of the depths of the drifts; many lambing ewes that became engulfed were quite protected in small caves, and gave birth successfully. Farmers were able to pick them out through darker patches in the snow above, caused by their warmth and breath.

The next depression tracked slightly further north, and the south was first plastered by heavy snow, but this soon turned to rain and for the first time temperatures rose substantially. Nevertheless, this rain all fell as snow in southern Scotland, which saw its worst blizzard of the winter. However, it became immediately apparent by 11 March that, with such huge volumes of snow, the rapid thaw and torrential rain were going to cause flooding. Sure enough, as the sudden thaw reached Northamptonshire and pushed on north, the River Trent led hundreds of rivers in quickly bursting its banks. Railways and roads were cleared of snow, only to become submerged underwater. The dramatic floods swept north and soon created another national crisis.

With the freeze gone, calculating its cost proved tricky; precise figures were hard to accurately calculate in terms of lost production, because the country was in such a weak economic state. However, the decimation of livestock and the human cost in terms of suffering and deprivation were extremely severe, and this is worth considering. In today's world, would we cope better in such an event? Most likely we would, but only careful planning and recognition from consumers, commuters, motorists and air travellers alike that severe weather can scupper the best-laid plans will really enable us to learn how to manage a changing and erratic climate.

5

The Record-Breaking Winter of 1962/63

Not since 1740 has a winter comparable in length and severity to that of 1962/63 been experienced in the UK, and, since 1659, only the winters of 1739/40 and 1683/84 were colder. In the twentieth century, although 1947 was a very severe winter and certainly had more snow, the bitter weather only began late in January and it was not as cold. This severe winter left the nation feeling traumatised and exhausted, and convinced several experienced climatologists that the climate was taking its first steps towards a new ice age.

In all, 120 people died as a direct result of the cold[7] and half the bird population perished; £150 million in industrial production was lost; many schools in England closed from Christmas time until February; and power failed time after time across all areas. There were also a lot of strikes and industrial disputes by key workers, which added to the difficulties faced by everyone in the country.

Most severe winters have been pre-empted by cold weather in November (though cold winters don't necessarily follow cold Novembers), and 1962 is a good example of this. Some severe weather struck the country quite suddenly from mid-month. While it was Scotland and the north that bore the brunt of the cold weather, snow fell across much of England and Wales as well. On 18 November, snow fell heavily across much of Scotland and a good part of the north, and in particular across north-west England. Traffic and shipping were badly hampered as the powerful northerly blast spread south, with heavy snow and gales focused largely on the west. With pressure high to the west of the UK, initially the east remained more sheltered from the strong northerly airstream. To the west, a mail train got stuck in drifts at Castleton in Roxburghshire, an Admiralty tanker grounded on the Devon coast and two climbers on Snowdonia, caught by the blizzard, died on the mountain. The A66 was closed, and many roads in the Lake District were blocked all day before the snowploughs liberated them. On 19–20 November the cold moved east; snow fell in Kent and even London before the temperature rose. Though not exceptional as a cold spell, it was a telling prelude of what was to come.

At the beginning of December, pressure rose sharply in northern Europe and high pressure centred over the UK. The result was some very cold, clear nights. Less welcome was the fog that accompanied the cold and which, in London, led to the last truly lethal smog of the century. Thick fog became widespread by 5 December and temperatures stayed below freezing in London. However, at Folkestone on the south Kent coast, 11 °C was reached under clear blue skies and these enormous variations in daytime maxima continued for days. On 5 December London only reached -2 °C in the dense fog, but the coasts of the south were described as 'spring-like' by the papers. Inland, the fog was so dense it brought about accident and injury. In Bradford, fog was blamed when a car ploughed into a bus queue and injured thirteen people. Disruption to traffic and train travel was reported from the foggy areas.

Nowhere else, however, would have to face the problems London was about to face. The fog quickly combined with dense industrial particulate matter circulating in the light winds. This proved hard to budge, especially as the low temperatures created an inversion; this means that the cold air and smog sank below a layer of warmer air above, and became trapped at ground level. As the weak December sun could not reach through this toxic mix and burn it off, the fog stayed all day.

This intense particulate smog proved deadly. Those prone to chest, lung and heart problems suddenly saw a vastly increased chance of severe breathing problems, in many cases serious enough to be fatal. This was starkly demonstrated by the deaths of sixty people in London on just one day, 6 December, as a direct result of the smog. I have heard friends and relatives describe these smogs as rather eerie and as having a foul odour. A thick brown haze dirtied windows and would slowly creep through cracks and under doors and hang like an unwelcome visitor in people's front rooms. Despite the Clean Air Act of 1956, air pollution had increased fourteen times above average during the smog, a level that was agreed to be intolerable. Swift action was needed to ensure far better air quality in the capital. Industrial production was stopped in many areas in and around London, and workers were sent home early in the day lest they get stranded. Deliveries were also stopped. Whether this contributed to an improvement in air quality is unclear, but on 7 December the smog thinned, and on the 8th the weather changed abruptly to an Atlantic pattern. Any frost and fog were quickly swept away on westerly winds.

There was mild and wet weather for much of the next two weeks, apart from some sleet and snow on the 12th. With 13 °C reached in Sevenoaks on 15 December, the mild Atlantic continued to dominate. (Much the same pattern of weather was in evidence in December 1978, when a strong anticyclone gave way to mild weather that preceded the most intense cold.) High pressure had begun to build rapidly to the north and east of Europe just after mid-month, and this spread gradually south and west. The influence of this anticyclone reached the east on the 23rd with a big drop in temperature in London, from 6 °C on the 23rd to a frosty maximum of 0 °C on Christmas Eve. This was the beginning of a nine-week freeze that was to leave the country reeling.

For the second Christmas in a row, the south of England experienced an ice day, with maxima at or below freezing. At first the anticyclone covered all of the UK until, on Christmas Day, pressure dropped to the north as a low frontal band began to slide southwards down around the western base of the high. The polar maritime air mass established over Scotland was at first mild enough to produce rain but as it slipped south it met the continental cold and turned to sleet and snow. Snow fell on Glasgow, giving it its first white Christmas since 1938. The continental air dug in further south, stalling the front, which moved increasingly slowly. Across the north of England, the precipitation fell as heavy snow, giving significant accumulations and leaving behind very icy roads.

On Boxing Day, it was only -3 °C at noon in central London. Skaters enjoyed the ice on Hampstead Heath, theatregoers went to pantomime matinees and many took their constitutional post-Christmas walks while large crowds braved the cold and cloudy weather to see the Formula Junior cars compete at Brands Hatch in Kent. Light snow gradually spread across the Home Counties and south into London in the early afternoon. The snow settled immediately on the deep frozen and frosty ground. Those leaving cinemas and theatres in London that evening were surprised to see a covering of snow on their cars, and the snow intensified as the front stalled over the south-east. A maritime air mass had raised temperatures in Scotland after the snow, but pressure thereafter rose spectacularly across much of the northern hemisphere. An intense anticyclone spread south from Greenland, turning the north of the UK very cold again. Low pressure across northern France brought a virtual halt to the snow across south-east of England and people were surprised to wake to see the heavy and continuous snow still falling on the 27th. Roads were now swamped with deep snow, and the snowfall continued all day long. Snow now covered much of the country, and the resulting poor visibility was blamed for a massive train crash just north of Crewe that killed eighteen people and injured at least fifty more.

By 28 December the full extent and impact of the snow was apparent. The Lake District was 3 inches deep in a snow blanket that extended all the way to the south coast. At that stage, the RAC reported treacherous icy roads and dense fog, as well as snow in most areas, and Birmingham and Manchester airports were shut briefly on Boxing Day. The papers stated that temperatures had risen slightly after the snow, which meant pipes across the northern counties began to burst and record demand meant power cuts in many areas. On a positive note, the RAC also pointed out that there was a big drop in road deaths that year – thirteen in 1962 compared to twenty-two in 1961 – because of the ice and snow restricting travel. At dawn on 28 December, rather remarkably, the snow band still lingered over the south.

Most southern counties were now under deep snow, often 2 feet deep. Worcester had a 6-inch fall on the 27th and winds were starting to pick up. Kent and Surrey were widely covered in 20 inches of snow, and drifts were piling up to 3 feet or more. Commuters attempted to get in to work in London for the first time since Christmas Eve and, on average, trains from Kent were three hours late. Other services from most areas were delayed, if they ran at all. Tunbridge Wells recorded over an inch of rainfall in the previous twenty-four hours, and the areas of deepest snow in Kent and Sussex measured depths of at least 28 inches. *The Times* showed the A25 near Westerham with cars stuck or abandoned in the deep drifts. During the day on 28 December the snow fizzled out. Thereafter things improved, if only gradually, and by the 29th the worst appeared to be over. Roads and railways began to be cleared, and slowly the situation eased. A BBC summary of the winter broadcast towards the end of the season described this as the 'fun part of the winter. It was the holidays and everyone was able to enjoy the Christmas snow.'

The freeze was widespread across Europe, and even the Mediterranean coast of Spain was not spared. Barcelona was cut off from the outside world for two days from 26 December by a huge fall of snow measuring 2 feet in places. It was the worst fall there since the 1860s, with emergency food supplies having to be flown in. By 29 December temperatures across even the far south of Europe were unusually low. The freeze was firmly entrenched and even the French Riviera barely climbed above freezing. The Netherlands, Belgium and Germany were all experiencing unusually severe conditions, with key waterways frozen over and snow blanketing most areas. In Brussels, as in London, this was the winter with by far the longest run (and total number) of snow-covered days since records began.

After a quieter spell of weather, a depression that had been deepening in the Bay of Biscay for a period of several days began pushing northwards. By 29 December it reached the south-west of Britain. Many forecasters thought this might bring a rapid thaw; however, it soon became apparent that the storm would not push far enough north for a thaw, and the cold air remained over all but the extreme south-west.

On the afternoon of 29 December, howling gale-force winds announced the arrival of this major winter storm. Lying snow was picked up and swirled around, reducing visibility to almost nil as soon as the storm hit. The blizzard conditions moved across the south that Saturday night and proved an impressive sight even in central London. It was hard to go out or even walk in these conditions, and a huge volume of snow fell.

Nevertheless, the south-west bore the brunt. Deep drifts, often more than 20 feet deep, cut off many towns and villages almost instantly, and the storm brought power lines and trees crashing down, cutting power and communications on a widespread scale. This blizzard cut off my mother's family at Bradford-upon-Avon in Wiltshire, and left them with drifts covering the roof of their freezing bungalow. My granddad had to cut a tunnel out from the kitchen door at the back of the house in order to come and go.

This situation lasted for weeks. London and the south-east saw much the same scenario, but the deep snows that had fallen unchecked since Christmas now meant that many places were no-go areas, and drifts over 20 feet high kept them unreachable. My parents, who had gone to spend New Year with my father's cousin and his family in Finchley in north London, ended up staying there for two weeks as the opportunities for travelling back to Cambridge, where my dad was studying, were nil. When they did return to Cambridge, such was the cold they were able to walk into town along the frozen River Cam. My dad clearly recalls seeing all the fish frozen solid in the ice below. The river did not thaw until the end of February, which is quite remarkable.

The morning of 31 December 1962 was perhaps the bleakest of the entire winter. Several people had died in their cars, notably an elderly couple that were stuck with their grandson and daughter in deep drifts. The younger pair were rescued, but passed a traumatic night before help came. Towns from North Devon, Somerset and Wiltshire, right across to Sussex, Kent and Surrey saw the pattern of normal life totally disrupted and they had to be sustained by airlift. Peaslake in Surrey, which is in a deep valley but not more than a few miles from Guildford, was unreachable by car or train from that weekend until 6 March. Remote spots in Dartmoor, Exmoor and the Salisbury Plain were similarly isolated. Following the 30 December snowfall a busload of seventy-one passengers from Evershot in Dorset had to be rescued by helicopter, along with other stranded motorists from a roadside café in Devon. Okehampton, Tiverton and other Devon towns were among numerous communities where people had to be airlifted to safety, and the Ghurkhas and other troops saved many people trapped in vehicles and in need of medical help.

Troops had to be used to clear deep drifts to liberate military and civilian infrastructure in Kent as the heavy snow moved northwards. In Sunderland the star and co-star of a Newcastle performance of

Cinderella disappeared on the way home and were found unconscious but alive under drifts in their car on the A68 at Jedburgh.

Since 1963 this level of national paralysis has not been repeated in the UK. As the New Year of 1963 dawned, a feeling of helplessness was offset by a gritty determination to 'carry on'. The wartime spirit returned to a degree, and many individuals and organisations went to great lengths to keep the country going. However, some saw the disruption as an opportunity; industrial strife suddenly increased in key services, ending in power cuts for many parts of Britain.

Meanwhile, in agricultural terms, farmers were realising that the deep freeze threatened many vegetable crops. For example, in East Anglia the cold had frozen the entire celery crop, and the quality of what remained was far from assured after a thaw. The head of the National Federation of Fruit and Potato Traders made a statement warning that supplies of cauliflowers, sprouts and carrots would be short in the coming days, and prices of all other fruit and vegetables would rise.

The depression that buried so much of the south brought with it some warmer air at higher levels on 30 and 31 December, but temperatures on the ground stayed at or around freezing. This resulted in sleet, hail, further snow and freezing rain. The freezing rain and drizzle caused less disruption than it would otherwise have done, as it fell on snowy or already icy roads, and many people were choosing not to travel unnecessarily. For a time, it looked like this warmer air would gain ground. Rain did begin to fall in the far south-west, but the expected thaw failed to show up anywhere else. The cold air then pushed back; by 2 January the south-east and London were well below freezing again, the deep snow remained and sleet and further snowfalls added to the gloom. At midday, freezing drizzle was falling at -2 °C in central London, icing over streets, cars and vegetation. Heavy falls of snow also reappeared from Kent across to Hampshire and Dorset in showers, driven on an unstable easterly airstream later that day. Strong winds once again set in along the channel coast, and the police at Folkestone were quoted as saying, 'The snow is blowing in the wind and drifting; it looks like we are in for more trouble.'

Conversely the north of England saw the overall situation ease slightly. Supplies were getting through to moorland villages by helicopter, and many of the main roads began to reopen. Nevertheless, anywhere above several hundred metres was a lost cause, as snowploughs were failing to cope at higher altitudes; the snow and strong winds were just too much.

Sport took a massive battering. In the two weeks after Christmas, few matches of any kind took place. Where they did, conditions were terrible; the ground remained deep frozen underfoot even where snow had been cleared. Thousands of miles away, however, in the heat of an Australian summer, Yorkshire fast bowler Fred Truman was enthralling crowds in Melbourne at the second Test. England were poised to deliver a celebrated win over Australia; it was a welcome distraction and a glimmer of warmth for an embattled nation.

That same week, the renowned climatologist Professor Gordon Manley made a press statement that conditions were the worst since the blizzard of January 1881. He added that the unusual longevity of the cold could make the overall event more severe than 1881 because February that year was not a cold month. If the cold continued into a second month of 1963, records would fall. On a positive note, however, the following weekend saw a slight rise in temperatures, especially to the north. Nevertheless, the snow remained deep on the ground, thawing only slightly in places by day.

The second week of January saw the three largest unions backing a strike by power supply workers. Their complex demands were closely linked to demands and settlements of other industrial disputes and wage patterns of the time. The severe cold had become an invaluable bargaining tool. Unions were so powerful in the 1960s and 1970s that Britain's economy was often vulnerable to large-scale industrial disruption. Allowing industrial and domestic supplies to fail was seemingly not an issue for them, and the unions refused arbitration. From the weekend of 5 January, official and unofficial strikes burgeoned, cutting power across the country. A new-born baby froze to death during one of these power cuts in a hospital in Essex, and the harrowing details of this and other horror stories were splashed over the papers the following week. The physical distress to ordinary people was reported to be terrible; many people used bar heaters and electric fires as their only source of domestic heating, which normally extended to a single room. Central heating was still considered rather exotic. Those who used coal as an alternative heat source found supplies were dwindling fast. When they did arrive by train, the stacks were frozen solid and had to be hacked apart before the coal could be sold. The negative publicity and public anger over the increasing death toll from power cuts meant that by 11 January, with a work-to-rule still in effect, the main union voted for arbitration. Nevertheless, the entire country still experienced power failures due to ongoing action, and more lives were lost.

The cold continued unbroken into the second weekend of the year, with only cricket occupying the sporting pages of the papers. Just a handful of football fixtures were played, and the pools panel sat again. Surprisingly, the Five Nations England *v.* Wales rugby fixture at Cardiff took place on a well-cleared pitch. England won fairly convincingly, with a final score of 13-6, in a biting and 'frequently straw-laden' wind as farm debris left behind by farm vehicles drafted in to clear the pitch circulated round the stadium.

The Scandinavian high went from strength to strength over the following weeks, only losing its grip on a couple of occasions. At these times, temperatures clambered reluctantly to just above freezing in the snow-laden south. Scotland and the north, closer to the high pressure, saw slightly less cold temperatures and snow than the south. Nevertheless January saw little material change in conditions across Britain. Snow fell on occasion in most areas, but many people remember how clear and sunny the winter of 1963 was – in stark contrast to 1947, where there was very little sun at all. Apart from fog, which appeared quite often in freezing form, dazzlingly sunny days and stunning Christmas-card scenes dominated over gloomy grey skies.

Unsurprisingly, wildlife of all kinds suffered. At a moorland cafe in Cumbria, bands of starving sheep began circling around the car park and cafe, desperate for food. Although many lorry drivers fed them, the café owners tried to drive them away, as they were becoming a hazard. The RSPCA complained, however, and in response the owners suggested the RAC use their markings to find the owner of the sheep and take control. Members of the public did their best to look after local birds by breaking ice and laying out food. However, the toll on the avian population in Britain – as in much of northern Europe – was immense. It took many years for some species to recover, and it is estimated that 50 per cent of all birds in the UK perished.[8] Some species, however, flourished by feeding off the carcasses of other birds. Less aggressive species were almost wiped out; wrens suffered such a fate, only to come back during the sixties and subsequently become Britain's most common bird.[9] Many experts believe these natural events, although devastating in the short term, can actually help many species adapt and become stronger. Any early lambing was a disaster, though, with vast numbers perishing in the drifts, especially in the more remote locations.

The sea was frozen along much of the south coast, and a 'polar slush' was evident for several miles out into the English Channel. The Thames froze up to Kingston and, although some major rivers were kept open, the canal network froze over pretty much in its entirety. While frozen ponds and lakes were bad for wildlife, they were good for skaters, and people took the opportunity to skate wherever they could.

The normally lush, green landscape took on alpine characteristics and dangers. Walls of drifted snow 5 feet high lined the roads in the north and south of the country, and on the weekend of 21 January an avalanche killed two walkers in the Chew valley near Oldham. A third missed death by inches and raised the alarm.

That same day, 21 January, while Gatwick had to close again because of ice on the runway, the RAF undertook its biggest ever peacetime evacuation, from the government's Fylingdales installation high in the north Yorkshire moors, where nearly 300 staff had been stranded for weeks.

This rescue took place on the same day that a test of the state of the roads at either end of the country was reported in the media. From Manchester, then a 35-mile drive, 5-foot drifts, trapped snowploughs and high winds caused huge delays. The journey took six hours and one main route, the A616, was totally blocked, leaving the A6209 as the only available road to Sheffield. Some main roads had been cleared from London to Brighton, but others were far from clear and many were treacherous. Perhaps the state of the key routes in the south was better than many imagined, because the high streets were deserted and the roads clear; on days such as this, when no substantial snow fell, travelling was easier. However, everywhere above 150 metres saw vast drifts hold fast and it was possible to see the layers of each snowfall where diggers had cut through them.

As January wore on the freeze continued, and the prospect of the slight thaw that had set in on 20 January becoming widespread quickly disappeared. The cold air once again pushed back across all of Britain. A largely sunny regime became established but it was interrupted by occasional snowfalls. With these came continuing disruption to travel and transport, and both the press and the public began to get very agitated about Britain's continued inefficiency at snow clearance. Rural communities stayed cut off, and the impact on livestock worsened. Sheep, ponies and other livestock continued to perish in the deep drifts and biting winds. After long periods of starvation, many animals still died when food reached them because their digestive systems had shrunk and could not hold any food down.

The sea continued to freeze in many places; early February saw the sea frozen as far as the eye could see at Whitstable and along the north Kent coast. Pancake ice floes appeared in the Mersey for the first time since 1895, and pack ice congested the Solent and the Channel. The sea was even frozen a hundred yards off shore at Eastbourne and in places up and down the southern English and Welsh coasts.

Late January was quite dry and the snow gradually diminished in many areas. By the first week of February, it seemed that the worst was over. However, just as people dared to think a change had come, from 3 February the south, east and west of England, South and Mid Wales, and much of Scotland were all affected by falls as great as, if not greater than, those at New Year. Cornwall and Pembroke were almost unreachable that weekend, and the RAC dubbed the day as 'snowplough Sunday'. Box Hill in Surrey and Wrotham Hill in Kent became ski slopes, and winter sports, especially skating, were now activities that could be undertaken in most areas. The emphasis of snow shifted on 6 February to northern England, where, for a time, severe blizzards cut England off completely from Scotland for the first time since 1947. At the same time, another temporary thaw produced severe flooding in the far south-west, most notably at Boscastle in Cornwall, where major flood alerts were raised.

By the following weekend, 10–11 February, a total of 420 football matches had been cancelled or postponed since December. Murrayfield's heated rugby pitch was cited as a possible solution to weather-related sports cancellations. However, the necessary investment of £7,000–£10,000 was beyond the means of most clubs back then. Only a thaw would bring a solution.

Then, on 14 February, a more widespread and meaningful thaw did spread in across Devon, Somerset and Cornwall, and flood plans had to be implemented there on a wider scale than in January. Fears of a repeat of 1947-style thaw floods were heightened, and the deep, drifted snow across much of the country certainly held great potential for serious flooding.

However, this concern proved unfounded. Once again, the thaw ended and colder weather spread back west accompanied by much snow. In Perth and Inverness, a fresh blizzard delivered 15-foot drifts that caused the worst disruption of the winter in eastern Scotland and left the area paralysed.

Just as many people thought the freeze would never end, the very first signs of a real change in the weather pattern emerged on 22 February. The anticyclone that for so long had sat to the north and east sank south-eastwards, and easterly winds veered southerly. Snow stopped falling, and brilliant sunny days brought slow daytime thaws in towns and cities. However, night time still saw the ice return. One family member, who was at school in Bromley at the time, summed up the end of the freeze nicely: 'The fields around the school turned into lakes of cold, dirty water and slush during the day in the bright sun, but froze overnight and would be covered in ice again each morning.' Huge drifts remained in upland areas and in the countryside, but most main roads were opened as the calmer weather became established. This cycle continued until March arrived. As the meteorological spring began, the sun continued thawing the snow and most towns and cities gradually became clear. Finally, on 5 March 1963, the first frost-free night since 22 December was recorded in Britain.

The general thaw and the bright sunny weather during the first weekend in March provoked a gigantic exodus to the coast, something comparable to a summer bank holiday. Roads around many of the south coast resorts jammed as families packed into the cafes and funfairs at their favourite spots and enjoyed their liberation from the confinement and gloom of nine weeks of snow and ice.

The conclusion of the winter was that Britain could do better. Nevertheless, a sense of proportion was urged in government and local authorities, given that this winter was so exceptional. Investment was soon made in snowploughs and better snow-clearing equipment; however, the papers were even more concerned that our power infrastructure needed to be dramatically improved. A range of agencies and charities clamoured for improvements in domestic heating. Storage heaters and affordable central heating would also reduce peak demand and consumer's bills. In fact, by the end of the 1960s, many of these improvements had been largely achieved, and the country was in a far better position to weather severe cold. Better insulation of pipes also became more common as the bitter experience of unlagged pipes bursting stayed fresh in people's minds.

After the long winter, it was also recommended that the third-rail system, while too expensive to replace all at once, should be phased out and replaced by the type of overhead lines that enable our colder European neighbours to keep trains moving through severe winters. Interestingly, with no comparable winter since, this change has not been effected. The issue of the third rail remains a thorn in many a rail commuters' (and rail operators') side, with only Eurostar and some inter-city and high-speed lines benefitting from overhead power. The 1960s saw a good deal of cold winter weather, and each winter had some severe spells, with only 1966/67 being mild. This helped improve snow clearance procedures and equipment. However, the 1970s were a mild decade, and all the lessons learned began to be forgotten. By the time the severe winter of 1978/79 came about, the infrastructure had again become outdated, and the same debates began all over again.

Across much of England, 1962/63 ranks as the snowiest winter on record. In Kent, Goudhurst recorded sixty-five days with lying snow against fifty-five in 1947, but in central London, Kew recorded fewer days than 1947, with forty-five against forty-seven. Birmingham had seventy-five such days in 1962/63 against forty-nine in 1947. Notably, however, Birmingham actually recorded an impressive sixty-two days in 1978/79, largely attributable to its relatively high elevation. Meanwhile, Hastings on the south coast recorded fifty-four such days in 1962/63 against only sixteen in 1947 and nineteen in 1979. Height clearly alters the situation, as shown by Buxton in the Peak District, which recorded seventy-one snow days in 1947, seventy-four in 1963 but eighty-two in 1979. Across the border in lowland Scotland this was an extremely dry winter, so much so that grass fires broke out in the Highlands in February and March. There was less snow generally than further south. At Edinburgh there were fifty-six days with lying snow in 1962/63, fifty-two in 1947 and thirty in 1979. However, the latter total was also recorded in 1986, 1955 and 1941, demonstrating that there are often substantive differences between British locations when it comes to snow. In fact, Braemar in the Highlands, Britain's coldest and snowiest spot, holds the country's record for snow days in a winter with a remarkable total of 107; but this was achieved in 1940/41, which was not comparably snowy across England.

January 1963 was the fifth-coldest January since 1659 at -2.1 °C; only 1795, 1684, 1740 and 1814 rank ahead of it. February was ranked seventh in the CET record. When all three months of the 1962/63 winter are combined, analysis shows this to be the coldest winter since 1740; only 1683/84 was colder still. The return period for such a winter now looks far longer than previously calculated because of the rapid warming we now face, so, to the joy of some and the chagrin of others, it may well be a very long time indeed before we experience a winter anything like as long and severe as that of 1963.

6

The Kent Miners' Blizzard, March 1970

Not for the first time, the Met Office got into trouble for failing to predict heavy rain or snow in March 1970. A polar low that crossed the UK on 4 March 1970 delivered a major, un-forecast blizzard to the Midlands and the south-east of England. This was one occasion when neither satellite imagery, computer data nor human instinct were able to predict an extremely severe snowfall event.

Predictions on the radio and in the papers that morning called for cold and bright conditions with the chance of light snow showers. In fact, that morning saw a deep depression over Scandinavia drag bitterly cold arctic air over the UK and much of northern Europe. The strong northerly airstream looked as if it would deliver dry weather, especially over areas sheltered from the north wind to the south. However, a small kink in the low pressure just south of Iceland was the telltale sign of what is termed a 'polar low' forming in the circulation. Given the strong northerly flow, all the indications pointed to the low dropping south across Ireland and into north-west France.

Sure enough, the polar low formed but pushed down in a south-easterly direction, clipping Northern Ireland and pushing into Wales and the Midlands early on 4 March. Snow began falling heavily across these areas, and in the morning it became apparent that something unusual was happening. The snow reached south-east England later in the morning. Heavy snow fell thickly in strong winds, reducing visibility to almost nil, and traffic became disrupted almost immediately. The unexpected blizzard caught police unawares and traffic chaos resulted. Police halted traffic from entering arterial routes, such as the M1 at Luton, because the strong winds and heavy snow were making the carriageways impossible to negotiate safely. The south ground to a stop.

As the afternoon wore on, the snow continued at full pelt, lasting twelve hours in most places. In the Midlands it was said that no snowfall had been so severe there since 1947. Birmingham, Luton and Stansted airports all succumbed to the blizzard and were closed. Heathrow was also closed for a time as crews battled against the elements. However, as was so often the case during events in the 1960s and 1970s, industrial action was a factor. On this day, firemen at Heathrow had decided to strike, and this meant even greater havoc. Most flights from the south-east were diverted to Manchester. It then proved impossible to move the diverted passengers back to London by road or rail because of the continuing snow and blocked roads. A total of 1,500 people had to be accommodated in hotels up to 50 miles out of the city.

Train delays averaged four hours into the capital, but two trains from Manchester took twelve hours to reach the centre of town. The snow intensified as it moved over Kent and Sussex, and by 2 p.m. the villages and towns on the east and north coasts of the county were experiencing gale-force winds and blinding snow.

At this time, there were three major mining sites in this area: Snowdon and Betteshanger near Deal, and Tilmanstone near Dover. The blizzard took out the power in all three at 2 p.m., leaving three morning shifts of men trapped in the mines. Attempts to repair the mains proved fruitless as the conditions worsened and increasingly frantic rescue efforts above ground continued. As the night wore on, the miners remained trapped in damp, cold conditions and complete darkness. Some food, water and blankets were winched down but it was not until the early hours of the morning that the nearly 700 men were finally rescued. Emergency equipment was used to winch the men up until the power was restored by about 2.30 a.m. All the men appeared safe and well, a great relief to their wives and families, and the government minister in charge. However, with many local towns and villages completely cut off, many of the miners now faced the prospect of staying the night at the pit – but above ground, at least.

In the papers, there was some pretty widespread criticism of the Met Office for failing to get even a hint of the risk of a dramatic snowstorm. Across a large swathe of England and Wales, level snow was at least 12 inches deep and large drifts in places made transport difficult for some days. Further heavy snow fell in the subsequent days and traffic dislocation remained particularly severe in south-east England. March remained cold for the first two weeks of the month but warmed considerably after mid-month, ushering in a welcome start to spring.

7

White Christmas 1970

Christmas 1970 saw the last overall white Christmas in the UK, with snow falling before, during and after the big day. What is particularly notable about this event is how widespread across Britain the snow was. Cars were trapped and massive dislocation was reported from Cornwall to the Midlands and Scotland; several deaths in car accidents were blamed on the snow. The cold air had spread all the way down to southern Spain, and snow was reported on the Mediterranean coast, much to the consternation of those holidaymakers who had tried to escape the blizzards in the north of Europe.

From a meteorological perspective, the synoptics for late December 1970 must have seemed eerily close to those for December 1962; the prospect of a bitter winter must have looked very real. Pressure had risen sharply over the UK just prior to 25 December and had pushed sharply northwards, settling into a ridge stretching from Greenland to Finland. This classic winter scenario brought a fairly strong and moist easterly flow right across the UK. Snow showers fed into the east on Christmas Day, intensifying on Boxing Day and progressing west. Low pressure across northern France caused Kent and Sussex to receive falls of 8 inches or more on Boxing Day. London experienced maximum temperatures below freezing from 27 December, as did Cardiff and Manchester. However, Scotland stayed milder; snow was less widespread and rain fell at low levels from 28 December.

The 1970 disruption came at a similar time as that of December 2010, when Heathrow was brought to a close by heavy snow in the weekend immediately before Christmas. The media then sought to punish the authorities for not keeping runways open. However, the manual clearance of hundreds of thousands of tons of snow and ice from the runways was a vast task. It was the timing that was unfortunate.

The 1970 snow also coincided with my family moving house. On Christmas Day my mother had to drive us to Orpington in Kent to stay with our grandparents for the duration of the move. I remember the journey well. It snowed very heavily all the way there and we had to stop on a number of occasions so my mum could get the snow off the windscreen. I remember having to be carried indoors from the car, such was the depth of the snow, which measured nearly a foot at Orpington by nightfall.

By 28 December the snow had begun to significantly impact most of England, largely through holiday travel disruption. The headlines that day were grim, with classics such as 'Blizzards Bring Road, Rail and Air Disruption, More to Come' being typical during the Christmas week. The RAC estimated that 150,000 miles of roads had become treacherous or impassable, bringing about the worst transport situation for eight years, and the Met Office made clear that at least three more days of harsh weather were to be expected. The impact of the widespread snow was described as being as bad on the high ground of Exmoor and Dartmoor as it had been in January 1963. Gatwick was closed several times, and staff had leave cancelled to ensure the airport stayed open.

A real worry for the authorities in 1970 was industrial disruption. Thousands of key manufacturing sites, including the major motor production facilities, were given several days' additional leave due to the snow, and production lines were at a standstill. To add to the disruption, most shops, including major department stores and large chains, remained closed. Luckily the freeze was not to be a repeat of 1963, but nevertheless the government remained very nervous about any hindrance to the economy in the volatile climate of 1970. In fact, since 1979 there have luckily been no successive months where national paralysis has been an issue in the UK. The new economy of the twenty-first century also offers working from home as an option for many stranded workers, which has mitigated the impact of snowfall in recent times.

The Met Office yet again came in for heavy criticism over the fact that it had not accurately forecast the snow. This hostility only intensified when the country prepared for blizzards forecast for 28 December, only to be met with rain and sleet. The next day, a forecast thaw turned out to be another unpredicted heavy snowfall, this causing Gatwick to shut unexpectedly and bringing widespread travel disruption. The freeze also spread back northwards and lingered across the whole country into early January. Further significant snow fell in some places early in the New Year but was increasingly confined to the north and Scotland. On 6 January, however, mild air finally flooded in from the Atlantic and a far warmer period ensued.

Up until the present time, 1970 is the last Christmas in which widespread, disruptive snow fell on Christmas Day and thereafter. The Christmas periods of 2010 and 1981 both saw plenty of snow on the ground throughout, but none fell on the titular day. Therefore, this scenario of heavy falling snow on the day itself remains very elusive indeed.

8

The Highland and South-West Blizzards, 1978

The period January to February 1978 was an eventful one in terms of weather. After a calm and sunny start to January, a deep depression, taking a similar track to the disastrous 1953 east coast storm, struck in the early hours of the 11th. Taking a slightly more easterly track than the 1953 storm, it spared the coastline further north from the worst. Nevertheless, at King's Lynn the storm surge was higher than that of 1953. This was the second gale in a week, the first of which, on 3 January, spawned a destructive tornado at Newmarket. On 18 January the south and Midlands were blanketed by deep snow, causing traffic disruption, but on the weekend of 28–29 January things took a more unusual turn. One of the worst blizzards to affect Scotland in modern times paralysed large parts of the Highlands. Five people died, and the widespread impact meant hardship for thousands as the country tried to cope. In a region used to the strongest winds and coldest temperatures that Britain can offer, this storm came as a shock. This was followed two weeks later by an equally fierce blizzard at the other end of the country, in England's south-western corner.

Following the deadly Glasgow storm of 1968, the authorities in Scotland prioritised the creation of an effective early-warning system for gales, devised to avoid a repeat of the high death toll from that single storm. Completed in the early 1970s, the system had proven itself to be useful several times before January 1978. Following this very severe event, however, a call was raised to implement a similar warning system for blizzards, one which would be able to warn of the types and levels of danger faced across the varied terrain of the country.

Nevertheless, the storm was well forecast and early warnings of heavy drifting snow and severe gale-force winds were put out across all broadcast channels from Friday 27 January. However, these warnings went apparently unheeded by a great number of people, who carried on regardless with planned activities, in some cases leading them into great danger, even death. Later, this apparent lack of public concern caused a lot of debate among forecasters and the emergency services both in Scotland and across the rest of the UK.

Low pressure began to cross the Midlands early on the afternoon of Saturday 28 January. The tightly packed isobars meant an easterly gale began to blow across Scotland, while a pool of very cold air was pulled into the flow. Snow began to fall in strong to gale-force winds, and by evening there were severe conditions right across the Highlands of Scotland.

Seemingly oblivious to warnings of severe conditions, on Saturday many people embarked upon routine activities that would determine their fate. Low, dark, snow-laden clouds raced across the sky and snow fell thickly into gale-force winds. Deep drifts quickly began to pile up, and visibility was reduced to almost zero in treacherous whiteout conditions.

Nicholas Quinn set about his normal Saturday routine in Farr, near Inverness, when the blizzard began. With shocking speed, his car was hopelessly stuck in deep drifts. As he waited to be rescued; deep snow would have started to pile up against his car windows. Sometime later, he panicked and decided he could wait no longer for rescue. He decided to walk to find help, but was soon hopelessly lost and succumbed to the conditions. The next day, his body was found not far from his car.

Meanwhile, George Cameron from Dingwall decided to leave on a planned business trip. At Helmsdale, his car was quickly stuck in deep snow that buried it. He, too, was found dead, trapped in his car, the following day. Christine Bruce and her husband James set off to visit her critically ill father in hospital, and they became stuck in large drifts at Ord near Caithness and perished in the bitter winds. A message was actually sent from the hospital just after their departure to say that Christine's father had died and urging them not to attempt the journey. In the Peak District, also affected by strong winds and snow, a young student, Robert Friar, was found dead the next day as well.

All these people appear to be victims of a level of danger they did not really understand, or at least seriously underestimated. In fact, the death toll could have been higher but for several lucky escapes, and some courageous heroism.

John Sinclair was a shepherd living near the summit of Slochd, on the A9 running to Inverness. As the snow enveloped and trapped all the cars on that stretch of road during Saturday afternoon and evening, he ventured out alone into the blizzard over and over again to find those trapped and rescue them. Trudging through sometimes waist-high drifts, he single-handedly managed to bring around sixty people to safety in his own cottage, where he kept them safe and warm until further help came.

So why were warnings of exceptionally severe weather so widely ignored? One view is that the tone of a forecast might be more important than the facts. For instance, it was suggested in the media that if the forecasters in 1968 had read out, 'The worst winds ever recorded in Scotland are likely to cause a high death toll in built-up areas', the impact on listeners may have been more dramatic when compared to the actual warnings of 'gales or severe gales'.

As for near misses, that evening four cadets who had been attending a ski-training centre had gone out to a disco in the town of Aviemore near Cairngorm, 7 miles away from where they were staying. After sheltering overnight at the local police shelter in the town, they set off early Sunday morning to get back to the lodge but were soon overwhelmed by the blizzard conditions. Convinced they were going to die, the boys huddled together under some trees and soon neared unconsciousness, too weak to move. Only a stroke of luck saved them; a party of skiers spotted them in the afternoon and a successful helicopter rescue followed. All of them recovered in hospital.

Another lucky escape befell a couple returning to Yorkshire from a family visit to Ullapool. Their car became completely buried by the snow and the desperate pair were so sure they would perish that they wrote a will. At their most desperate hour they were saved by a passing punk rock band who had spotted the roof of their car sticking out in the blowing snow and dug them out. After his rescue, Bernard Foulstone, who was in his fifties, declared, 'I will be a punk fan from now on.' Another couple, Frank and Celia Eadie, who set off from Inverness with their five-month-old baby, were luckily spotted and rescued by helicopter after a night in the freezing drifts.

The Scottish Saltire Branch of the RAF performed rescues non-stop from 28 January until 2 February. One of their first missions was to evacuate the passengers from a derailed train near Tain. As they reached the scene they saw that the windward side was already buried; panicked passengers were attempting to walk the 5 miles to the next station in clothes 'totally unsuitable for even a short hike in such conditions', and many lives were saved. In the following days, the service rescued 372 people from 'hostile' situations and completed 85 searches during 305 hours of continuous effort, as well as dropping fodder and supplies to isolated farms and communities.

Both the scale and severity of the blizzard only really became apparent by Monday, after the worst of the snow had stopped. Nevertheless, the fact that so many people had felt no trepidation in taking journeys into remote areas in such extreme conditions was still a great shock to the rescue services. It was also not until Monday that perhaps the luckiest and most resilient survivor was found. Bill Sutherland, a sixty-one-year-old travelling salesman, had been on his way from Wick to Inverness when he got stuck in his car at Ord in Caithness, the scene of most of the fatalities. By Sunday his car was buried under 20 feet of snow, and he was forced to spend three nights in icy darkness. His instinct to survive took over; he stated at the time that he was driven by a desire to 'finally get to draw my pension'. Using a metal spanner, he managed to drill an air hole in the snow to allow himself to breathe. He also used his consignment of female apparel, consisting largely of tights and underwear, to keep himself insulated. He was found by one of a series of rescue teams that were by then scouring the area for survivors. Bill Sutherland became somewhat of a local celebrity afterwards, not least because of his survival by undergarment.

Certainly one of the most exceptional blizzards in Scotland's history, it was twenty-three years before a comparable snowstorm challenged the emergency services to such an extent again, albeit in a far smaller area. Nevertheless, it is hopefully going to be much longer before a more violent and widespread blizzard strikes the country and exacts such a great cost in terms of human life.

Less than three weeks after the Highland storm, another blizzard arrived; this one was to ravage the south-west of England in a similar fashion. Just like its predecessor, this storm was well predicted and affected a wide area, including Dorset, Somerset, Devon, parts of Wiltshire and Hampshire and much of South Wales. Cornwall largely escaped, with the warm air sitting just over the south-west approaches giving substantial rainfall there instead. However, it was in these first three counties, especially over the moors, that the effects were felt most severely.

February was a cold and snowy month on the Continent, and the cold spread over much of Britain at times. In the first week of the month, high pressure had built up over Scandinavia and the far north of Europe, bringing about a strong easterly flow. The very cold air spread westwards over the British Isles and the Low Countries on 8 February, bringing heavy and continuous snow over Brussels and the Low Countries. In this flow much of the UK was initially dry, but low pressure pushed north out of the Continent the following week and heavy snow fell in the UK, especially over the eastern counties. Sevenoaks, for example, saw around 15 centimetres lying on the 10th. By 15 February the cold pushed back west, driven by the same anticyclone sitting over Iceland. The cold dug in and pressure began to drop. Towards mid-month, unusually warm maritime air, originating near the Azores, met the very cold air circulating around high pressure to the north and east. England's West Country then became a battleground between the two air masses, generating an intense depression.

The storm, which broke on the weekend 18–19 February, was initially forecast to spread further east but the depression stalled over Dorset, greatly exacerbating the severity of the snow in the west. On 15 January, heavy rain across the south-west of the country slowly began to turn to snow. Temperatures continued to drop overnight, and by the 16th most areas had a covering of snow several inches deep. On Friday 17th, it now looked as if a deep depression off Biscay would extend across much of the south of England, bringing heavy snow and gales. This scenario would have most likely brought a rapid thaw to the south and west, but the stronger, colder, drier air to the east and north held the storm in an almost stationary pattern and it became stuck over the south-western corner.

An eyewitness account vividly describes the arrival of the storm-force winds and the biting, blinding blizzard. It very clearly illustrates how and why the dangers posed by this type of storm can easily be underestimated by the inexperienced. It also shows how panic can quickly ensue and lead to confusion when such conditions are experienced for the first time. At midday, the eyewitness and his friend, a local from Dartmoor, drove out of Tavistock and went high up onto Dartmoor and parked their car. They readied themselves for a bracing walk out into the gale to experience a once-in-a-lifetime event: a blizzard on Dartmoor. Once parked by the roadside, the two companions set off into a Force 8 easterly gale and light snow, eager to experience the arrival of the blizzard:

> To the west, the horizon was blotted out. I was totally unprepared for the next minutes. Nothing I had read in literature prepared me. Neither tales from the Arctic, the Cairngorms nor Dartmoor itself. In an instant we were enveloped in a freezing white hell and a screaming wind that tore at us in all directions. We were literally stopped in our tracks unable to think, walk, talk or see. In an instant we were blinded, struck dumb by elemental forces beyond our imagination. The real terror was the inability to breathe. I was sucking snow into my lungs and my nostrils were furred up with encrusting snow.

The snow spread past Southampton on the south coast all the way up to West Sussex. In a line running east of Guildford to Basingstoke and up to Swindon and Stroud, there was no snow at all. The higher elevations of the south-west, on the other hand, saw 60 centimetres exceeded widely and drifts over 24 feet were recorded in some places. South Wales, including Cardiff, Bridgend and Swansea, all the way to Tenby, saw 10 to 30 centimetres and severe drifting. Towns along the North Devon coast were particularly severely impacted. Minehead and Barnstaple were cut off for some considerable time, as were Ilfracombe, South Moulton and villages on the high ground in northern Cornwall. By Monday 20 February, the government declared all roads in Devon and Dorset closed and most in Somerset impassable or passable only with difficulty. Unusually, roads into Devon were actually sealed off to incoming traffic, and the RAC described the area as 'a Siberian wasteland' littered with abandoned cars, stranded livestock and isolated towns and villages.

Dennis Howell was appointed as government 'Snow Supremo' and given responsibility for handling the authorities' response to the crisis. Even towns such as Dorchester, Poole, Swanage, Weymouth and Bournemouth, located towards the normally mild south coast, found themselves under deep, drifting snow and were littered with abandoned cars. While comparisons to 1963 and 1947 were made, the unprecedented local severity of this situation was highlighted by the fact that, on the streets of these major towns and cities, private transport was banned; an unparalleled event before or since in peacetime Britain. The streets were only accessible to emergency vehicles, which effectively meant that these areas were entirely isolated from the outside world.

Two hikers from Bristol, who had set off on Saturday on a trek across Dartmoor despite being well aware of the warnings of dire weather and blizzard conditions, ran into trouble and, not surprisingly given the above account of the conditions, quickly fell into mortal danger. They dug a snow hole, and the stronger of the two braved an eight-hour trek through the blizzard on Sunday to alert the emergency services to the plight of his companion. The rescue workers, fearing the worst, found it unlikely the man would have been able to survive the night exposed to such a severe blizzard. However, they persevered and eventually he was found, barely alive, in the snow hole that had doubtless saved him, and was taken to safety. All weekend, a fleet of RAF helicopters from its south-west base at Chivenor rescued those trapped in cars or in need of emergency help. By Monday, they had rescued more than eighty people, a total larger than all the rescues undertaken throughout the whole of 1977.

On Tuesday 21 February, a spokesman for RAF Chivenor spoke of the enormous task his colleagues had faced and of the experiences of some of those they had saved: 'Some of the people we rescued had been in their cars for twenty-seven hours. We only found one car on the A361 near Brampton because the occupant had stuck a red umbrella through the snow. Some people on the same road had spent the previous night in the back of a container truck. We have flown five kidney patients to hospital and an eighty-year-old woman suffering from hypothermia.'

The snow was, at first, widely compared to the New Year blizzard of 1962. However, the RAF believed the snow was far worse than that of 1963 because the winds were stronger and had driven giant walls of snow across major and minor roads. These created almost solid barriers though which no snowploughs or emergency equipment could pass, rendering all available snow-clearance equipment useless, leaving local authorities helpless to liberate those communities trapped by the mountainous snows. To illustrate the amount of precipitation that fell during the 1978 storm, rainfall readings from towns such as Teignmouth in Devon recorded over 110 millimetres of rainfall during the storm, which comprised more than just a single fall of snow. This is why the level total of snow exceeded 60 centimetres at a number of locations.

When the thaw came, during the last week of February, it was very rapid and was accompanied by unusually mild temperatures. The significance of this is that it was this same warm air stream that produced the blizzard in the first place. The deep cold, entrenched over England for so long, was quickly displaced and temperatures at the surface shot up to as high as 16 °C in twelve hours.

Interestingly, neither January nor February 1978 were especially cold months overall in the UK; January's CET value was 3.4 °C, not far from average; February's was somewhat lower at 2.8 °C, making it slightly colder than average. However, what stands out is that very cold air was close by the UK pretty much throughout the winter, and when it did arrive it certainly left an impression. After some very mild winters in the 1970s, in retrospect it does seem like the harsh weather and wintry spells experienced early in 1978 were indeed a foretaste of the far harsher winter that was soon to come.

9

The Winter of Discontent, 1978/79

The seventies was a decade of mild winters, but the winter of 1978/79 was the most severe since 1963 and coincided with a run of increasingly severe industrial disputes that eventually toppled the Labour government.

A noticeable alteration of winter weather patterns began in the previous winter, although the winter of 1977/78 was not really remarkable at its outset. However, during February a spectacular blizzard in the West Country led to severe drifting that rivalled the great Victorian blizzards of 1881 and 1891, as well as those of 1963. To the north, 31 January saw the Highlands of Scotland experience an almighty blizzard and gale that also paralysed large areas and brought much destruction of livestock and agriculture. This was the most severe weather for fourteen years, and the sudden cold was mirrored across the Atlantic as some extraordinary episodes on the eastern seaboard of the USA occurred, including the great east coast blizzard that killed twenty-three people and caused urban snow drifts of up to 40 feet. Of particular meteorological significance was a daytime snowfall in Miami in February 1978 that saw a judge halt a trial so everyone could watch aghast as snow fell and settled on the coconut palms. Almost immediately, speculation began of a climatic downturn.

A heatwave in May and early June 1978 was not followed by a good summer. I recall several very wet days in August, with flooding in Kingston, where I was from mid-July until 1 September. July had a dismal CET value of only 14.8 °C, and only July 1988, at 14.7 °C, has since been cooler. Whether this awful weather was the opener to a long-term colder spell is hard to say. In fact, the autumn was notably mild; Brussels and London recorded temperatures in the low to mid-twenties as late as early October. On a trip to London in late November, night-time temperatures at Heathrow stood at a remarkable 14 °C. However, on the morning Radio 4 weather bulletin the next day, Saturday 25 November, Michael Fish reported that flakes of snow had fallen in London early that morning and the temperature had dropped to zero from 14 °C in just a few hours. Under blue skies, after much autumnal gloom, this change to crisp, icy cold weather in retrospect marked the beginning of a long cold period.

It has often been the case for notably cold winters that November includes a cold spell, and back in Brussels Monday 27 November was cloudier and wetter than England had been, but also bitterly cold. Hail, sleet and snow showers fell in gusty winds from a northerly airstream accompanied by lightning and thunder. These airstreams are frequent in the Low Countries in winter and spring, and can deliver heavy snow, hail and torrential rain. The next morning there was a deep covering of snow and the roads were treacherous. As high pressure built, 1 December saw thick fog and sub-zero temperatures settle across the Low Countries. High pressure now became increasingly dominant across much of northern Europe, just as in the first week of December 1962. The slack easterly flow and moderately depressed upper-level temperature profile meant largely dry and cold weather persisted for some days, with heavy frosts and fog. A brief wet and mild period began mid-month, but this was not to last. An anticyclone developed that stretched from Scandinavia across to Greenland and the week before Christmas saw another rapid drop of temperature in London, and light snow began to fall, firstly from a heavy mist as snow grains and then as light snow from overcast skies and on light easterly winds. Snow was on the ground in small amounts, even in London, immediately prior to Christmas. To my disappointment, shortly before the big day it once again turned mild and wet, and continued that way through much of Christmas week. In fact, the temperature in London did not drop below 10 °C from Christmas Eve until 29 December.

Events elsewhere, however, gave signs that something exceptional was brewing. The aforementioned anticyclone brought severe cold across all of the east and north of Europe, in particular Scandinavia. Helsinki recorded spectacular cold, with -36 °C in the daytime, and Baltic ice was making its first appearance for years. From 27 December, the really exceptional nature of this cold pool became apparent on the synoptic charts and it must have been clear to forecasters that this deep cold could move south.

In the event, the change took place literally overnight. In the Low Countries and northern France, temperatures, having reached mild values of 6–9 °C on 31 December, began to plummet in the evening as revellers set out for their New Year's parties. The drizzle turned to snow and a gale-force easterly wind changed the calm weather in to a choking blizzard that paralysed traffic and trapped many people who were out. Within three or four hours, Brussels, Paris and Amsterdam were under at least a foot of heavy, drifting snow and temperatures had plunged to between -8 and -10 °C. The weather station at Brussels Airport saw a drop of 17 °C in five hours that evening, and it continued to fall the next day, settling at -14 °C the following night. My father, in Brussels, had gone to friends for dinner at 8 p.m. in a cool drizzle, emerging at 1 a.m. to the great shock of -10 °C, a raging blizzard and a car that would not start. Northern Europe was not to recover from this severe cold until the end of February.

In London, it was the night of 30 December when the snow came. Although not quite in the dramatic fashion of the near Continent, the change was broadly the same. The day was clear and cold; frost remained on shaded roofs and grass all day. A weather warning on ITV sometime after the early evening news warned of exceptionally heavy snow that night but it was not and until after 11 p.m. that the snow swept across the south. Howling winds whipped the snow into eddies that swirled past the streetlights, and soon the city streets were under several inches of snow and complete silence reigned in the normally busy urban sprawl.

New Year's Eve dawned with Britain transformed. From Scotland to Devon, towns and villages were cut off. Despite intensive efforts, many North Devon towns such as Ilfracombe remained accessible only by helicopter, and in Scotland two trains were completely stranded near Stirling with 300 passengers on board. It snowed all night across the south, but during the morning the sun came out. However, the day was exceptionally cold; Heathrow only reached -3 °C and the snow stayed intact. Great icicles formed on many buildings, bearing testament to the rapid drop in temperatures the night before. Such was the cold abroad that some towns in West

Germany banned all forms of private travel due to the deep snow and high winds; Paris was clogged with abandoned cars, hampering any efforts to clear the streets of snow, and Moscow woke up to -41 °C that morning.

Sports in the UK were decimated. There was no rugby at all and only three League football matches took place over the New Year period. The RAC expressed horror at the fact that so few roads had been gritted or cleared, and laid the blame squarely at the door of local councils. The councils in turn stated that lack of staff and a whole gamut of industrial issues meant they were not able to carry out the work. The strong winds also took their toll, with several coastal districts reporting flooding and breaches of sea walls. Further snow fell that week, and on 4 January Plymouth found itself cut off. Newspapers reported that shops were running low on fruit and vegetables, especially away from town centres. Nevertheless, Dennis Howell, then Minister of State, had sought assurances that local authorities would use all resources available to them to keep roads clear. Their governing body, the AMA, reported that they had been able to satisfy the government with assurances that they were working hard to overcome their problems. However, it was clear, even from the busy suburbs, that only the main roads were going to be cleared. A lorry drivers' strike that had begun in December had now also spread, leaving thousands of rural dwellers without gas or oil and ensuring that the misery of the public was fully maximised.

Some horror stories also emerged. On 3 January, three men drowned in the pond on Hampstead Heath. Five of them had ventured on to the ice and gone through. A passer-by was only able to rescue two of them. All aged between eighteen and twenty-one, they had been out in Hampstead at a local pub drinking and making merry that night, and had then decided to try the ice. My brother went through the ice in February 1978 after venturing onto an area of a lake that looked thick and sturdy. However, water was kept running from a sluice underneath the ice on the part of the lake he was on, and it gave way. My dad was able to reach down and grab his coat before he vanished, and pulled him out. It was snowing hard, and even on the way back to the car he went blue and was shaking badly. That day has taught me that, drunk or sober, walking on ice is not to be recommended.

In southern England, the cold relented after ten days and, unlike

January 1963, there was a thaw, followed by some mild, damp days. However, anywhere at altitude saw no release from the cold. Upland Britain remained in real difficulty, and day after day helicopter pictures showed stranded livestock vehicles and communities cut off from the outside world. It wasn't long before the cold reclaimed the south. After just under a week of milder weather, the cold continental air mass slipped back across the whole of the UK, and the bitter weather returned; snow, sleet and freezing rain all played their part, with some heavy periods of snow and easterly winds across most of the south.

On 22 January a belt of freezing rain spread across much of England. That night I remember clearly the rain turning to ice as it hit my bedroom window, and the pinging noise it made as it fell away. Colder air cut in under the warmer air and again there was a rapid drop in temperature. By midnight, the rain turned to snow and fell for the rest of the night. At daybreak it continued to snow heavily, once again putting huge pressure on the already crippled infrastructure of Britain.

Inflation was running in double-digit figures and had been for some time, putting huge pressure on the government for wage increases to mirror these inflationary pressures. One memorable headline on the 24 January read 'Freeze Piles on Agony for Labour'. This time the snow had coincided with a national rail strike, and the frustration of the nation was reflected in the lack of any optimism in that week's media. After three weeks of cold, January saw 90,000 people go on to the dole because of the industrial paralysis the bitter weather and the widespread squabbling over wages caused.

From this point on, the milder weather did not become truly established again; although there were some slow thaws and February saw less cold days and nights than January, snow fell again and again, sometimes on easterlies, sometimes in random showers, and ice on roads became a menace. Out in Sevenoaks, at my grandparents' house, the snow rarely thawed and I was able to sledge with my dad at the end of January and again in February.

Just before the middle of February, the weather became more benign. Bright sunshine and frost brought talk in the media of spring and an imminent thaw, despite the fact that patchy snow and ice remained. As is so often the case, however, human instinct proved false. The bitterest phase of the winter swept all of northern Europe mid-month, paralysing most of the Continent and delivering gale-force easterly winds of ferocious strength. The Netherlands and Belgium really suffered in this period, with wind chill factors that would not have been out of place in the Yukon.

By this time it was so cold that the ice on the Pen Ponds at Richmond Park was thick enough for skating to be officially permitted for the first time since January 1963. Hundreds of people turned up at the weekends, with or without skates, to enjoy the ice. However, the renewed snowfalls of late February badly affected the high ground of the west and north, and once again helicopters had to be used to feed isolated communities. Travel disruption became widespread owing to the strong winds that piled snow up in huge drifts. Even in rural areas, drifts piled up against walls, hedges and doors.

Meanwhile, high inflation was prompting big wage demands, which only served to worsen the situation. Almost every sector seemed to be in crisis, and strike after strike was announced on the news. For the media it was a time of deep-seated despair, and the epithet 'the winter of discontent' appeared around this time. Nevertheless, life went on pretty much as normal for most families despite the numerous strikes. Even so, after weeks of snow and cold, people began to feel frustrated and run down and could only talk of when the snow would end and life would get back to normal. Unlike 1962/63, however, there were relatively few power cuts, and essential services, outside of rubbish collection and gritting in city centres, largely still worked. Supermarkets remained well stocked in urban areas and the motorways mostly stayed quite clear, so goods moved better than in 1963.

On 22 February, one headline read 'Snow Everywhere'. Driving to Dover on the A2 that day was like gliding across an arctic landscape, with the soft peaks of towering drifts sculpted into shapes of beaten egg whites. Across the Channel, snow lay deep but fairly uniform across the flat lands of Flanders. The cold was bitter and the far lower temperatures in northern France and the Low Countries gave a remarkable average monthly temperature in Brussels of -2.7 °C in January and 0.3 °C in February. The thaw that began at the very end of February was by no means the end of the winter. March saw several snowfalls, some of which were very heavy and caused particularly severe disruption again across the high ground of the west and north. Scotland saw some heavy snowfalls, but nothing too exceptional occurred. By mid-March the higher temperatures experienced in the day meant the worst of the snow did not last long, and any disruption was short-lived.

Rather like 1947, the overall cost of this hard winter in Britain is probably difficult to quantify, given the fact that much of the key industrial infrastructure was crippled by strikes. The country was in need of a change of some kind; that much was clear. It soon came in the form of the first Thatcher government, whom one can credit with standing up to the powerful unions and tackling the crippling industrial malaise of the time. The fact that the cost was largely a human one would become brutally apparent in the years that followed. One thing that was noticeably absent was the endless media criticism of snow clearing that has followed every snowfall in the current decade. It seems the RAC was at the forefront of the gritting lobby but had an uphill struggle on its hands, given the terrible state of industrial relations in general. Anyone who remembers that winter will recall that roads often weren't gritted and salted as much as now, but traffic paralysis was not the key issue for the news teams of the time. There was less traffic and less reliance on road freight; that, coupled with what I would term 'low expectations' due to the constant strikes, may have contributed to this.

One impact of the cold that seemed to be common to both the UK and other affected countries was that weeks of snow and frost ruined the roads. Potholes, cracks and fissures appeared on most roads and quickly worsened.

However, the meteorological impact of the winter was far less severe than 1962/63 because the cold was generally associated with low pressure, which meant more variability in temperature. It was also a fact that high pressure was centred to the north in the 1963 winter, meaning the lowest temperatures were to the south and east. In 1978/79, it was upland and northern Britain that were the coldest regions.

In the CET record, which dates back to 1659, January 1979 ranks as the seventeenth-coldest month, with an average monthly mean temperature of -1.4 °C, while February ranks thirty-first at 1.2 °C. While overall it was only the twenty-eighth-coldest winter (December to February) period in the long record, at 1.3 °C it was the third-coldest winter of the twentieth century. There have only been three sub-zero months in the last fifty years, of which January 1979 was one, and the combined average of January and February 1979 is

-0.1 °C, a figure that has not been neared for any two-month period since. Thus, only February 1986, at -1.1 °C, and December 2010, at -0.7 °C, have been sub-zero months since January 1979.

The 1979 winter met with much discussion of an impending Ice Age, as did the winter of 1963; indeed, 1976 caused worries of desertification in Europe, and a rethink on water supplies. It seems science is strongly affected by the prevailing conditions of the time. As a temperate country, it appears that Britain will experience climate change in a form that reflects the immense variability of its existing weather and climatic patterns. For my money, that will almost certainly at some stage include a bitter winter, a prolonged drought, gales and flooding rains. Just exactly when these will occur is anybody's – and I mean literally anybody's – guess.

10

Heavy Snowfalls and Record Cold, 1981/82

The years immediately after the bitter winter of 1978/79 saw no severe winter weather in lowland Britain. After two fairly mild winters, the rigours of that period were largely forgotten and autumn 1981, in particular November, was most notable for being very, very wet. The rugby fields at my school were quagmires, and, as Tuesday 8 December dawned dark and grey, it was no surprise to anyone that persistent rain was falling yet again. That morning it felt quite cold as we walked to across the quad to breakfast at school, where I was a boarder, and I noticed snowflakes in the rain. On the way back, the rain had turned to heavy snow and surprisingly had already settled on the grass. Thereafter, an intense snowstorm, which lasted all morning, brought ever stronger winds that began to whip the snow up into drifts. Snow was knee-deep by lunchtime where I was, and indeed across much of the south of England. The temperature, which at midnight had been about 3 °C, fell at breakfast to 0 °C and by the afternoon sat at a bone-chilling -5 °C. Great surprise was expressed on the radio that there was no warning at all, even as the rush hour began. This unexpected snowfall caused widespread travel disruption, especially on the trains.

I wonder what the reaction would be today should such a substantial event occur totally unannounced. I was extremely surprised at the time and checked the day's newspapers in the school library that evening; all of the forecasts reflected the Met Office forecast of 'bright and sunny with isolated wintry showers', with no mention of widespread snow. Even the outlook did not mention the large amounts of snow that were to arrive later that week. While this is less likely to happen now, with the powerful computer power available, one can barely imagine the media and public reaction.

It is therefore even more interesting that there was a rather low-key reaction in the following day's papers, with headlines that included 'Snow by Stealth Smothers Britain'. In the quality papers, at least, the conclusion was that the temperature in the lower atmosphere had been two degrees lower than the Met Office had expected at 5 a.m., turning rain to snow and catching 'forecasters and gritters alike off-guard'.

British Rail (BR), however, were far less sanguine. A spokesman moaned, 'We rang the Met Office at 4 a.m. and there was no mention of heavy snow!' BR had taken flak from all quarters when a train succumbed to a frozen point outside Clapham Junction. Commuters, desperate not to be late for work, had got out of the train, as one could then, and walked along the live rails (750 volts) the short distance to the station. BR, realising what was happening, had to switch off the power, paralysing London's busiest junction at rush-hour and causing a big backlog. They refused all the waiting passengers' refunds and accused the commuters of 'lunacy', risking death and causing worse chaos for everyone else.

The roads suffered as well, because the local authorities had not been warned. The M4 was blocked by jack-knifed lorries, the A12 and A127 in Essex were impassable because sheet ice had developed under the snow, and the M1 on the stretch running from London to Northampton was running on a single lane; the M11 and M2 were also blocked in parts, and at least twenty-five accidents in the south-east had resulted in injuries. Heathrow stayed open but only because managers took over from clearance drivers who refused to drive due to a demarcation dispute (whatever that may have been).

The high pressure pushing out of Scandinavia asserted itself further during the day and, as the cold air filtered south and west, the rain turned to snow across much of France, Belgium and the Netherlands as the polar airstream introduced a sudden rush of very cold air. Daytime maxima from 9 December sank below freezing, and would stay there until 27 December.

Back in England, the transformation of the town and landscape around my school in Leatherhead provoked an unusual sense of excitement and carnival feeling throughout the school. Despite the disappointment of not being able to attend the annual varsity match at Twickenham, the sun had come out and we built a proper igloo on the 1st XV rugby field.

The cold remained firm in its grip on Britain and was considered the most serious early December snow since 1967. By Friday morning, however, it began to snow again. During the afternoon, the snow became heavy and incessant. By mid-afternoon the school resembled a Dickensian Christmas scene and everything looked spectacular. This day of heavy snow closed Heathrow for five hours and Gatwick, Manchester and the East Midlands airports (then called Donnington) were closed periodically throughout the day. A major train crash took place at Gerrard's Cross, with the driver and three passengers killed, but it was not clear if this was caused by poor visibility. Mrs Thatcher capitalised on the snow by pelting journalists with wet snowballs on a visit to a racecourse, and the motoring organisations took their opportunity, as they always do, to warn everyone 'not to venture out unless absolutely necessary'. The weekend brought brilliant sunny but bitterly cold weather to a snow-covered country. There was almost no sport played at all that weekend, with the exception of a Scotland *vs* Wallabies rugby Test match played at Murrayfield and nine League football matches.

On Saturday 12 December, the evening weather forecast warned of an 'arctic front' bringing more snow the following day. The clear night of 12/13 December proved bitterly cold. Across most of the UK, double-digit minus figures were measured. Exceptionally, -25.2 °C was recorded in Shropshire. The following evening it began to snow hard, but the forecasts were wrong again. This time, the snow turned to rain. The next morning was sunny, milder and very slushy. However, to the east of Britain there was a rather different outcome. The mild air did not reach East Anglia, and snow went on through the night in gale-force winds, causing 10-foot drifts that buried livestock and cars alike. The south-west took the brunt of even stronger winds, with trees blown down and up to half a million homes in Devon, Cornwall and the Severn valley without power. Trees tore down power lines and blocked roads as snow whipped up into drifts before the subsequent thaw and rain began to flood some of the areas that had been swamped with snow. The north stayed cold and dry as the warmer air to the south battled with the colder air that held to the north.

The warming, where it happened, did not last long. After three days of 3–5 °C in most places, the cold air filtered back; by 17 December any wet snow that remained in London was solid ice. Temperatures in the south dipped back below freezing, although in the north it had remained bitterly cold throughout. Braemar in Scotland, well known for its record low of -27.2 °C in 1895, recorded its coldest month ever, with a mean average temperature of -3.4 °C, during which the daytime maxima did not exceed -10 °C on some eleven days.

The return of the cold and severe frosts across the whole of the UK came without the snow of the previous incursion. Nevertheless, we did not have to wait long until it returned. On 20 December, rain, sleet and snow, accompanied by strong winds, swept the UK, with the south-west again being battered by severe gales. A young girl was killed after a wall blew down on her in London, and power still had not been restored to many south-western homes after the gales and snow of 13 December. Forecasters on 20 December now assured the public that an imminent thaw would arrive nationwide as the wet weather was expected to spread east by 21 December, bringing an end to the cold spell. The bookmakers were very relieved that the threat of a White Christmas had seemingly receded.

However, to the horror of the media and those caught up in it, instead of a thaw, for the second time that month the Met Office failed to predict a rush-hour blizzard that paralysed the capital. The low they thought would move east slid south down the Scandinavian high pressure, pulling down very cold air once again. On 21 December, London was again totally unprepared at rush hour; train and bus services were decimated because of a lack of preparation. In fact, London Transport declared it as one of their worst days 'ever'. This time, many parts of the north shared in the worst of the snow with Yorkshire, along with Britain's other eastern counties coming to a veritable standstill. Kent and Essex saw the A2 and M2 closed for the whole day, with abandoned cars littering the roads. Many thousands of commuters were stranded, and it suddenly became clear that it was going to stay cold for some time to come. The reaction of the Met Office on this occasion is intriguing; a spokesman stated, 'We did not get it wrong in total. We have been warning for a couple of days that things were on a knife edge but the wind turned more easterly which is why the snow was more dominant. Perhaps our emphasis could have been better.' The press were rather less forgiving on this second occasion, and the criticism was intense.

With odds on a White Christmas at 4-5, the bookmakers closed off bets on the 23rd, claiming that a payout for them was a 'dead cert'. In the event, however, they did not pay out a bean. Snow lay across much of the country, giving what the populace would consider a very white Christmas; however, the official bookmakers' definition is for a single flake to fall on the roof of the London Weather Centre. As it was, the day was dry and sunny so the bookmakers were saved substantial pay-outs.

Further snow fell across Wales, the West Country, the West Midlands and many eastern counties on 27 December. However, this was the last cold day, and the Atlantic began to make major inroads from this point on, with milder air filtering right across Britain.

The New Year was particularly mild, and in the first days of January it remained so with 11–13 °C and much rain, especially in the north and west. As the lying snow and frozen ground thawed, the rivers swelled and floods spread across many prone areas in the north of the country. It had been quite a month for winter weather but it was a sorry, soggy end to the long period of cold. Indeed, the floods worsened into the following week with three people drowned. Yorkshire and Northumberland saw some of the worst floods in years, with troops having to assist police evacuating stranded householders in the towns along the burst River Ure, notably Boroughbridge.

On 5 January, a sharp drop in temperature across Scotland heralded a return to cold weather. London saw an unusual ten-degree drop in temperature over the following twenty-four hours. The next day, negative temperatures became established right across the UK. This sudden return to cold brought a remarkable escape for both Selby and York, where the Ouse had threatened a disastrous incursion. The river and floodwater froze solid, halting a rise in the water levels and sparing the towns the worst. The news that night was memorable, with rescue boats evacuating householders around Selby and having to break through the ice to keep moving. Fresh snow also followed close behind the cold. On Friday 8 January, Wales woke up to a blizzard. Snow had begun the night before and continued through the day with temperatures well below freezing. Cardiff Airport recorded over 50 millimetres of rainfall, and more than 20 inches of snow or more fell in the south, with 7 to 15 inches further north into Mid Wales. The snow began in the south on Friday afternoon and continued through the night. That Saturday was dark and very windy, and snow fell heavily throughout a second day without a break. Walking along the river in Kingston that afternoon presented a bleak prospect; the powdery, drifting snow hissed as it snaked along the banks of the Thames and stung as it blew against your face on the freezing wind. The snow continued most of the night, only dying out on Sunday morning. The temperatures then really dropped under clearer skies. As early as 6 January, temperatures of -22 °C had been recorded in Scotland and the strength of the cold grew as the snow began to grip and disrupt much of England and Wales. On 10 January, the all-time record low for the UK was equalled with -27.2 °C reported in the highlands at Braemar. Even Gatwick had two consecutive nights below -14 °C. England also recorded its lowest-ever temperature on the same night, dipping to a remarkable -26.1 °C at Newport in Shropshire. For a few days, the deep freeze really set in and there were some stunning snow scenes in the bright sunshine of the following week.

The weather relented slowly. Bright sunshine and warmer air spread from the south-east, then the south, and daytime temperatures and low humidity this time delivered a very slow thaw. Night frosts remained for much of the month, but by 17 January only patches of snow remained in southern counties before it finally vanished. Even on the high ground in the north and Scotland, the snow slowly melted away.

It wasn't until 2010 that there was another Christmas with lying snow on such a wide scale; strangely, on that day, just as in 1981, not a single flake fell on the roof of the London Weather Centre, and the bookies again avoided a payout to a disappointed public.

11

The Great European Cold Wave, January 1985

Most of the winters in the 1980s up until 1987 saw spells of cold and snowy weather, but 1985 stands out due to the sudden intensity and length of the cold weather.

November and December 1984 were mild, and December saw hardly any frosts at all in southern England. On New Year's Day it was damp and mild where I was, at my parent's house in Brussels, but the following day, 2 January, we woke up to a thin covering of snow and bright sunshine. The snow thawed a bit during the day but the next morning a covering of several centimetres had fallen, and snow showers fell off and on through the day, building up the depths on the ground and covering the trees, grass and roads. High pressure that had sat over southern Europe through much of the winter had suddenly moved west into the Atlantic. It then began to squeeze itself northwards. A trough over Scandinavia began to sink south over eastern Europe, dragging down bitterly cold air, and several disturbances formed on its western flank that began to push out towards the west. This pool of bitterly cold air reached Belgium during 2 January on a strong north-easterly airflow. That same day, the cold air also reached south-east England but the lighter north-easterly flow there delivered clear, sunny skies.

By Friday 5 January, the increasingly cold and disturbed airstream began piling on the snow over the Low Countries. At least 10 centimetres of fresh snow fell that morning in Brussels, and by early afternoon the thermometer in the city centre was showing -10 °C. Extremely heavy snow soon began and continued to fall all day. The snow had become so severe that even the normally efficient Belgian train services, which ran on overhead cables, started to break down in the deep drifts.

The next day in London saw clear frosty conditions over most of the UK, as had been the case for much of the week. The forecast for the night of Saturday 6 January was for a change to unsettled weather, and heavy snow was forecast to move from west to east late in the night and much of the next day.

The next, morning much of southern England woke to a winter wonderland. Snow was falling thickly and a good 10 to 15 centimetres had covered everything in rural Surrey, where I was visiting friends, including the roads and the railways. Back in London that same day there was less snow but it was still cold enough for the snow to remain in the parks and gardens, and the Thames riverbank at Kew looked marvellous the next day after a heavy frost. Thus began a run of very low temperatures.

The -16 °C isotherm was sitting over Belgium at just over a kilometre up in the lower atmosphere level, and the snow had piled up to over 30 centimetres at my dad's house, night-time minima of -17 °C or -18 °C being recorded across several nights. At Gatwick, with a clear sky and snow on the ground, it fell to a more modest -10 °C, but that was cold enough to freeze all the major ponds and lakes in southern and eastern Britain, where the coldest air refused to be driven out by milder air to the west. The following week was a cold one. There was only light snow in London, but the cold intensified and all of Europe began to see exceptional minima. It was the south-east of Britain that was most affected by the snow that week and, unusually, Scotland experienced fairly mild conditions; only light sleet and snow fell across some parts of Liverpool, Humberside and North Wales, while in Kent, Sussex and East Anglia the easterly winds brought in frequent snow showers that whipped up drifts several feet high, especially along the coasts.

The deep cold had, most unusually, spread all the way down to North Africa, such was the power of this northerly blast; and with such low temperatures it was not surprising that snow was widespread in the south of Europe. Not only this, but temperatures were far lower than in 1963, 1940 and 1895, when the bitter cold also reached the Mediterranean coasts and beyond. The French Riviera experienced its heaviest snowfall since 1963, with over 30 centimetres falling on 6 January at Nice, weighing down the palm trees with frozen snow. Meanwhile, Paris recorded an almost record-breaking daytime high of only -11 °C, the coldest there since 1956. Most of Germany experienced deep snow and extremely low temperatures, colder in many places than those of 1963. On 7 January, a deep low passed to the south of the UK, bringing some snow showers and light snow to the far south. This depression deposited a further 20 centimetres on top of the 30 centimetres already covering Belgium much of northern France and the Netherlands. My dad and stepmother had driven in to work that morning in the Belgian capital; by home time that evening the car had to be abandoned, only barely visible in the drifts.

In Paris, the temperature had stayed below -9 °C for four days by 8 January; twelve people were reported frozen to death. The normally balmy Basque coastal resort of Biarritz was blanketed by extremely deep snow and the cold was intense across the whole country. Metéo France, the French meteorological office, reported that this was the coldest spell since 1895. On 8 January, lowland stations in central France were reporting -32 °C and the olive growers' associations in both France and Italy began to express concern that it was too cold for many olive trees and that crops would be under threat if the cold went on; an all-time record -41 °C was recorded in eastern France the following night. That same day, -32 °C was also recorded in Munich, and here the low temperatures trapped unwelcome industrial pollution at low levels. An emergency warning was put out for children not to 'eat snow'. Blizzards swept most of Italy, reaching down to Rome, with snow so deep by midweek that buses there were forced to use snow chains for the first time since 1969. The cold air also pushed down across the whole of Spain, with severe cold and snow reported throughout the country.

In the UK, the Met Office said they were not sure how long the freeze would last, as Britain had become 'the battleground between warm Atlantic air from the west and the bitter cold over Europe'. 'If the Atlantic does win out, it is likely to be only temporary,' they commented on 8 January.

The Atlantic made some inroads into the UK, especially in the south-west where rain fell, but it was only temporary; the east and south remained remarkably cold and snow fell widely here, especially along the south coast. By the end of 9 January, many cars became trapped after incessant snow, driving winds and high drifts; each vehicle had to be bulldozed out so the occupants could be taken to safety. Heavy snow also began to affect the north significantly for the first time, paralysing the Lake District and upland routes for days. I met my dad at his club in London that week as he was over for business, and he recounted tales of the extraordinary snow on the Continent. That night, 10 January, there was snow, ice and frost even on the roads around Oxford Circus; however, during 11 January the cold eased a little over the UK but offered no respite on the Continent. The Paris police had begun rounding up all vagrants at night and taking them to shelters for their own protection. A further eighteen homeless people had died in Paris by midweek, and the authorities also began leaving underground metro stations open at night to offer shelter to those they could not find.

On 12 January, however, rain and sleet over the south-east soon turned back to snow. By pub closing time that night a couple of inches of very icy snow lay on the roads, and driving home with friends on treacherous icy roads was a memorable event. The next day, after a clear start, the winds picked up from the east once more and much of eastern England, as far north as Lincolnshire, saw a long spell of heavy snow that lasted from 13 January almost without a break until 17 January. Temperatures in this period dropped remarkably low across the east and south; Gatwick only reached -5 °C on 16 January, with a night-time low of -14 °C, and this was under heavy cloud.

Despite the snow, the cold had dropped from the papers for a few days in the aftermath of a huge gas explosion in Putney and a serious run on the pound. However, the fierceness of the gales and snow had become so intense by 15 January that the disruption being caused once again took over the headlines. While Folkestone on the south coast saw temperature readings no higher than -3 °C that day, nearly half an inch of rain fell. The result was 12 inches of fresh, level snow being widely reported from Essex and Kent, with drifts at Maidstone topping 10 feet in places. Very little snow fell outside of the SE, but nowhere in the SE was spared; a fact in which some newspapers took a strange delight! The coldest day of the entire spell was 16 January. Temperatures failed to rise above -4 °C in central London and -6 °C widely across the south-east, with night-time minima below -10 °C in many places. Paris did not exceed -13 °C, and even Barcelona stayed below freezing. Deep snow blanketed Dublin and much of eastern Ireland. There was no end in sight for those areas still in the grip of this deeply entrenched Europe-wide cold spell. My grandparents, living in Kent, returned from holiday during this week to find much of the living room roof of their bungalow collapsed, such was the weight of the accumulated snow. The thaw could not come too soon for them, and it began on Sunday 21st with a little sleet and higher temperatures. The following week saw a general thaw and temperatures in double figures.

A cold January is often followed by a wet and mild February, and the start of the month was wet. However, on 9 February a sharply defined cold front pushed south across all of the UK, with the accompanying heavy rain turning to snow as it pushed southwards to then be followed by nearly two days of relentless snow. On this occasion it was the Midlands that bore the brunt of the snow. Nevertheless, the north and Scotland all experienced a period of deep snow and freezing temperatures. My brother, who was at college in Stafford, at the time, saw some of the deepest snow of his life, with drifts covering his friend's car completely on 10 February. To the south of England the snow was about 8 to 10 inches deep in some places and drifts dislocated whole communities, with deep drifts blocking even some of the major routes for a time. However, the cold was nowhere near as intense as in January. Winds during this snowfall were strongest to the south, and the snow and gales battered the south coast with particular ferocity. Folkestone harbour closed because the ferries were being tossed around in the wild seas and boarding would have been too dangerous. East Grinstead was cut off from the outside world by deep drifts, and the A23 and M23 were closed, as was the exposed A303 in Wiltshire and London's orbital route the M25. Sadly, nine people up and down the country were killed in a variety of accidents attributed to ice, snow and poor visibility. However, this second wave of cold only reached as far south as central France, and much of Italy and Spain escaped completely, in sharp contrast to the January freeze.

This very cold weather lasted another week before there was a gradual thaw. There were some further snow showers in the south and east, but in general the weather was cold and quiet. The slow thaw continued over the following week, and on the second Saturday of February we were back playing our standard rugby fixtures and nationwide sports fixtures went ahead uninterrupted. Nevertheless, it was still cold enough for snowmen and ice on the ponds to remain near Esher racecourse on the weekend of 23 February. The following week, however, saw a sharp jump in temperature. The last of the snow vanished overnight. With very mild weather and brilliant sunshine, spring was finally in the air.

12

The Great Easterly Outbreak, January 1987

A small article appeared in the *Financial Times* at the beginning of the second week of January 1987. It concerned an 'arctic spell' of weather that the Met Office had been predicting for some time, which would be affecting Britain in the coming days; it was described as one of the most severe for many years. It grabbed my attention and was the first I had heard of any impending cold spell that winter. Over the next few days this began to be mentioned elsewhere, and by the end of the week the cold weather looked imminent.

The cold had been affecting Scandinavia and western Russia for some days, and the northern capitals of Europe had become exceptionally cold. Finnish meteorologists said it was the coldest spell there since the great 1939/40 freeze. They expected the all-time record low of -46 °C, set in 1940, to be broken shortly. In polar Sweden, the temperature had already fallen to -52 °C – extremely exceptional. Helsinki's daytime maxima had dropped to -27 °C earlier in the week and central Stockholm measured -21 °C, with thick ice covering the harbours, seriously hampering shipping and ferry services. Poland was also shivering. Temperatures of -34 °C were recorded there, and the increasing cold was threatening their all-time record low, set in February 1929, of -45 °C. Further east in Russia, Moscow's daytime maxima were at around -25 °C. This bitter cold affecting the east and north of Europe now sank south into Greece, where one of the worst blizzards in years killed three people and cut off numerous mountain communities in the north of the country.

The first really cold air reached London on Saturday 10 January. The forecast was for severe frost and some localised snow, but on the ground the general picture was one of clear skies and sunny weather. The weather was bitter, however, and light snow crystals fell out of a virtually clear sky in London as the temperature dropped throughout the day. The winds were still quite light, but what breeze there was had a bone-chilling effect; it simply felt too cold to spend much time outdoors unless it was totally unnecessary.

Snow, in the form of heavy showers, began to fall across East Anglia and some parts of the east of England from about midday on Saturday, but it was not widespread and much of the country remained mostly clear. Towards the evening, however, the most notable aspect of the weather was the increasing intensity of the bitter cold. That night central London was at -5 °C, unusually low for the city centre. Out in the countryside in Surrey it was so cold the lock of my friend's car froze. The temperature here fell below -10 °C quite widely, especially out of the wind, and the frost became permanent and severe.

The next morning was clear, bright and sunny but extremely cold. The thermometer did not rise above -3 °C in London that Sunday, and in Kent, East Anglia and other parts of the east heavy snow showers were developing over the sea and pushing progressively further inland, borne on gale-force easterly winds. The Met Office had somewhat underestimated the instability caused by the exceptionally cold air and wind strength passing over the relatively warm North Sea. The weekly *Countryfile* 'weather for the week ahead' programme on TV had offered one of the coldest and snowiest outlooks I had seen up to that time. They were talking of heavy snow throughout the week. Sure enough, as the day progressed the localised flurries of Saturday became far more heavy and widespread. By the end of Sunday, large parts of eastern Britain, from Scotland all the way down to Kent, including Essex, Suffolk and Norfolk, were under a deep blanket of snow.

During Sunday night, the snow pushed inland for a time, and much of the east, including London, woke up to a covering of snow a couple of inches deep. Despite the sunshine the Met Office was clearly warning that much of the country should brace for long-lasting severe snowstorms, gale force winds and very low temperatures. The temperature struggled to reach -6 °C in London that day, and the eastern coastal counties, especially those to the south, were already getting buried according the news programmes, which showed lorries stuck on the way to and from Sheerness.

The cold in Europe was intensifying. On Sunday, Helsinki failed to get above -30 °C and the most extreme pool of cold air was spreading south and west. The maximum temperature that

Monday in Stockholm was -23 °C, in Moscow -27 °C, Brussels -10 °C, Paris -8 °C, Copenhagen -15 °C and Munich -15 °C. These were maximum temperatures, and the minima were even more bone chilling. The cold across western Europe mirrored that of the extreme cold of January 1985, but in Britain and further north it was much colder. By Tuesday, nearly sixty people were dead from the cold in the Soviet Union, with temperatures that, according to the news agency TASS, were 'below -60 °C' in Siberia, and unusually deep snow was isolating numerous communities across Scandinavia. Such severe cold has not occurred since in northern Europe, and shipping was seriously disrupted as the seas around the Baltic began to freeze.

The Met Office warnings soon proved accurate. On the night of Monday 12 January, snow began to fall heavily shortly after dark. In a short space of time, the roads were covered. I was living in a tower block in Woolwich, in student digs, and had the most fabulous bird's-eye view from the Woolwich Arsenal all the way to central London. For now, all I could see was the twisting and spinning eddies of snow howling past the tower block at high speed, and visibility became limited to a few blocks; nevertheless, it was fascinating to watch the snow take over the streets during the following hours.

Overnight on Monday, deep snow and strong winds covered most of eastern England. Drifts were 6 to 8 feet high in some areas by Tuesday morning, and the main roads began to suffer as much as minor roads from the blowing, drifting snow. The police were horrified by the amount of accidents being caused by speeding and negligent drivers on the M25 in Essex in particular, recounting how 'Go Slow' police cars in the middle lane, aimed at slowing drivers down in heavy drifting snow, were being overtaken by speeding cars on both sides. The AA said similar behaviour on the M20 led to numerous accidents, all due to negligence and a refusal to slow down in potentially lethal conditions.

Further afield in Wiltshire, a lorry convoy carrying nothing less than nuclear waste slid down a hill on a minor road near Salisbury. One lorry overturned on to a field and the other was left hanging over an embankment. Two locals walking their dog witnessed the accident and went to offer their assistance. To their surprise, they were arrested and questioned by military police. The farmer who owned the field expressed his amazement that a transport of this nature would be undertaken without stringent checking of the route first. Two anti-nuclear activists rushing to protest at the scene were also detained. No apology or regret was expressed by the MOD, but luckily no detectable nuclear material escaped from the wreckage. That same morning, the Isle of Sheppey had drifts over 20 feet deep and for a while was cut off from the mainland before snowploughs liberated the access bridge. Most of the Medway was under feet rather than inches of snow, and in Yorkshire the A1 was shut in places, the police installing hot drinks facilities to warm up freezing motorists waiting to move.

Tuesday 13 January saw the weather take an even more serious turn. The heavy snow showers began to band together, giving long periods of continuous snow that lasted across London and Kent until Wednesday. The winds became even stronger, and drifts began to exceed 15 feet on the North Downs. I remember the intense snowfalls made it hard to make out objects not far away in east London, and even the A2, one of London's main routes to the coast, running from the Blackwall tunnel, became hopelessly blocked that morning. With barely a car in sight and the roads deep in snow, that night the centre of London became virtually silent as the local news announced temperatures as low as -16 °C. Even glum Woolwich looked pretty covered in a thick layer of deep, powdery snow.

That night, with heavy snowfall in a deserted London and deep, powdery, blowing snow piled up thickly on the Strand and drifting shin-deep on the pavements, walking to Charing Cross was an unforgettable experience. Unusually for a busy road like the Strand, there was no slush or ice because it was so cold. However, the strong wind made the cold almost unbearable. The cold and heavy snow spread further and further west until, on Wednesday 14 January, the entire country was below freezing; even the Scilly Isles in the warm waters off the south-west coast succumbed to the snow, and the temperature fell below freezing by day for the first time in many years. By then the south had not exceeded -3 °C for four days and a reading of -15 °C in Sussex was recorded overnight. On the near Continent, the daytime figures were closer to -10 °C by day but the deep snow was not impacting our near neighbours as much as it was the UK. The cold had eased a touch in Finland, with only -22 °C in Helsinki, and the signs were that Scotland would see higher temperatures in the following twenty-four hours.

In the meantime, snow depths in the south of England had built up to incredible depths. West Malling in Kent saw level depths over 75 centimetres, with Rainham and Sevenoaks at around 60 centimetres; these kind of depths were repeated along both sides of the Thames Estuary, and across the North Downs drifts of 17 to 20 feet had built up along the more exposed areas. Trains were badly affected, and there were general cancellations in most regions, especially towards the south and east. A lot of commuters stayed home for much of that week.

The RAF had to ferry emergency patients to hospitals in Northern Ireland, Newcastle and Kent. Gas and electricity supplies held, despite record demand over a sustained period, and the Thatcher government began to give signs that they might improve Cold Weather Payments to prevent the numerous deaths from hypothermia reported across the country. Waterloo station actually shut its doors and packed up; with large amounts of rolling stock trapped and abandoned in deep snowdrifts, and passengers heeding advice to stay at home, the situation was hopeless as long as the snow kept falling. Thursday, however, saw the snow ease almost everywhere in the east. The very heavy snow shifted emphasis and began to impact the south-west and west of England and much of Wales. Heavy snow fell in Somerset, closing numerous roads, and in Bristol it fell all day, leaving motorists trapped on the Severn Bridge, while many parts of the M4 were closed to traffic west of Swindon. It remained cold over the next five days, and the lying snow stayed intact; any thaw only really got underway towards the end of the following week.

After the harsh weather had begun to loosen its grip and the snow began to fade, the government was furiously criticised by the WMO and a variety of experts, including many key charities, for ruthlessly ignoring a detailed WMO report published in 1979 that had recommended all Western governments take a variety of measures to protect life during severe weather. These measures included setting up a meteorological research agency that would ensure the government was up to speed and fully prepared for such events. Britain was apparently the only country in the developed world to ignore every single recommendation, and as a consequence the death toll was enormous. One day alone saw at least twenty elderly or vulnerable people wiped out by the cold. Dr Nick Parry, a social expert from Birmingham University, said, 'Our domestic arrangements for cold weather are extremely poor. For example, we don't even warn people to insulate their homes.'

A further report on the consequences of severe weather, commissioned by no less than the UK government itself in 1986, was also ignored on the basis that it would be far too costly to implement. It urged the linking of economists, meteorologists, charities and other agencies to ensure that information, funds and resources be linked to put processes and preparations in place that would save lives. This woeful lack of response from the UK government, even to its own report, resulted in not just a high number of unnecessary deaths but also a lack of warning for key agencies such as the RAC, AA and local councils. It also provoked the need to call in troops to manage food distribution to isolated communities, and emergency measures to release millions of pounds in Cold Weather Payments for vulnerable groups. The situation was summed up rather well by one of the national papers, which stated, 'As the city makes vast sums every day and drinks champagne, not even a mile away people have frozen to death.'

Statistically, the relatively short duration of this intensely cold spell means it is not well attested to in any monthly records. The average temperature for Gatwick for January was 0.5 °C. However, this included eleven ice days, fifteen days of falling snow, eighteen with lying snow and twenty-two air frosts. Between 11 and 20 January the temperature never rose above freezing, and on the 12th it never rose above -7 °C, which is very exceptional for the south of England. The period was similar in intensity to the severe weather of February 1895, and had it continued for some weeks it would have rivalled some of the coldest winters in the instrumental record.

The rest of the winter was fairly mild, and there was no more general snow across the UK for over four years. This spell also brought to an end a fascinating run of winter cold snaps that ran through much of the 1980s. However, the experience of such severe weather, although etched deeply onto the public consciousness, made very little long-lasting difference to centralised efforts to alleviate the widespread poverty and homelessness in Britain's crowded urban landscapes, despite the spiralling wealth being generated in the City at the time. Nine months later, a violent gale devastated large swathes of south-east England and also shut London's markets down for a day, creating shockwaves through the global investment community that, combined with a range of other factors, caused a major panic on the global markets, resulting in billions being wiped off the equities markets, decimating some of the legendary fortunes made in the city during 1987. The irony was not lost on the British public.

13

The Wrong Kind of Snow, February 1991

After the very severe January freeze of 1987, a series of extremely mild winters followed, and these coincided with the first robust debates in the media and among scientists about global warming. Predictions of rapid changes in sea levels, an explosion in British wine production and montages of palm trees lining the Blackpool promenade all entertained the media, while CFC usage began to be curtailed after a vast hole was detected in the ozone layer over the North Pole.

At that stage, climate modelling and the available levels of computer power were still fairly basic compared to now; however, natural climatic fluctuations, which are always at work, have become increasingly important factors in determining regional weather, bringing scientists and climatologists to differing conclusions. Nevertheless, the debate had begun. A very rapid warming clearly took place through most of the twentieth century, but a sudden cooling in northern Europe that began around 2008 has shown that variations in weather patterns and more extreme weather would be a key factor in the warming process; the term climate change has now largely replaced global warming to account for these uncertainties and differences of opinion.

The winter of 1989/90 was the third very mild winter in a row. February and March of 1990 were unusually sunny, dry and warm. Indeed, the summer of 1990 saw the second drought and blazing hot summer in a row, and included record-breaking heat in early August. During November, the weather suddenly went cold; watching Mrs Thatcher leave Downing Street during a very cold foggy and wintry spell in November, I wondered whether it were possible that we could actually get another cold winter.

This question was partially answered during the first weekend in December. Forecasts predicted that snow would affect many areas from the Midlands southwards during the first weekend of the month. In the event, this snow brought with it some severe traffic chaos. Despite accurate warnings of snow, people went about their normal Saturday routines. Perhaps this was because the day began with heavy rain early on and people thought the forecasts were mistaken. This early rain and sleet served only to wash away the grit that had been laid first thing, most notably on the M6, where the wet, cloying snow and gale-force winds blanketed major and minor roads alike with black ice, overlaid with deep snow. Some cars were stuck all day. The high winds also produced such a strong wind chill that snow froze solid onto every surface as the temperature dropped. Snow even blanketed our area around Kingston in south-west London on the Sunday and fell again that night. Although it became milder later on, there were several further cold snaps in December and January, and snow fell on a couple of occasions in the south towards the end of January when it turned cold and frosty.

On the last Sunday in January, the *Countryfile* forecast for the week ahead suggested that high pressure would take a similar position to that of January 1987 late the following week. The following edition, shown on 3 February, has become something of a winter classic. Very cold air was forecast to sweep in from the east on tightly packed isobars under a vast anticyclone centred over Scandinavia. In 1987, a vigorous anticyclone drove strong winds that caused such instability over the North Sea that blizzards buried many eastern coastal areas for days. The 1991 setup had the added feature of low pressure close to the south, which meant that the snow would possibly be more prolonged. Nevertheless, it appeared that it would largely be the same areas that would be affected in eastern and southern Britain.

Monday 4 February was my grandfather's funeral. The day was dark, grey, bitterly cold and windy across Sevenoaks in Kent where the service took place. The wind was piercing and pushed the low, scudding clouds quickly across the rolling hills and fields from the east. The darkness alternated with some brighter moments, with crepuscular rays of sun occasionally lighting up the landscape. A slight frost accumulated throughout the day and high pressure rose to the east and north, squeezing the isobars ever closer, causing a boisterous easterly wind to set in. As this bitter wind freshened, the stage seemed set for snow. The next day, the sky over London darkened suddenly. The first flurries of snow and hail swept across the streets, but, despite the cold ground, it failed to settle for long. However, towards the east coast, snow had already begun to fall in heavy showers and accumulations built up rapidly. During the afternoon the snow moved west and fell in heavy showers, settling across much of the south and east of Britain. It snowed on and off all night, and by Wednesday 6 February there were substantial depths of snow in many places. Kent, Essex and much of East Anglia had over 12 inches in places and some drifting began in the fresh winds. It was another dark, cold grey day, and snow fell in sharp showers throughout. The winds, however, became lighter and that evening there was very little traffic. The Christmas-card scenes of that evening transformed the London suburbs into places far more magical than they had any right to be. It was unusually cold, though. So much so that the snow was powdery and light, the type with which it is difficult to make a decent snowball.

On Thursday 7 February, the low pressure that *Countryfile* had predicted moved north across the south. The snow intensified. It was almost dark on Thursday morning, and the snow piled up in the suburbs of London, covering the roads and pavements in a deep, powdery layer of snow that settled to surprising depths, even in central London. East Anglia, Lincolnshire and Yorkshire all had 6 inches or more, with drifting snow beginning to draw a serious halt to most forms of travel. The Home Counties now had between 12 and 18 inches of snow and there was much drifting. Road, rail and all other forms of transport now ground to a halt and commuters were largely persuaded to stay at home. By Friday it had become very cold and Gatwick saw maxima fail to exceed -5 °C, dropping down to a very cold -12 °C overnight. The snow continued on through Friday, and it was not until Saturday afternoon that it turned back into showers. Some of these in the south-east fell as hail in a strengthening east wind, but there was no sun or brightness over the entire weekend. By this time, central London had 10 inches of level snow; much of southern England was under 18 inches or more.

Further north, it became apparent that Scotland and Northern Ireland had escaped the worst of the weather and, despite the cold conditions, there was relatively little snow. Nevertheless, all the ski resorts had plenty of snow, in stark contrast to a year previously, when even the highest mountains saw virtually no snow at all. It was a very different story in much of the north and east of England. Here there was deep snow, with disruption widespread. Leeds and Manchester airports sporadically closed. Flights were already being diverted there from Gatwick and Heathrow, both of which were closed at various times between Wednesday and Sunday, and huge delays began to build up; soon many flights had to be cancelled altogether. Mid Wales suffered more than other parts of the principality, with rural communities widely cut off, but it was clear that this spell was neither as cold nor as snowy as that of 1987. Most of the motorways stayed open, which had proved impossible in 1987. It was rail travel that seems to have been worst affected.

In fact, the railways became an immense battlefield in the media over the weekend of 9–10 February, and later even in Parliament. On Tuesday 5 February, British Rail had made the fatal mistake of declaring that they would keep the railways running despite the snow. By Thursday morning, the network was paralysed. Frozen points and fine, powdery snow blowing into the engines shorted them out and badly damaged many of them. A rail spokesman declared that their promise had been thwarted by 'the wrong type of snow'. The media rounded on this unfortunate but entirely accurate assessment with such venom that it still resounds with many today.

An Old Bailey judge, Justice Alliott, apparently so exasperated by the closure of nineteen courts due to staff absences caused by the failure of the railways, was widely reported as stating that 'the reaction of the authorities to keep London moving is pathetic'. This frustration at Britain's struggle to maintain a transport network when hit by the white stuff seems almost as old as the horse and carriage, and is much in evidence in this book. It is worth remembering that the heavy, wet snow Britain normally gets is harder to manage than the lighter, powdery equivalent many European and North American nations often experience; nevertheless, disruption can and does happen everywhere, and will continue to do so for some time to come.

The rail paralysis was quite short-lived. More trains were running by the weekend, but many commuters opted to stay home the following Monday despite the limited improvements. Schools were largely closed and supermarket shelves emptied of all the basics. The manager of one store in Hampshire described how more than fifty people were queuing at the door on Friday morning, leading him to comment that 'it's just a bit of snow, not the end of civilisation!'.

Saturday on the M25 was described as grim. Hollow-eyed commuters sat frozen in endless jams and many abandoned their cars and walked. One weeping couple, found at an A3 petrol station, pitifully described the five hours they had taken to get from Paddock Wood to Gatwick only to find they had missed their flights to Val d'Isère, where they were supposed to be skiing. While some roads were blocked with traffic, others became treacherous with ice. Five people were killed in car accidents at the weekend, while a further five more were injured in climbing accidents in the Lake District alone. The cold spell was no record-breaker, but daytime maxima remained below freezing for ten days. A group of exchange students staying with us at the time from California had been told to expect mild, wet weather. They arrived to over 18 inches of snow and temperatures below -10 °C. Some of the group actually went back immediately, such was the shock.

By Tuesday, however, the snow had stopped, and bit by bit things returned to normal. One of the main things that became very evident in this severe cold spell was the number of homeless people on the streets. In fact, contemporary accounts put the number at 100,000, and the government admitted that it could do little in the short-term. An additional 500 hostel places were found in the capital, but one homeless man sleeping out in deep snow in London was quoted as saying, 'The worst thing is never being sure you will wake up. Perhaps it would be better if we didn't.' Just as in many other cold winters to this day, many elderly and vulnerable people died from lack of heat and food. However, 1991 sharply highlighted the fact that Britain lagged far behind all its European neighbours in saving its poorest citizens from this fate. Even the USA, not known for its welfare system, fared better. It is surprising to learn that only 78 per cent of people in 1991 had central heating, and safe to say that those who didn't were among the old and most at risk.

Soon the newspaper headlines moved away from snow to war. As the snow began to melt, Britain and the USA responded to Saddam Hussein's decision to invade Kuwait in August 1990 with a bombardment of his forces, and so began the First Gulf War. A fresh heavy fall of snow affected the south-east on 12 February, but this was the last one of the season. Thereafter it became dry, and by the weekend of 16 February a thaw set in. It was only a gradual one, and many ponds still remained icy for some time. However, this severe spell was also to be the last truly notable winter event across all of Britain until December 1995. From 1991 until 1995 there was no generalised snow in Britain at all.

14

The Record-Breaking Cold and Snowy December of 2010

Not since the Victorian era, namely 1890, has such a cold December been experienced in the British Isles as that of 2010. Even more astonishing is that, before 1890, no colder December had ever been recorded, in a record going back to 1659. This includes the harshest winters of the Little Ice Age. At -0.7 °C, this was England's very first sub-zero month of the twenty-first century, and the first since 1986 – a full twenty-four years. This remarkable month came in the midst of a spell of colder winters that followed an exceptionally long run of mild winters, which had appeared to mark a sustained period of winter warming.

Suffice to say, since the blistering heat of July 2006, summer weather had equally seen a downturn with a run of disappointing, below-average summer months and above average rainfall. In fact, while the winter of 2011/12 was mild and unusually dry, the following summer was a washout, with repeated deluges and floods ending in the second-wettest year in England ever recorded (after 2000). These erratic meanderings of the British weather are nothing new, but over the previous decade, from a statistical standpoint, the number of extremes has increased. In the last ten years, a surprising number of records for cold and wet weather have been established. Nevertheless, December 2010 and its extreme cold came as a big surprise to both the public and the meteorological community alike.

The story actually begins in November 2010. The month did not begin unusually in any way. It was not particularly wet or dry, and temperatures were mostly average. On 4–5 November it reached

18 °C at Heathrow and it was at this point that the computer models first picked up unusually consistent and strong signals for a very cold period of northern anticyclonic blocking over Europe. Often, these signals can get close in terms of realistic time frames but then suddenly 'flip' into a milder and 'un-blocked' pattern. In this case, however, the charts became progressively clearer and more consistent; cold, dry weather was on the way.

The cold, dry weather duly arrived on 24 November in the south-east and a bit earlier in the north. Snow showers soon fed in on a north-north-easterly flow. In Leeds, it dropped below freezing on the 26th and recovered little for some days, with snow falling every day for five days. During the final week of November, very low temperatures were recorded in northern England and Scotland, and the north-east coast began accumulating large amounts of snow; as much as 2 feet of snow was recorded at several locations. In the south, the sun shone brilliantly out of cloudless skies but there were some very hard frosts indeed. At Gatwick, -5 or -6 °C was registered each night in the dry northerly airstream. On the 28th, the anticyclone sitting to the north of the UK, which stretched from Norway to Greenland, moved slightly further north and flattened out. Meanwhile, pressure was dropping over northern France, creating a strong easterly flow over the UK; to the south, in particular, the isobars tightened, and the airflow became unstable over the relatively warm waters of the North Sea.

Soon, the snow was to begin. On Monday 29 November, after days of clear skies and calm winds, an easterly wind picked up and cloud moved in by evening. During a birthday meal for friends, the smokers came back into the restaurant damp with snow. It had begun to snow moderately, and the cold ground and lawns were covered over immediately. Following some bad experiences of being caught in the snow, those living in other towns left early. The snow continued with varying intensity through the night, and about 2 inches had accumulated by 7 a.m.

It was still snowing around midday, and the fall had doubled to around 4 inches, but in areas higher up on the downs there was a deep covering. Central London had no snow at all. During the afternoon, a stream of heavy snow showers that had given huge snow depths in the north-east turned into a heavy, persistent snowfall through much of the south-east. Leaving London Bridge that night, it was soon very clear that the heat island of central London had greatly reduced the amount of snow on the ground. By Lewisham, the snow was deep, and constant blue sparks were lighting up the rails as we progressed increasingly slowly. Once into the suburbs, there was well over a foot of snow as it had actually snowed to the south and east of London without a break all day. I was stuck all night at Orpington on the train and it was only by a stroke of luck that I got a taxi home from there the next day in 14 inches of snow.

The deep snow paralysed most places outside central London. At Orpington, lorry drivers and motorists alike had abandoned their cars, some of which were blocking the roads. This meant that any snowploughs that came would be unable to pass. The M25 motorway was blocked and the police weren't letting people on that morning as vast queues had built up and any new traffic would only add to the problem. My car was under about 14 or so inches, and the snow reached up to the handle of our front door, which would not open. I had to use the kitchen door at the side. I began to dig out paths to and from the door to the driveway. The snow, which had begun on Monday 29 November, fell across Kent until Friday 3 December. By that time I measured 28 inches of even snow, in light or calm winds, on the lawn outside. These depths were obtained right across the North Downs and locations in Essex, Sussex, Kent and Surrey saw the deepest snow measured in the UK since 1987. Falls on the north-east coast reached 24 inches or more in many places and piled up for days on end. There was, however, one major difference between this event and 1987: the wind. Gale-force winds piled similar amounts of snow into 10- to 20-foot drifts in the worst-affected areas in 1987. There was almost no wind at all during these snowfalls, so drifting was fortunately never an issue.

The easterly flow slackened on 5 December as a warm front passed through and pushed the temperatures up just enough to give rain for several hours in the south. The rain and thaw did not reach as far north as the Midlands. Huge puddles of slush formed in the towns and cities of the south where there had been deep snow. As it was only just above freezing, however, most of the deep snow cover remained largely intact.

This thaw lasted less than twenty-four hours, and the next day it was back below freezing. It stayed bitterly cold for some days thereafter, but without any further snow. From 10 December, the temperatures rose in the daytime and a more general thaw set in. Frosts remained early and late, and the days were misty and grey. By 16 December, only patches of snow still remained outside of the towns and villages, especially over the higher ground of the east and north of the country. That day a band of heavy rain sat over Scotland and the anticyclone that had brought the intense cold began to reassert itself across Scandinavia. Far colder air was pulled down behind the rain band from the north as the high moved west and south, turning the rain to snow. The snow fell over London and the south-east during the rush hour and, although not that long-lived, it once again covered everything. The Christmas feel was inescapable.

The ground was covered with snow on the morning of Saturday 18 December, which was set to be the busiest day of the year for Heathrow, with a packed schedule of flights ready to take people to their home countries, and holidaymakers off to the sun for the big day. During the morning, it began to snow but only lightly. Christmas shoppers went about their business in a very traditional yuletide atmosphere. Chestnuts were roasted in the streets and hot wine bolstered the spirits of carol singers in the freezing high streets as the hustle and bustle of Christmas shopping went on. Snow was forecast in the afternoon across most of England, particularly in the south.

Sure enough, by about 10 a.m. the radar picked up a major band of snow moving north-east and this duly arrived at around lunchtime. The light winds became strong and boisterous, it went as dark as night and all hell broke loose. Blizzard-like conditions tore across the landscape and set in for the afternoon, dumping between 10 and 20 inches of snow across the whole region in a few hours. London was not spared any of the ferocity or depth of snow from this storm. Christmas shopping plans were largely abandoned and an ordinary afternoon turned extraordinary as roads ground to a halt and anybody out and about found themselves battling against elemental forces.

The snow was so heavy and accumulated so fast that the airports could not clear the snow off the runways fast enough. Millions of tons of snow had to be cleared manually from Heathrow's runway, causing disaster for those travelling abroad. This was also the case for the other south-eastern airports including Gatwick, leaving thousands more travellers stuck fast – some with nowhere to go. Heathrow became overwhelmed with a backlog of flights it could not shift and thousands of furious passengers desperate to get home before Christmas. It was not until the next day that Heathrow had moved all of the snow, piling it into vast mountains near the runways. The paralysis of the airports left many dumbfounded by the chaos that it brought. Some of it was around timing, and there is little doubt that our airports run at capacity most of the time and were at full capacity that weekend with no margin for delay. It was perhaps the worst Christmas disruption from snow since 1970.

For the rest of us staying in Britain, it was a memorable time. The snow stayed for Christmas, and it was an icy and snowy holiday. A slow thaw began around 27 December and accelerated into the New Year with heavy rainfall. By New Year's Eve, the snow was gone from Kent and, although not mild, the end of December was cool and damp, and most areas saw an end to the cold of the previous four weeks. Any fears – stoked largely by the tabloids – that it was to be the 'worst winter in 1000 years' proved false, and the rest of the winter was mild and mostly free of snow.

In conclusion, the infrastructure of the country groaned under the weight of snow in December 2010, but, despite the severity of the month, the food shortages, power cuts and hardships of previous severe winters did not materialise. The most severe transport disruption actually took place in Scotland, when the M74 was gridlocked overnight. Nevertheless, in my view the country held up rather well. The media would never accept this, but a glance back in time shows that today's expectations are based on a belief that the weather cannot and should not be able to govern our lives – but it does, and far more than we think.

This was the second-coldest December in nearly 360 years, and temperatures dropped very low. Northern Ireland recorded -18 °C, an all-time record in the Province. A temperature of -18 °C was also recorded in Powys in Wales, in late November. Combined with the subsequent daytime maxima of -5.6, these are the coldest such readings outside of Scotland ever taken in November. Although the last severe December, in 1981, saw some spectacular snowfalls and severe cold, some milder interludes ensured that it was not a record-breaker. December 1981 emerged with a CET mean average of 0.3 °C – the coldest of the twentieth century. Taking the thirty-day period from 28 November to 27 December 2010, the result is a remarkable

CET of -1.5 °C mean average – the coldest-ever pre-New Year cold spell. Only the last few mild days raised this reading somewhat higher. The month of December ended with a CET mean average of -0.7 °C, the coldest since 1890 and the second-coldest in the entire CET.

As far as 2010 is concerned, the Christmas airport closures will probably be what people remember best of this remarkable month – rather like the 'wrong kind of snow' summing up the February 1991 snowfalls. For me, it was the unexpected night on a train, as well a delightful sunny White Christmas that will be etched on my memory for some time to come.

15

Spring on Hold: The Snowbound Spring of 2013

An unusually cold March brought paralysing blizzards to much of Britain in 2013, and, with snow still falling in April and May, spring was held back several weeks by continued episodes of cold temperatures, snow and frost.

The winter started relatively late. By the end of December, it looked as if the winter of 2012/13 was going to be a mild one. December itself had been largely on the mild side, with only one short, sharp cold spell that brought a little snow to the east of the country early in the month. From then it became very wet, and flooding yet again plagued the UK after what had turned out to be a very wet year; the second-wettest on record, to be precise. Christmas, New Year and the first week in January were very mild, but a sharp frost on 9 January heralded a change. From that point onwards, it got progressively colder from the east as a blocking high set up to the north of the country, and easterly winds began to set in. However, the real story of this winter was not just that that there was a lot of snow; it was the dominance of easterly and northerly winds. In London, of the ninety days from January to the end of March, sixty-six had an easterly or northerly component. Average temperatures were below normal in most places, and March was perhaps the most severe winter month of all three of these months, despite technically being spring.

In much of eastern Britain, heavy powder snow fell all day on 20 January, delivering 11 centimetres in temperatures well below freezing. This was the culmination of a week of cold weather, and the snow lasted for many days. In point of fact, snow fell on thirteen days at my weather station in January, and lay for twelve. In February, it fell on twelve days and lay for five, and in March it fell on fourteen days and lay for twelve. Of these ninety days, therefore, snow fell on a total of thirty-seven, and lay for thirty-nine. Given some of the colder winters experienced since 2008/09, these are some of the highest totals.

As March began, there was an expectation that winter would end and spring weather would bring blossom, daffodils and buds as usual. The start of the month was deceptive. On 5 March spring was in the air. Clear, sunny skies and light breezes saw temperatures lift across much of the country, with 17.1 °C recorded in Gravesend, and 16 °C widely reached across the south-east. However, the sun lasted only a couple of days before cloud and rain took hold; it also became markedly colder as winds swung once again in to an easterly and northerly pattern. By the 10th, snow was falling across much of Britain, even in London.

On Sunday 11 March, a winter storm approached Britain from the south, where light snow fell during the day and left a covering in much of Kent, Surrey and Sussex. The heavy snow reached the south coast on Monday. Towards mid-morning, gale-force winds and driving snow hit Folkestone and Dover, reducing visibility to a few metres and causing widespread traffic disruption. In France and Belgium, reports of 50 to 70 centimetres of snow were widespread, and some towns were cut off for the first time in thirty years or more. During the day, the end part of the M20 became a horror show, with jack-knifed lorries blocking the main routes and slip roads. Even heavier snow in France closed down Eurotunnel, meaning the lorries that were still functional were backed up for miles on the M20 as the dreaded 'operation stack' was instigated. That evening the snow spread north, reaching the southern suburbs of London, but it was particularly severe across Kent and East Sussex. The evening rush hour on Monday was horrendous. In Folkestone, where drifts on the higher parts of the town and the A20 now approached 6 feet or more, the surrounding towns became gridlocked and outlying villages unreachable.

Gale-force winds buffeted my car on the commute home that evening, and the snow lasted all night without much of a break. By morning I measured 17 centimetres of level snow in my garden and, even in this relatively sheltered spot, there were drifts almost up to the tops of the fences. News footage showed evidence of vast drifts and Facebook and Twitter were full of stunning snow scenes from across the south. Traffic problems were diabolical well into the night, and many people were stuck for hours.

Milder air pushed into the south on 13–14 March and a thaw began. It seemed as if this rather exceptional event would now give way to more spring-like conditions. However, as a depression approached from the SW on Thursday 21 March, the blocking high over Scandinavia pushed cold air back south across the UK. Once again a bitter easterly flow set in, and severe cold returned with a vengeance, bringing with it more heavy snow, this time to the north and the Midlands. This depression in fact brought the most dramatic snow of the entire winter. Accompanied again by very strong winds, the snow persisted in many places for three days. Over the weekend of 23–24 March, thousands of communities were quite literally buried. East Anglia northwards was worst hit, with high ground and moorland bearing the brunt. Yorkshire and Cumbria northwards, right up to Dumfries and across much of Scotland and Northern Ireland, was buried in deep snow and under vast drifts. Power cables became heavily iced in the raw winds and began to come down, leaving tens of thousands of homes without power. Arran was without power for days while locals were often buried in drifts up to the eaves. One road that made the news in Cumbria had drifts 18 feet deep, and rescue service vehicles, lorries and cars vanished under the gigantic drifts and blowing snow.

The snow reached the south-east again the next night, and Sunday was an ice day over large parts of Britain. Approaching the last week of March, snow persisted over central parts and East Anglia until Monday, and it seemed that winter was only tightening its grip. In the vast, arctic-like landscapes of the northern moors and uplands, lots of farmers were able to rescue poorly lambs and keep them alive but some did not have the money to invest in such facilities, and the lambing was a disaster. One of the worst-hit areas in terms of losses of sheep was the Isle of Man. Drifts 15 feet deep in places buried thousands of pregnant ewes. Although this scenario was repeated across many other parts of Scotland and upland northern Britain, one Shropshire farmer told the BBC that he expected to lose 4–5 per cent of lambs to the cold; on the Isle of Man, the loss of whole flocks was becoming a reality. However the local communities rallied and people from all walks of life, be they schoolchildren or prison officers, all helped desperate shepherds locate their animals.

The cold spring of 2013 clearly showed that the severe cold more typical of the Little Ice Age could easily be matched in the modern age. Holding the number-one spot for March cold is 1674. With only 1.0 °C for a mean average, it rates alongside many bitter winter months and is remembered in Scotland for a thirteen-day blizzard known as 'the thirteen drifty days', which wiped out vast numbers of sheep, while East Anglia had lying snow from the third week of February right up until the end of March. The coldest March of the twentieth century was 1962 at 2.8 °C; however, 2013 came in at 2.7 °C, beating it by one-tenth of a degree. As two other March averages equal 2013 in the CET – 1892 and 1784 – this means the last time a March was colder was back in 1883.

The strong north-easterly winds strengthened as April began, and on 4 April snow fell all day in places in the south-east, with temperatures creeping up not more than a degree above freezing. Snow continued across many areas, quite widely and sometimes heavily on several days up to the 6th, and high ground in the north of England, Wales and Scotland saw the deep drifts lying unmoved in the cold, dry air. By the second week of April there were no daffodils anywhere in London, nobody was able to put out any bedding plants and crops were not being planted. On a trip to Manchester on the train in mid-April, large drifts were still in evidence throughout the countryside; here spring was even more recalcitrant, and April felt more like March. Over the Easter break, from Good Friday (which was exceptionally late that year) most garden centres reported business at half of normal levels, and stock running into millions of pounds was left unsold. Severe night frosts persisted, as low as -10 °C in the north and -2 to -4 °C in the south, and there was little gardening to be done. Not a single bud appeared away from the south-west, and May showed little promise of change. In fact, at the beginning of May, frost was still impacting areas north and south, limiting the growth of flowers, plants and leaves. The last unpleasant sting this unusual spring delivered was another widespread snowfall, this time in the middle of May, which swept across the higher elevations, blanketing many upland areas from Devon all the way to the north of Scotland.

In the twentieth century, the cold Aprils of 1917, 1922 and 1986 rank eighth, fifteenth and twentieth respectively in the CET in terms of cold. The all-time top spot is held jointly by 1701 and 1837, with a dreadful average temperature at 4.7 °C. Cold Mays seem more frequent in the last hundred years, with eighteen Mays colder than that of 2013, which had an average of 10.4 °C. Indeed, as recently as 1996 a very cold example occurred with an average of only 9.1 °C, ranking fifteenth. The coldest ever was 1698 at 8.5 °C. Nevertheless, when looked at seasonally, the spring of 2013 ranks thirty-first at 6.87 °C – colder than many bitter springs of the Little Ice Age – and was the coldest since 1888, 116 years years prior. However, the award for the coldest spring overall goes to 1837, which stands out far ahead, offering a dismal combined average of only 5.63 °C.

May was a month of continued disappointment. Even as late as the 24th, a daytime maximum of 6 °C was accompanied by hail and rain in the south-east, showing just how late springtime cold can actually occur. Luckily, after an average June there followed a glorious flaming July, with temperatures regularly hitting the 30 °C mark and a long run of clear, hot, sunny days. Only then did all thoughts of blizzards and snowdrifts become a distant memory.

16

The Little Ice Age

The term Little Ice Age was coined by climatologist Francois Matthes in 1939 while he was investigating changes in European glacier length and came across some rather unexpected results. Matthes saw a clear increase in the length of most northern hemisphere glaciers during a particular historical period, and then significant retreats in these same glaciers throughout the twentieth century. This contracting ice is a phenomenon that not only continues today, it has accelerated to such an alarming rate that it now looks likely that many of these glaciers will no longer exist in the not-too-distant future.

While scientists do not agree on exactly when this episode of great cooling in the northern hemisphere began, NASA has completed a significant study into the periods of most significant cold. There are three distinct decadal minima, all separated by warmer interludes. These are the 1650s, 1770s and 1850s. For our purposes here, the term Little Ice Age covers the period defined by renowned climatologist Hubert Lamb. This stretches from approximately 1550 to 1900. This cooling was not initially a constant process; it came in fits and starts, being at its most intense in the late seventeenth century. Additionally, it seems that major cooling was initially most keenly felt to the north of the northern hemisphere and gradually spread southwards. Sea ice and some glacial expansion were therefore observed to the north long before the period of greatest cold. This in fact began as early as 1250.[10]

This gradual and sporadic cooling process accelerated with time and began to affect the populations of northern Europe noticeably after a significant transition from 'reliable warm summers'[11] in the period prior to 1300 to the extremely poor summers that began with the first of NASA's three periods of climatic minima in the 1650s.

Of particular significance is the major change in winter climate in northern Europe. Here, the temperate winters of the north-west were replaced by increasingly frequent freezes. These reached a maxima towards the end of the seventeenth and start of the eighteenth centuries but lasted right to the end of the nineteenth century.

The transition to colder, wetter summers began as early as the fourteenth century when a rapid climatic downturn, with an appalling series of wet summers early in the century, marked a huge change from previous decades of reliable, stable summer weather. Studies of this change have indicated that the extended wetness, along with greater oceanic trade, prompted large migrations of rats from east to west. Lamb mentions research that shows how persistent deluges in China drove rat populations further west and south, taking with them plague-bearing fleas. One escape route would have been on to ships. This seems to be at least partly responsible for the spread of bubonic plague into Europe, which wiped out whole generations in the Black Death outbreak of 1348–49. In his book *Climate History and the Modern World*, Lamb emphasises that the Little Ice Age is the most significant cooling event in the historical record and, although the causes are up for debate, the impact it had on a range of northern hemispheric countries was enormous.

One of these was Ireland's disastrous potato famine. Persistent rain during 1844 and 1845 left most Irish crops poor in yield and quality. This coincided with a new strain of potato fungus that, combined with cold summer temperatures, lack of sunshine and drenching rain, decimated the staple crop, potatoes. These failed each year from 1845 to 1848.[12]

In that period, the Irish farmers were often tenant famers on large estates. On poor, rocky soil, potatoes proved to be a resilient crop. Unfortunately, this created a vast dependence on a single food source, which proved ruinous. When crops failed, rents could not be paid and families were evicted from their traditional farms, losing their livelihood. Any political influence of the native Irish population had become negligible in this structure as, since the union in 1801, Catholics had been banned from political influence and disenfranchised. Landowners were generally wealthy English gentleman or Irish protestants and largely absentee. Westminster's reaction to the crisis was therefore, to put it mildly, extremely slow and very limited. When the famine struck it took hold fast, and for the agricultural majority it worsened progressively. Within a year, villages and streets became littered with the dead and the dying. People of previously good character and stable backgrounds found themselves expelled en masse from their homes, living rough with only nettles and berries to eat. The younger children usually died first, and the adults slowly followed.[13]

By 1848, a million people were dead. While Robert Peel's administration sent a trickle of relief to slow the death rate and the ravaging of the island's economy, his successor, John Russell, called a halt to any relief going to Ireland, stating that 'the market will provide relief', which of course it didn't.

Where local relief was made available, anyone with a third of an acre or more was not eligible and the *Górta Mor*, or 'great hunger', worsened still. This episode led to the formation of the Land Leagues in Ireland, the first popular groups to resist this feudal system, making challenges in the courts against many of the lawless and random decisions that destroyed so many lives. The cold, wet weather continued into 1849, by which time up to 20 per cent of the population were dead or dying. The only option left for many of those that survived was migration to the Americas. Another million people migrated to the USA during the famine, leaving behind a broken and crippled society that would not fully recover for a century.

Ireland was not alone in suffering from this climatic and agricultural catastrophe. Scandinavia, Germany, the rest of Britain, the USA, Russia and Poland all saw enormous impacts from the climatic downturn. During the harshest phases, as many as 10 per cent of the entire population of these nations perished while the increasingly wealthy and burgeoning middle classes just looked on.

Iceland suffered particularly badly in the Little Ice Age. After a series of devastating volcanic eruptions that decimated their agricultural world, the winters grew harsher and longer, and soon the seas were frozen right around the country during the winter months, trapping fishing fleets in for much of the season and forcing people to eat their precious livestock. As the winters got worse, Denmark, of which Iceland was a part at that time, was helpless to send relief because of the great distance and the fact that the seas were choked with ice and often unnavigable throughout winter and much of the spring. When Laki erupted in 1783, the ensuing crisis killed most of the remaining livestock on the island as well as a quarter of the population. Visitors are often shocked to find that Icelandic delicacies include parts of sheep that most English people would blanch at: sheep's head in jelly, pickled testicles and eyes. These all stem from this period when hunger and famine were a fact of life and nothing could be wasted.

From the 1660s, when diarist Samuel Pepys was active, right through to the 1760s, some of the coldest winters of the instrumental era occurred. Statistically, the coldest is that of 1683/84. A description of this winter appears in the novel *Lorna Doone*, which gives a detailed account of the effect of the terrible cold, describing how birds died in great numbers, and the frost was so severe that it split oak trees open.

Diarist John Evelyn described the great frost fair that took place on the Thames that year thus: 'January 19, 1684: I went across the Thames on the ice now become so thick as to bear not only streets of booths in which they roasted meat and had divers shops of wares, quite across as in a town but coaches, carts, horses passed over.'

A vast area of high pressure controlled Britain's weather from mid-December until 19 February 1684, when a thaw set in. However, the general pattern itself remained, and two years of low rainfall and severe summer drought followed.

It seems that the Atlantic and the ocean currents were very weak at times, and one suggestion[14] for these cyclical changes is that sunspot activity was heightened at this time. These areas on the surface of the sun reduce infrared radiation dramatically and thus the amount of heat radiated. This could have disrupted the cyclical biannual tropical-zone stratospheric wind flows,[15] known as the quasi-biennial oscillation (QBO), reversing this and changing the weather progressively downstream. This link between the QBO and sunspot activity was made by scientists Labitzke and van Loon in 1988. Dryness and drought often occurs during such periods of reversed QBO flows, giving Britain a far more continental climate. The impacts of a reversed QBO may explain the recent cold winters from 2008 to 2013, and perhaps the unusually 'continental' weather of years such as 1947 and 1995.

After 1683/84, a long series of regular sub-zero winter months and mixed summers followed until 1739–40, when another extraordinarily severe winter occurred with a frozen Thames providing a frost fair. Further extreme winters also occurred in 1671, 1677, 1695, 1697, 1698, 1716, 1766, 1780, 1784, 1785, 1780, 1795, 1814, 1820, 1823, 1830, 1838, 1845, 1879, 1891 and 1895. After 1895, there was no severe overall winter until 1940, and a big upturn in summer and average annual temperatures suddenly began.

The five worst summers ever measured – 1695, 1725, 1816, 1823, 1860 – all took place in the Little Ice Age era.

Any simple explanation into the length of this downturn will have to look further than the QBOs and their ability to shape the jet stream's upstream patterns. The sheer longevity and severity of the period must have been driven by other complex factors to sustain the change. Volcanic impacts have clearly been at play to some degree, such as the vast eruption in 1815 of Tambora. The cooling effects of such eruptions produced ever-greater volumes of sea ice at the poles as more of the sun's radiation was reflected back out into space. This is a likely contributing factor and it has also been suggested that several large eruptions in the late mediaeval period had a cooling effect that was not fully reversed. However, climatologist Hubert Lamb is more convinced that the earth's changing elliptical orbit around the sun is a more fundamental underlying cause and responsible for the longer-term dramatic shifts of climatic regime the earth experiences. As the Earth orbits the Sun in an ellipse (giving an oblong rather than circular orbit), relatively small changes in our distance from the sun can increase or decrease the amount of radiation we receive over time. In the same way that the tilting of the Earth drives the seasons, the impact on the climate in the longer term can be large, and could be the cause of the Ice Age maxima our planet experiences. In terms of past patterns,[16] the Earth should now be heading towards a long-term cooling phase that will eventually end in an Ice Age.

Whatever the cause, research does show one clear fact. In the last 12,000 years, there have been three periods of major cooling, with roughly similar warmer periods in between. The last of these was the Little Ice Age, so it may be that there are specific cycles of cooling that already form a wider climatic pattern. Despite the human effects on climate that we are now experiencing, it seems logical to conclude that eventually nature will prove unstoppable, and the movement of the great ice sheets will once again draw the poles down to lie across where our familiar cities, towns and landscapes now stand.

17

White Christmases

Long before the festive season can reasonably be said to be in sight, images we associate with Christmas appear, and snow is an almost universal element of them. There is no doubt that this is a powerful, romantic and deep-seated association; yet when most of us in Britain look out of the window on Christmas morning, it is unlikely we will see snow falling. In fact, when I think back to Christmases from my childhood through to the present, most were mild – some frosty, but very few snowy.

Historically it has been suggested that it was Charles Dickens's images of snowy Victorian Christmases conjured up in his novels that began this trend; a world of bonneted carol singers, roasting turkeys and warm hearth fires– all of which are pictured against a backdrop of cold, snowy weather. Although these images seem largely responsible for our expectations of snow at Christmas, is there more to the association than Dickens alone?

This quintessentially idyllic Christmas seems rather a long way from the reality of modern life. Nevertheless, Dickens experienced some very snowy Christmases, such as that of 1836 (see chapter 54 on the Lewes Avalanche), or 1859, when Nottingham recorded -24 °C on Christmas night. The nineteenth century was the last of the Little Ice Age but was fairly typical of this climatic period in terms of winter climate. The previous three (sixteenth to eighteenth) centuries would all have seen some very cold Christmas Days. Furthermore, before 1752, when Britain moved to the current calendar, Christmas actually fell ten days later, so would have taken place on 4 January. There have been more snowy 4 Januarys than snowy 25 Decembers since 1900. So perhaps these factors explain why our recent ancestors must have associated the Christmas period with snow and cold, and how this association has become so deep-seated, despite today's warmer world. Indeed, the power of the White Christmas remains immense, and much of the population waits in hope of seeing one as the big day approaches every year.

As mentioned before, snow does not often fall in December in lowland Britain, although there have been some notable exceptions in recent years. The meteorological winter may begin on 1 December, but in general the cold deepens into January and February, when snow becomes more likely.

So, how many White Christmases have there been since 1900? The answer is far from straightforward, as the definition of a White Christmas is, in itself, a tricky concept to pin down. For the bookmakers of Britain, the official definition has been established as the fall of a snowflake on the roof of the London Weather Centre, reported by the official observer, at any time in the twenty-four-hour period. Bets will be taken either for London, or for the same scenario to be reported in other cities. For the general public, however, this definition seems absurd. Most people would say that a convincing covering of snow, most especially in the daylight hours, and seeing snow falling, is what they would categorise as 'white'. This means the popular definition is rare indeed, and has only been seen three times in London since 1900 in 1927, 1938 and 1970.

The snow of 1938 took place during a strong easterly incursion that ran from the middle of December and ended just before the New Year. In many parts of England, snow fell on pretty much every day on the run up to Christmas Day itself and in the south-east and London, deep, powdery snow, persistent snowfall and Christmas-card scenes gave something quite rare – a truly Dickensian Christmas. It was thirty-two years before this was to occur again, and the very snowy Christmas Day of 1970 (see White Christmas 1970), which began a little later than the 1938 event, carried on through the New Year period and delivered many days of heavy snow and deep accumulations. Many people assume that Christmas 1962 was a white one, but this was only the case in Scotland. The snow only made it to most of England on Boxing Day, so it was not a national event.

Less well known, but still a remarkable meteorological event, was the blizzard that hit the south on Christmas night 1927. A depression that year moved south-east across Britain on Christmas Day, delivering a band of torrential rain that became slow-moving across the region. Behind the depression, a wave of cold arctic air was drawn down into the disturbance and the colder air soon caught up with the warmer air in front and undercut it. After dark, as the air mass cooled rapidly, the torrential rain turned to snow. The rain was enough to rattle windowsills in the capital during the day, but for those who were in the theatre or at social gatherings that afternoon, a winter wonderland awaited as they stepped out into the evening. Outside of London, however, the snow was fierce. As it fell on gale-force winds, visibility was reduced almost to zero and travelling became impossible. The immense snowfall continued all night and some of the following day, before trekking its way into the Low Countries and northern France. It left behind drifts 15 to 20 feet high on the downs and hills of the south-east. The snow completely paralysed an area to the west and north of Canterbury. The areas east of this line got sleet and torrential rain. In fact, so heavy was the rain that it caused widespread flooding, and the River Stour burst its banks. The snow lasted until 6 January, when renewed heavy rain caused severe flooding, particularly along the Thames.

In order to get a national view of Christmases that can be considered white by every definition, we need to look at the records of both falling and lying snow in three of our key cities: London,

Glasgow and Birmingham. As records are variable before 1900, I have used that as a starting point for our purposes here.

1906
Snow fell west and south of London on Christmas night but only reached London after midnight, where it left a substantial covering.

1916
This year saw sleet fall in London, and some snow in Birmingham, but no lying snow on the day.

1923 and 1925
Both these years saw snow on the ground, and falling, in Glasgow alone.

1927
This saw a great blizzard strike London and the south-east; Birmingham also saw snow falling and lying but not in such great quantity. Glasgow saw wet snow and sleet, but it did not settle.

1938
In Glasgow, there was deep snow but no snow fell on the day. In London and Birmingham, it snowed and there was a good covering of snow of around 15 to 20 centimetres.

1956
Snow fell in showers across much of Britain on this occasion but no snow settled in central London. However, Birmingham did see 2 centimetres of lying snow. Sleet fell in Glasgow.

1962 and 1963
In Glasgow, a weather front gave a covering of snow during the day but the snow turned to sleet and rain before it died out. The following year the exact same scenario occurred. Neither years saw snow in London and Birmingham.

1964
London saw snow showers on Christmas Day, but not enough to give a covering. This year saw a major snowfall event across France,

Belgium and the Netherlands, with 24 centimetres in Brussels. Glasgow saw no snow falling but there was an existing covering of snow.

1966
Glasgow saw a covering of lying snow.

1968
London saw several sleet showers, and snow fell in the suburbs. Snow also fell more heavily to the north; Birmingham woke up to 10 centimetres of snow, and further snow fell during the day. Glasgow saw no snow that year.

1970
There was deep snow across much of England and Wales in a major wintry outbreak that lasted through into January 1971. Surprisingly, however, Glasgow only saw sleet falling on the day as milder air sat to the north and west of Britain.

1976
Snow fell in London on the day but did not give a covering. However, not long after midnight, more substantial snow fell in the east, with Kent, Surrey, London, Essex and many northern and eastern counties receiving several inches of snow.

1980
Glasgow had several centimetres of lying snow, and wet snow fell during the day.

1981
Deep snow was reported in London and Birmingham but the day itself was clear and cold. No snow was reported in Glasgow.

1990, 1993, 1995, 1996, 1999
These years saw sleet or snow falling but none lying at Birmingham and Glasgow. Only 1996 and 1999 saw this happen in London. However, there was one exception; Glasgow had a covering of snow in 1995.

2004

This year saw no snow falling in London; however, snow fell and settled in both Glasgow and Birmingham.

2010

This was a replica of 1981, if not quite a bit colder. Thick snow covered almost all of the UK, and had done so for much of December. The weekend before Christmas saw a vast snowfall in London paralyse the airports, and much disruption was experienced. Christmas Day itself was clear and frosty.

PART II
HEAT AND DROUGHT

18

A History of Heat and Drought

Detailed weather records are a relatively recent phenomenon in historical terms, and instrumental data even more so. Nevertheless, both research and ancient documents do exist, and there are some good sources that have enabled meteorologists to draw some decent indications as to how the climate has evolved in human history.

In relatively recent prehistory, in broad terms, the northern hemisphere came out of the last Ice Age gradually from around 6000 BC, and temperatures rose into a climatic optimum, or warmest phase, between 4000 and 3500 BC. During this period, forests grew at higher elevations than they do now, and the climate of Britain may have been a full 2 °C warmer than it is today.[1] Britain was initially connected to mainland Europe by a great plain that stretched out across what is now the North Sea. Mammoth tusks and other evidence have been dredged up over the years, both by accident and design. These intermittent discoveries have slowly been enabling archaeologists to build a picture of this extraordinary landscape, which has been named 'Doggerland', after the shipping region that inhabits a good part of it. As the climate warmed, often in peaks and troughs, the great rivers that ran across the expanded European landmass to the east and north began to grow into ever-wider estuaries. As these widened, they gradually merged with the sea, forming marshy landscapes in what are now the North Sea and English Channel.[2]

Over time, these areas began to flood with increasing regularity, and the great rivers began to expand yet further, consuming dry land and marsh. This must have sometimes happened gradually, and at other times in great flood events and storm surges. By 4000 BC, the geography of Great Britain had changed beyond all recognition and it had become an independent island group. On mainland Britain, the hunting-based cultures that had inhabited it since the Ice Age, or longer, became isolated. They had to adapt to a reduced habitat as the resources of Doggerland vanished. However, the climate now gradually declined until around 850 BC, when a famously terrible winter, recorded in ancient Nordic sagas as the 'Fimbul Winter',[3] was felt over much of the northern hemisphere, its impact perhaps lasting some years in the form of a significant climatic downturn.

After about 600 BC, a further, gradual warming began. This accelerated from 200 BC and lasted throughout the Iron Age until the end of the Roman period after one slight downturn.

It is in the Roman period that Britain's weather is first mentioned in the historical record, by Julius Caesar in 55 BC. It probably won't shock anyone to hear that severe gales and strong north-westerly winds were the subject of his record. Caesar's legions were stuck on the coastline of Gaul for much of the summer of that year, and, though they get across at the end of August, bad weather sank a great number of their supply vessels crossing into the Dover Straits and all but a few ships on the shoreline were wrecked. Julius Caesar withdrew, but in 54 BC once more tried to invade. Again, he found his forces badly affected by weather at sea. Caesar's armies left our shores before the winter and it was another ninety years before the Romans successfully invaded Britain, in AD 43.[4]

After the Roman invasion in AD 43, there are occasional accounts of major weather events. This is in the midst of what is termed the late Roman cool phase,[5] although heat and drought still played a role in this era. In AD 139,[6] it is recorded that a 'great drought' struck the south of Britannia, taking the Thames to such low levels as had never been seen before; in fact, historical accounts say that the river dried up completely, but this is open to interpretation. The river at the time was also part of a wider, marshy landscape, rather than the highly banked river of today. It may have been dry – or appeared so –in certain places while the flow remained extant in others. A further drought in AD 155 caused a major fire at *Verulamium* (St Albans) because of the parched ground.[7]

The next climatic phase, the late Roman warm phase, began around AD 200. Drought and famine are mentioned during this period as occurring in AD 362 and 374, and again several years after the Romans left Britain in AD 439; many deaths and episodes of severe drought are described. While the detailed impacts of such a drought are unclear, for an event to be mentioned and singled out in the records one can assume it was exceptional, especially at a time of massive social upheaval. As the Roman army left, the native Britons were thrown on the mercy of the invading Germanic tribes, who eventually came to dominate Britain as they gradually spread west.

Now began the Dark Ages cool phase. This commenced in earnest after the huge volcanic dust veil of AD 535–36 and lasted up until the ninth century.[8] Many historians agree that thousands of Britons poured into Brittany as refugees at this time, just as the Angles, Saxons and Jutes poured in from the east and north of Europe. Further into Anglo-Saxon times, a lengthy period of drought was recorded in AD 605 that lasted through the winter, which itself was bitterly cold, and from AD 664–65 another significant drought is recorded. A major dry period began in 676, culminating in three parched years in a row that lasted from 679 to 681. This saw the recurring failure of crops, and great hardship across the land. While a three-year drought sounds hard to believe, such dry periods in Britain are not that unusual. Between 1989 and 1991, two very hot summers and persistent drought were followed by a dry winter in 1991 and another relatively dry year. By 1992, many lakes and rivers were running low or even empty right across Britain and the media and some politicians were discussing piping water from the wetter regions of Wales and Scotland. It wasn't until the end of 1992, after prolonged rains, that the situation returned to its previous state.

Between 720 and 741, a further series of hot summers and regular droughts brought a far more arid regime; remarkably anticyclonic patterns dominated British and Irish summers and winters from 759 to 764. The year 763 is singled out as causing major water shortages after a roasting summer, with most springs and wells dried up, and we can assume that the great hardship for agriculture this must have caused lasted well into 764 after a spectacularly cold winter that saw the Bosporus frozen over. In 764, widespread heath and grass fires caused devastation at Winchester, Southampton, Cirencester, York and in the City of London.[9] Dry weather of great note returned in 822–24, but with little of the devastating effects of the previous century, and the period is largely characterised by warmer, wetter weather.

The medieval optimum period[10] saw a general upturn in the climate that lasted from about 900 to 1300. The 980s were a decade of progressively more severe drought, beginning in 986. Each year after that had hot summers and progressively more severe droughts and water shortages that affected Ireland and Britain and only ended in 995. This period included a four-month freeze in 988, implying a major slowdown in the Gulf Stream. An even more severe drought was reported in 1022 as taking a major toll in terms of livestock and people due to the 'excessive heat'.

A few years after the Norman invasion of 1066, many towns and strongholds in the south were reportedly ravaged by wildfires due to a prolonged drought. This happened in the very hot summer in 1078 and an almost equally severe drought occurred in 1089.

The thirteenth century recorded a tremendous rise of the incidences of hot and dry weather. This began in 1212 when a fiercely hot spring resulted in a huge fire in London, known as the first fire of London. This fire killed as many as 1,000 people and devastated the local economy. By August of that year, the weather had turned cold and wet. At this time it had warmed so significantly in England that vines were planted and provided fruit as far north as York.[11] The period from 1237 until 1288 saw an extraordinary period of regular heat and drought. Every summer from 1238 to 1241 was exceptional, and that of 1241 was reported to have had dry and warm, or hot weather from the end of March right through to the autumn of that year. Matthew Paris of St Albans commented on the summer of 1238, saying that 'the heat and drought were beyond measure and custom in two or more of the summer months'.[12]

In 1241, with the situation worsening, Paris noted even greater severity of the impacts, reporting that 'drought and intolerable heat dried up lakes and wide marshes, exhausted rivers, desiccated fish ponds and suspended the working of the mills; verdure perished and animals pined away from hunger and thirst'. One report from the coast of Sussex mentions people jumping from the cliffs on the coasts to save themselves from death by starvation. In the next forty years, eight periods of drought are reported, which included a range of warm and hot summers. In Ireland, 1252 takes particular attention because of the exceptional drought there recorded in the *Annals of Loch Cé*, which noted the 'great heat and drought in the summer of this year so that people used to cross the Shannon without wetting their feet ... the trees were burning from the sun'. The impact of this particular heatwave in England was also severe, and droughts continued through much of the 1260s; however, the incidences and severity lessened as the century progressed.

After a severe two-year drought that lasted from 1325 to 1326, the mid-1330s onwards saw a wetter, colder regime set in. This is known as the late medieval recession. Lamb points out that deluges across much of the northern hemisphere sent plagues of rats westward out of China and Asia, taking with them the dreaded bubonic plague that wiped out up to a third of the population of Europe. During the fifteenth century there were far fewer incidences of hot weather and drought, and wine growing in England gradually declined. Nevertheless, from 1473 to 1479, a series of fine summers were recorded; rainfall was very low during these years, although it appears that famine was also far less in evidence than during the catastrophic droughts of the thirteenth century.

Then, in the sixteenth century, what Lamb regards as the transition into the Little Ice Age (see above) began in earnest. In fact, it was in 1550 that this transition fully began. This year coincided with a major eruption in the Philippines of Mt Taal and brought a rapid downturn from the summer of that year, with extremely poor harvests. However, this was preceded, from 1538 to 1541, by an extremely hot and dry period that was felt all across Europe, with 1540 possibly being the hottest-ever summer in Europe of which we are aware. From February to September it only rained six times in London, and wells and major rivers ebbed ever lower. The heat was so prolonged and intense that year that, according to reports from Germany, 'the excessive heat continued into late October with the lakes of Bavaria still providing the only source for cooling off and the drought being exceptional from early spring'.[13] In fact, the Seine ran dry in Paris during the height of the summer, and people were able to walk across the mud to the opposite bank. In London, seawater that would normally be restricted to the Thames Estuary flowed up and beyond London Bridge for the first time in living memory. This polluted water caused the deaths of thousands of people and cattle from prolonged bouts of diarrhoea and dysentery in the area. According to contemporary records, drought was also fierce in Italy, where Rome recorded no rainfall for a full nine months. The spring and summer of 1541 were also dry and warm, although not as extreme as 1540. The Trent in England became nothing more than a 'runnel'. Rivers across Europe, already starved of water, ran dry, and conditions remained very harsh after three years of failed crops and below-average rainfall.[14]

In complete contrast, the following year, 1542, saw a complete reversal. The summer was very wet and cold, and from here on in this colder, wetter weather pattern continued, and along with the onset of periodically severe winters signalled a long-term cooling that would stay entrenched until the nineteenth century.

The Little Ice Age also produced periods of great heat and drought as the climate became more continental in nature, and the ocean currents appear to have weakened. In fact, as winters grew longer and colder, some being incredibly harsh, summer weather became ever more erratic. In 1583, a severe drought began in the early spring and ran through to the end of the summer, causing a great shortage of water, and a temporary upturn followed. However, 1586 saw yet another huge eruption, this time from Kelud in Java. This created a vast dust veil that caused a 'year without a summer' in 1587 and a renewed cold regime, and severe winters returned. Only 1591/92 saw drought conditions, though no great heat, before the next major eruption of Grimsvötn in Iceland strengthened the cold.[15]

As the colder regime of the Little Ice Age progressed, it seems the country also became drier, and not just in the summer months. Each decade until the 1630s contained periods of great drought alongside severe cold, but even these were interspersed with periods of extraordinary wetness. The year 1636 produced a long, scorching summer, as did the following two years. Between March and September 1636, some locations recorded barely any rainfall at all; crops failed and many trees shed their leaves because of the stress from lack of water and heat. Between 1651 and 1654, much the same happened again, with 1652 chronicled as an extreme drought and very hot summer. The 1660s were again extraordinarily dry. Most summers contained long hot and dry spells, culminating in the famous drought and hot summer of 1666 that provided the backdrop to the Great Fire of London. From there, 1667, 1669 and 1676 provided yet more of the same, yet overall the climate was cooling. The more erratic nature of the climatic regime was emphasised by the onset of another very hot and almost rainless summer in 1699 that began in June, and a period of aridity and below-average rainfall that began then continued up until 1701.

Although the eighteenth century saw some of the coldest and wettest summers of the Little Ice Age, long periods of great aridity continued, with a dearth of rainfall through winter and summer lasting from 1714 to 1716. Indeed, 1714 is cited as being the most arid year ever recorded, with only an estimated 280 millimetres of rain falling in England over the entire year. Thereafter, this trend for great swings of stormy cyclonic decades alternating with arid, anticyclonic decades continued. From 1731 to 1734 the dryness mirrored that of 1714–16, and 1738–41 saw not only exceptional dryness but bitter cold.

A far warmer interlude lasted from about 1770 to 1783, with two hot and dry summers, 1778 and 1783. Following the vast Laki eruption in 1783, there was an intense and prolonged winter and a major recession of the climate in Europe back to the seventeenth-century levels of cold.

The nineteenth century could offer no long-term change in the overall decline in climate, and an eruption in Indonesia in 1815 only exacerbated this by producing the coldest summer ever recorded, that of 1816. However, in the midst of this renewed climatic awfulness, which persisted through large parts of century, there appeared two extraordinarily hot summers: 1825 and 1826. Without doubt the summer of 1826 was, until 1976, the hottest summer ever recorded instrumentally – although 1540 may have been hotter, without instrumental data there is no way of knowing for sure.[16]

After a cold winter and a dry spring, June 1826 became very hot, and the period from mid-June to mid-July is still the hottest reported thirty-day sequence in the CET record. The three months of June, July and August saw mean average monthly temperatures of 17.3 °C, 17.9 °C and 17.6 °C respectively – a seasonal average of 17.6, only fractionally behind 1976. A full set of figures from Tottenham in London shows the heat in action. The resulting drought was not as severe in the east as it was in the west. Just as in 1976, high pressure was centred further west by the end of the summer. According to the papers at the time, the drought was by then most severe in Ireland and Wales, and water supplies were at desperate levels for cattle and humans alike across the normally lush and wet pastures of the Emerald Isle and Welsh valleys.

June was very exceptional. On 9 June, the temperature rose above 25 °C for the first time that summer, a value only two days in the entire summer failed to reach. For nine days it rose above 30 °C and twice higher than 33 °C. Apart from a little rain on 1 June, only one thunderstorm was reported on the 27th. The heat continued unabated into the start of July, and on the first ten days temperatures between 27 and 32 °C were measured. That month, 25 °C or more was reached on twenty days, seven of which exceeded

30 °C. Thunderstorms and some heavy rain were recorded between 22 and 30 July, but it was mostly hot and sunny. August was also consistently warm or hot, with twenty days above 25 °C and one of 31 °C.

After this superb summer ended, no whole summer season was warm or dry in any comparable sense for another forty-three years. This period saw some of the worst summers of the Little Ice Age in particular after a whole chain of volcanic disasters ejected a long-lasting dust veil that resulted in chaos and famine in Europe from the mid-1840s after five years of severe cold and wet seasons (see Little Ice Age). One of the driest periods of the nineteenth century saw a severe two-year rainfall deficit comparable to 1989–91 and perhaps drier still; this was 1853–54. In fact, over the five years from 1850 to 1855 there was consistent drought and this is one of the driest five-year deficits of the last 200 years. This also coincides with the third and last of NASA's decadal minima in terms of northern hemisphere temperatures of the Little Ice Age. The two are clearly related and are likely to be linked with a slowdown of the jet stream caused by shrinking differences between polar regions.

It must have therefore been a shock for the Victorians when the summer of 1868 came about. Clothing had become ever more austere, especially for women, in the cool climate after 1845, with tight black choking collars and furs. Extraordinarily tight undergarments and crinolines must all have made for desperately uncomfortable outdoor attire. The period of 1868–69, however, proved to be exceptionally hot and the summer persistent. The second half of July 1868 recorded nine days over 32 °C, with temperatures widely exceeding 35 °C on 22 July. In Tonbridge, Kent, a reading of 38.1 °C was recorded on the same day and for years most record books quoted this as Britain's highest temperature. However, this reading is no longer recognised; it was taken using an open-fronted Glashier stand and not a standard Stevenson screen. Nevertheless, it is estimated that, based on other local results, the measurement was still close to 37 °C, exceptionally hot for Britain. Furthermore, 32 °C was also recorded in every month from May to September, and drought became a progressively more significant feature of the weather, with less than 40 per cent of the average rain falling over the season.

It was not to last. A renewed regime of colder, wetter weather began again immediately thereafter and the late 1870s and 1880s were among the worst decades of the Little Ice Age for wet and cold, with 1880 and 1888 in particular comprising the depths of this meteorological nadir, with snow reported quite widely across the upland north of Britain in July 1888.

From the early 1890s, it appeared the worst was over. A much drier period began that lasted until around 1902. In fact, this period of very dry weather is responsible for Britain's record for consecutive days without rainfall. From March until June 1893 at Mile End in East London, no rain fell at all for ninety-three days. This drought was widespread across the country, with large parts of England and Wales receiving 30 per cent or less of their long-term average rainfall. The weather was particularly damaging to fruit, as it was not summer heat that brought the dryness, and the bone-dry air and low dew points brought persistent frosts in May, making the impact on agriculture considerably worse.

From here on in, every successive year offered a dearth of rainfall until 1902. Once again, 1895 proved very dry and delivered a further five-month-long drought that wrought havoc on the countryside. Before the century was over, the climatic regime also began to see a rapid long-term period of warming.

The post-1900 episodes of heat and drought are covered in their own right in this chapter. What one can conclude from the past history of heat and drought, however, is that, despite some really wet and cold regimes, at no time has Britain altogether escaped either phenomenon. To varying degrees heat has impacted agriculture and thus the fortunes of the population, and starvation has been a reality on many occasions since the Romans invaded the shores of our country and written records were kept. Whether they have been nationwide or local events, drought and heat have played a major role in every century.

19

The Great Coronation Summer, 1911

The summer of 1911 began early and, despite a few cooler and wetter periods, delivered the sunniest summer in the instrumental record, with record heat and drought conditions, especially in south-east England.

The first signs of summer weather began in May. After a rather cold start, the weather picked up fairly suddenly on 8 May and temperatures rose to 23 °C in the south of the country. The month proved to be a sunny one. The fair weather persisted through to about the 17th, followed by a cooler and cloudier interlude. The heat returned on 25 May and lasted until 8 June. On 31 May a destructive series of thunderstorms hit London and the south-east of the country, with a large number of people killed by lightning, in particular at Epsom where people were pouring out of the Derby on the exposed downs. Despite this stormy episode, temperatures in the south-east stayed warm, and 27 °C was recorded in the continued sunny weather in early June.

June 1911 was therefore somewhat of a disappointment. After the initial heat, the remaining three weeks were mixed, and some rain did fall. The weather had broken on 8 June, and a series of very cool days followed, with the worst of the weather coinciding with King George V's coronation on the 22nd. Just as at Elizabeth II's coronation in 1953, it was dull, cold and wet. Even right at the end of June, once the excitement and celebrations of the coronation were long finished, the temperature only rose to a depressed 15 °C as late as the 26th. Nevertheless, though a relatively cool month, June was dry and very sunny.

On 2 July, it once again turned hot. In fact, July turned out to be a classic month. Almost every day of the month brought clear skies, both south and north. An aircraft race run in London in the middle of July took place under clear blue skies and in great heat, at a time when the grass of the parks and fields was already dry, brown and dusty. Problems with milk increased, as, without refrigeration, such was the heat that milk was curdling before it got to many households; many children became seriously ill after drinking soured milk.

Soon the 'green pastures and hazy warmth' of May and June faded, the ground cracked and the grass began to turn brown, right across the country. Temperatures crept up. By 8 July it reached 30 °C at Kew for the first time. London reached 32 °C on two occasions in July and in Surrey on the 22nd a very high official temperature of 36.0 °C was measured at Epsom.

There were to be a further twenty days of 30 °C or more at Kew that summer, and the heat became progressively more widespread. Many places saw little or no rain during July; according the CET rainfall record, dating back to 1766, July was the nation's fourth-driest month, with only 15.8 millimetres, placing third behind 1911, 1825 and 1800.

Many people initially found the heat to be exhausting. However, with the humidity often low, some commentators pointed out that by the end of the month people became accustomed to the heat. Some fashion magazines at the time encouraged women to wear looser clothes and abandon the use of the tight girdles, while men wore light cotton jackets and straw hats even on formal occasions to mitigate the effects of the heat. Of course, this was not an era of sun worship – sun tans were still considered 'for labourers of the outdoor type'. However, the middle classes nevertheless enjoyed the beaches and resorts that access to the transport links of the day provided.

These modern facilities also allowed working families to enjoy the occasional day in the sun. Most British resorts were packed throughout the summer of 1911, and guesthouses could barely cope. Weekend traffic became blocked going into most south-eastern resorts such as Brighton, Southend and Margate, and amusement parks saw a huge boost in popularity. In the north, Blackpool and Scarborough enjoyed a golden summer at the very height of their popularity.

Along with most of the UK, London remained bone dry and sunny from 1 to 25 July. Saturday 29 July marked a change, however. The first rain for weeks fell on parts of the country, particularly to the west in the form of severe thunderstorms. That day London hit 32 °C – the third day in a row above 30 °C – and Bristol reached 33 °C. A violent thunderstorm broke in London with 'vivid lightning' and several hours of intense rain. At Caterham (then a very rural town), a house was struck and badly damaged and a passing pedestrian – the local postmaster – required treatment for shock.

Severe drought now took a major toll on farmers as grass for livestock had become scarce. Although 'agriculturalists' were delighted with the rain the storms of the 29th delivered, it was a short-lived event. The most intense summer for forty-three years saw the harvest reported to be the earliest since 1876.

The last weekend in July saw the ever-increasing heat's effect on the vulnerable come into focus. Several deaths from heat exhaustion were reported. Also, near Worthing, a man who had gone out to sea in a rowing boat was caught in violent thunderstorm and disappeared – the boat being found empty some time later. In Hanwell, west London, the annual fete at the village church of St Mellitus saw a more unusual cause of injury. As a thunderstorm broke, many people took shelter on a covered platform erected in connection with the fete. It soon became full, but people continued to seek shelter under the platform while the rain intensified. Suddenly, under the weight of the crowd, the platform collapsed. Three people were injured, one seriously, after being crushed by a piano and sustaining internal injuries. Luckily all the victims survived. July ended in great heat, and the average maximum at Kew Gardens for the whole of July was a stunning 27.6 °C. As July changed into August, the 'anticyclonic belt' remained firmly in place, and there was little sign that the weather would change its pattern.

The summer heat coincided with serious industrial unrest, in this case centred on both London's dockworkers and Liverpool's railwaymen. The strike meant produce could not be processed and distributed in London, nor could it be transported to and from the docks of Liverpool by rail. On the day of the most intense heat, and one of the hottest days in the last 150 years, the London dockers marched through central London. There were reports of intimidation and violence spreading, and the government had reason to be concerned as the strike in London was on a massive scale. Vast crowds gathered in the furnace-like heat to wait out the day and listen to the speeches and calls for action. The London men had in fact already got a pay rise and had all their demands met, but because this had been achieved 'far too easily', new demands appeared for longer mealtimes and holiday allowances (then a day a year). Further north, the Liverpool railway workers were ramping up the pressure too, and the strike spread to Birkenhead, creating a general strike for a day. Interestingly, the widespread industrial strife that plagued the summer of 1911 eased off rapidly as the weather cooled.

Away from this industrial strife, one commentator described the summer as 'magical'. On 9 August, the Wednesday immediately after the August bank holiday weekend dawned clear and exceptionally hot. By 9 a.m. it was already 27 °C in the London area; Kew reached 34 °C by noon, as did Nottingham and other locations in the south and Midlands. Maxima recorded that day were 35.1 °C at Kew, and 36 °C at Kensington and Camden Square in Soho. These values equalled the 36.0 °C recorded at Epsom in July 1911 – a record for the month of July that stood until 2006. Top of the pile that day, and indeed a new national record, was that recorded at Raunds in Northants – an official temperature of 36.7 °C, measured late that afternoon. Canterbury in Kent was close behind at 36.6 °C. This official record for the UK stood until 1990.

Interestingly, rather than bemoaning the heat, the papers continued to state that the heat was dry and that the very high temperatures had become such the norm that people adapted their clothing and routines to accommodate it, often taking the high humidity and sudden heat of August and September 1906 as an unfavourable comparison. Nevertheless, the dockworkers marching through London still wore waistcoats, collars, ties and jackets and some women still wore corsets in the intense heat; smelling salts would have been a must.

During the second week of August, the heat began to ease somewhat. Nevertheless, the weather remained largely dry and sunny, if not as hot. Temperatures in Manchester were not much lower than about 20 °C, and at Kew generally between 20 °C and 25 °C. The temperatures soon climbed again and the end of the month saw the searing heat return. Forecasters at the end of August were predicting a major breakdown of the heatwave, but the strong Azores anticyclone once again continued to extend northwards and eastwards over the whole country and, contrary to what was generally anticipated, the Atlantic depressions were driven back by the Azores high yet again.

Early September saw the heat return to the unusual levels experienced at the beginning of August. At Kew, 30 °C was reached on no less than five days in the month, topping out at an impressive 33 °C on the 9th. By this time, agriculture was in a very poor state. Famers were using the hay dried for the following year to feed cattle.

The countryside looked parched and brown, and many village greens and parks of cities and towns across England and Wales were devoid of grass altogether, with just dust and brown scrub having replaced once lush green grasses. Over a very wide area many rivers and ponds had actually run dry completely and stones and branches long swept away were exposed by the drought for the first time in many a year.

Of course, nothing lasts forever. On 13 September the maximum temperature reached 30 °C at Kew for the last time. The following day, the values dropped down to 17 °C and the long-awaited Atlantic depressions finally swept the hot air away. In the space of a few hours, the Mediterranean weather was replaced by grey skies and the more familiar wind and rain that blows across the British Isles in an average autumn.

Cruelly, but not unusually, the following year, 1912, saw one of the wettest and most awful summers of the entire twentieth century. It was a full nine years before another warm, dry summer took place, and it was not until 1976 that 1911 was convincingly beaten.

20

The Great Drought and Record-Breaking Summer of 1976

For those who don't remember 1976, this was the hottest summer of the twentieth century and the hottest in the entire CET record, which dates back to 1659. It was also the culmination of one of the driest periods of the last two hundred years, with a dearth of rainfall beginning with the hot weather of 1975 and continuing with an exceptionally dry winter and spring.

In fact, 1975 produced some very hot weather, with 32 °C in London reached in early August, which at the time was the hottest month ever measured in the UK. The warm, dry weather continued through into to September, as did the dryness that began that summer and lasted through the autumn and the following winter and spring. After a cold and snowy period at the end of January and early

February 1976, a period of sunny and mainly dry weather began in the cold of February and lasted throughout March. March was a remarkably sunny month, with day after day of clear blue skies and cold, misty and sometimes frosty mornings. The usual grey dullness that is such a feature of the northern European winter and spring was largely absent.

However, by April, signs of a serious drought in Britain became evident. April once again saw very little significant rain and it was around this time that the government, media and the general populace began to realise that further dry weather, combined with a hot summer, could spell disaster for industry, agriculture and the population of Britain at large.

After a warm, sunny Easter break in April, the first two weeks of May were gloriously hot. Very little or no rain fell over England and Wales, and at Heathrow 29 °C was reached. The grass began to die, becoming patchy and wilting into a generally straw-like state from which it did not recover that summer at all. The second half of May was not so warm, but the generally sunny weather persisted, and cloudy days were minimal; rain was still a rare event.

June continued bone dry and sunny. Rain refused to fall in any helpful quantity, and the first two weeks of June began to see some really hot days, with 30 °C being recorded widely across the UK. I was living in Brussels then and I remember being dismayed that my mother would stand by the front door as we left for school every day in June to make sure I took a jacket to school. As the days got hotter, the battle of wills grew until one day when it had become so hot, so early in the morning, that I bluntly refused to take the jacket off the peg. She admitted defeat.

Some heavier bursts of rain arrived on 20–21 June across most of England and into the Low Countries, frustratingly ruining my brother's eleventh birthday party, which had to take place indoors after weeks of sun. Nevertheless, the rain that weekend was the final general rain before the weather finally broke in the last week of August. The next day, in fact, the sun returned and, for the following few weeks, never really left. On 23 June, London reached 30 °C yet again and high pressure began to build strongly across southern Europe, extending quickly northwards. Scotland and the north of Britain continued to be influenced by low pressure initially, but here, too, as the influence of the high spread further north, skies cleared and thermometers began to rise. By 30 June, Edinburgh was up at 27 °C, Manchester 30 °C and London at 34 °C.

In early July, the heat reached its peak. Much of Britain was recording temperatures over 32 °C every day. The period from 24 June until 9 July saw 32 °C reached in the UK somewhere on each day; a total of sixteen consecutive days. The mornings would begin clear and warm, but temperatures climbed fast from late in the morning, leading to breathless, body-sapping heat in the afternoon from which there was no escape. I remember taking a bus home from school around the very beginning of July, when Brussels reached 36 °C several times, and thinking this was the hottest I had ever felt. Luckily, an end to school was called a full two weeks early because of the heat and we were shipped back to England for the summer.

Although the fine weather was uninterrupted, it was very occasionally punctuated by some memorable thunderstorms, especially in July. Some spots got close to breaking records as well – Southampton recorded 35.6 °C at the end of June – but it was concern over the dwindling water supplies that dominated the media. Ponds, rivers and lakes began to dry up fast and the nights were so warm that sleeping outside offered the only chance of relief for us at home.

As Britain became progressively more dry and parched, wildfires began to break out, sometimes on a large scale. Grass fires and forest fires became a constant feature right across England and Wales, and even in London many open spaces and commons saw serious fires. In Sevenoaks, smoky skies and the foul smell of burning alerted locals to a huge fire on the nearby downs in August; this was typical of the kind of wildfires that ravaged most of England in July and August, and the fire services struggled to cope.

The water crisis began to take an even greater hold of the government and the media's attention. The main concern at the time was how to meet industrial demand and what steps to take to ensure that it was not interrupted. A Water Bill was rushed through Parliament that enabled the government to take steps to protect and control supplies. This was completed in the light of advice by the famous meteorologist Dr Hubert Lamb, who advised the authorities that a more 'arid regime' was a possibility in the UK, and measures to better control and store water should be implemented. It was also not long before the use of hosepipes was banned in England and Wales for the first time. However, the restrictions did not go unchallenged.

Many journalists noticed that some in the water industry who were calling for a four-fold increase in water storage capacity were not following any solid pattern of evidence, and Dr Lamb also warned that nothing about our long-term climate is certain. One newspaper editorial pointed out that we surely couldn't spend a fortune on anticipating 'every climatic quirk' without any real knowledge of the future. Nevertheless, the heat went on and soon night-time shut-offs of the water supply joined hosepipe bans; there was also a request to put bricks in cisterns to save water.

While the Wimbledon men's final between Năstase and Borg was played on courts said to be exceeding 40 °C, the papers were headlining a statement by the EEC[17] that expressed hope that the heat would reduce the massive milk and butter 'mountains' through lower agricultural yields. In mid-July, the Met Office said the great heat would soon come to an end, with showers and thunderstorms to precede a return to average weather. Agriculture and industry held its breath, but the Met Office was far from the mark. The great heat continued, although less fierce than in the first two weeks of the month, and the Met Office were left scratching their heads as to the Atlantic's inability to break the drought.

It was reported that London's tourists were becoming more and more fractious in the intense heat. The tourist industry in London was suffering as people were refusing to pay extortionate prices for ice cream and drinks or to be whipped through the city at breakneck speed on a roasting-hot tour bus. Bookings fell rapidly as the heat intensified. However, outside of the capital, beaches became packed across Britain, and a huge boom in tourism saw visitors to British resorts in the sorts of numbers they could only dream of today. Cornwall and Devon were inundated with swarms of visitors looking for relief from the oppressive city heat, while these were the very areas (the south-west and Wales) worst affected by drought and water shortages. Water supplies were running critically low by July, and only half of Cornwall's 2 million gallons a day were getting through by August; there simply wasn't enough water.

On 16 July, a series of spectacular afternoon thunderstorms moved across much of south-east England and London. It was the only lengthy daytime storm of that month. In fact, this was one of only three rainfall events of any kind during July in the south-east, where we were staying in Wimbledon with my aunt. Just after lunch, the sky darkened until it was virtually black, and thunder could be heard booming from a distance. Soon after, almost continuous thunder and lightning, torrential rain and hail flooded streets and tore up flowers from their beds in a theatrical display that lasted for a couple of hours. The rain was of tropical intensity but afterwards yet another ridge built in from the Azores and the dry, sunny weather continued, with temperatures in the mid to high twenties. Despite this rain, the extent of the dry and dusty landscape is not something I have ever seen again in the UK, not even during the hot summers of 1990 and 1995.

There were no more major storms in England during August and the weather became even clearer and more consistent than at the end of July, with high temperatures sometimes cracking the 30 °C mark but generally in the mid- to high twenties.

The water restrictions remained stringent. The water supply was cut off overnight, and bathwater had to be shared in the evening. Every telegraph pole in the lanes of Cornwall, where we holidayed that year, had a notice nailed on stating 'Drought, Save Water!'; and it did the trick. My grandparents took the restrictions very seriously. As part of our evening routine, we would fill up bottles and jugs, the sinks and buckets in the loo before the 10 a.m. cut-off. Bricks were put in the cisterns to stop as much water filling them.

It is said that all good things must come to an end. During the week before the August bank holiday it reached 30 °C for the last time. That Friday, a cool breeze and light showers spread gradually from the south-west and the azure skies faded out of sight. The next day and throughout the August bank holiday the heavens truly opened, and it felt like nature was taking its revenge for having to stop up the rain for so long.

The impact on agriculture of the 1976 drought was considerable. There was a significant impact on crops, as aphid infestations decimated the wheat crops in several counties; fruit was dropping off the trees long before ripening because of the water stress of the trees, many of which were also shedding leaves for the same reason.

Dennis Howell was appointed Minister for Drought and courted controversy when he pleaded with 'concerned neighbours' of any transgressors of the water restrictions to report any offences, in secret, if necessary. One can imagine that many a petty score was settled and provided the basis behind neighbours being shopped to the council and fined. However, the media felt it was promoting an Eastern bloc-type informer culture that was most un-British. Howell responded by saying, 'I don't think of it as informing, it is seeking to achieve a responsible attitude; clearly people understand what it is we are trying to do. It's good people are aware of water being wasted.'

September was one of the wettest on record, and flash floods and deluges occupied the minds of the nation instead of drought; as the reservoirs and aquifers gradually filled up again and usage of water dropped from its high summer values, the crisis ended seemingly with some pace. Nevertheless, it was in fact several months, after an atrociously wet and cool summer in 1977 and a very wet winter, before the situation returned to that prior to the drought.

The summer was the hottest ever in the UK in records dating back to 1659. Mean CET temperatures for June, July and August – at 17.0 °C, 18.7 °C and 17.6 °C respectively – delivered an overall mean average of 17.8 °C for the summer season. This figure is unlikely to be easily matched, as is the desiccation of the 1975–76 drought period.

Without doubt, it is hard to envisage the challenges faced by government and populace alike in 1976 being faced again anytime soon. The country has changed in many ways since, in part due to the generally warmer summers we regularly experience. Air conditioning is now commonplace and long-term forecasts and general trend forecasting are much more accurate, potentially giving the authorities time to better prepare and plan.

One final thought. It is also worth considering the consequences for the UK if the dry weather of 1976 had continued into the autumn of that year. The impact would have been very severe indeed, and perhaps this scenario should be the doomsday drought benchmark for current and future governments to consider in planning for the next great drought crisis, which we will certainly face one day.

21

The Long Drought and Record Heat, 1989–90

After the stormy winters of 1988 and 1989, and a particularly dreadful summer in 1988, a period of great heat and drought began in May 1989 that struck a complete contrast to the wet and cold of the year before. Despite being followed by another stormy winter, culminating in the Burns' Day storm of January, the heat and drought continued for a second, even hotter summer in 1990. This, although not as serious as 1976, produced an extended drought that only really concluded in 1992.[18]

The winter of 1989 was a mild one, and very little snow fell across England, Wales and even Scotland. Typical of this mildness was Heathrow, with only 28 millimetres of rain, no snow and only four frosts. The spring, however, was not particularly warm, and the end of April was grey and rather cold. However, the May Day bank holiday was a day of transition. The weather was grey and quite cool, and there was a little drizzle across south-east London, where I was at university, in the morning. The next day, however, the sky was clear and sunny, and the temperature rose. Thereafter, a period of glorious sunny weather set in. After a minor break around 12–14 May, it then became very warm and sunny until the end of the month, with temperatures in London hitting 29 °C on 24 and 25 May. At this time, while the temperatures were at their highest, there were some severe thunderstorms; in various locations surrounding London, floods and deep accumulations of hail led to both damage and disruption. Nevertheless, the month was predominantly dry and sunny and a welcome break from the very poor weather of the previous summer.

By the first week of June, however, it had switched to a very cool and wet regime, a great disappointment after such a remarkably sunny and dry May. Rain fell very heavily on several days and it looked very much like it was going to be another cold and dreary summer. To everybody's great surprise, 10 June dawned warm and very sunny and temperatures right across most of the UK responded well. Between 10 and 27 June, the weather in London was either warm or hot. Daytime maxima sat between a sweltering 28 and 30 °C, memorably coinciding with my end-of-year exams and a tremendous party on Brighton Beach in fierce heat.

June was the second month in a row with below-average rainfall and above-average temperatures. Sunshine figures also began to creep up, and it was with some luck that I managed to get a holiday job that year as a postman, as almost every day dawned with bright sunshine and great heat.

July was the hottest month since 1983 in much of England and Wales, and with an average maximum value of 25.9 °C it was in the exceptional category – with an extraordinary monthly average of 20.2 °C. The first few days of the month began with average temperatures, but after 11 July the rest of the month was warm or hot yet again. Temperatures in London climbed above 25 °C on twenty-two days and above 30 °C on seven of those; in fact, 30 °C was reached on six days in a row from 20 to 25 July, reaching 34.2 °C on the 22nd. Only 9 millimetres of rain fell at Heathrow, and the countryside began to turn brown under the hot sun and increasing drought. The heat was on and, on this occasion, not restricted to the south as it had been in 1983. Leeds in Yorkshire saw the temperature rise above 31 °C on a number of occasions, and even the lush Yorkshire dales began to wilt in the sun. August also saw plenty of dry, warm weather, with an average maximum temperature of 24.2 °C in London, and it remained dry and parched until the beginning of September. The first half of September was warm or hot and, as late as the 21st, it reached 27 or 28 °C widely across England and Wales. Autumn temperatures weren't too exceptional after this, but October and November had below-average rainfall, especially in the south and east.

The following winter was extraordinarily mild, and January's average maximum was 10.1 °C in England. It was the second winter in a row that had been exceptionally warm, but the month also had a very stormy period, with the famous Burns' Day storm killing over forty people on 25 January.

By mid-February the weather was spring-like, and on the afternoon of the 23rd, 19 °C was reached in the east. March proved to be even more unusual. The weekend of the 17th saw a mini-heatwave, with 23 °C reached widely across the south. Easter was generally fine, but the middle of April saw an unsettled spell. After that, the sun returned.

The first genuine heatwave coincided with the May Day bank holiday. From 30 April until 7 May the weather was hot and sunny, and the beginning of May saw 28 °C reached across most of England under clear, Mediterranean-like azure skies. Although it cooled down a lot after this weekend, May was sunny almost all the way through. Day after day dawned clear, and it was almost a pleasure to get up and go into work in the morning. It was now getting very dry; May was dry for the second year in a row, with only 5 millimetres of rain during the whole month across England. It seemed that this long dry period would not end.

There was one notable exception to the very dry months of 1990, and that was the unexpectedly unsettled June. While the temperatures were about average, only two days exceeded 25 °C, and 42 millimetres of rain fell.

July saw a switch back to the dry, hot weather pattern. Temperatures climbed and it was mainly dry and sunny throughout. By 15 July, 30 °C was widely reached in England, with Heathrow reaching 31 °C that day as an example. From then on, it did not get cool again for some time. The rest of July was very hot, and as we moved into August the temperatures moved into the exceptional category. Only 9 millimetres of rain fell in July, so now the overall rainfall totals for the year had become woefully small.

On 1 August the heat began to reach its zenith, and for the first five days temperatures were between 32 °C and 37 °C in England. Wildfires were breaking out across the country, and water supplies dwindled. On 2 August, Big Ben got so hot it refused to chime. The heat caused the mechanism to fail, and most of the papers delighted in the fact that for once it was heat, rather than ice, that had caused it to fail in its duty. In Sussex, a swing bridge on the main road at Newhaven jammed shut as the wood expanded in the heat, and the rush-hour traffic stood waiting for hours as the fire brigade sprayed it with cold water to shrink it back and get it open.

The north-west saw its hottest ever spell as Leeds saw a temperature of 34.5 °C, the highest ever measured there, and the rain shadow provided by the Peak District had proved most effective in keeping things to the east of the Pennines bone dry. Almost no rain at all had fallen at Leeds since the end of June. The district itself was seeing a number of larger fires break out, even on the higher ground around the city and in the Yorkshire Dales to the north. In fact, the Peak District itself saw such paltry rainfall all year that, by August, it was assessed as one of the most vulnerable points for wildfires in England. From the week beginning 2 August, the Peak National Park was shut because the risk of fire was so great. This sent the Ramblers' Association into convulsions of rage; just as the best weather of the year had arrived, they were now stopped from enjoying some of the best countryside in Britain. One letter to a newspaper suggested that having ramblers there might actually stop fires as soon as they broke out; the writer argued that ramblers would be able to report any smoke they saw far more quickly to the authorities, rather than fire crews being alerted to fires that were only discovered because they had got so large as to be visible. A David Bowie concert due to take place at Milton Keynes on Friday 3 August was considered for cancellation because of the heat, but it went ahead on the understanding that the crowds would be hosed and free water given out at multiple points to prevent casualties.

At this point, the highest official temperature recorded in Britain was 36.7 °C, measured at Raunds, Northants, taken on 9 August 1911. On Thursday night it was reported that Worcester had reached 36 °C and that somewhere west of London could well break the all-time temperature record the next day. Friday 3 August was very hot indeed, and I took the day off work so I could go to a friend's house and enjoy their garden for the day. The morning was very hazy and the humidity relatively low; nevertheless, it felt extremely hot taking the train, despite going away from London and against the commuter tide, at a time when air conditioning on public transport was unthinkable. Those lucky enough to be on holiday were relishing the spectacular weather. There was almost no wind that day and the sky remained hazy until the evening, when it cleared completely. A number of different locations were cited as being the record-breaker that evening, but the next day it appeared as if Cheltenham had come out as the winner, with a new British record of 37.1 °C.

Some weather enthusiasts were disappointed the magic 100F mark had not been breached; 37.1 °C was only 99F on the Fahrenheit scale, used long ago in Britain but abandoned in 1960 by the meteorological community. However, perhaps most disappointed were the people of Nailstone in Leicestershire, which at first was thought to be the location of the record at 37.0 °C. They were pipped at the post by one-tenth of a degree, and any hope of the glory that comes with a national record soon vanished. The local postmistress there at the time, Joy Lawrence, was interviewed by the press when it was thought the record had gone to the town, and she reported that the extreme nature of the heat was manifested by the fact that customers were sneaking in to her shop, hanging around the freezer cabinet and then leaving without making a purchase. The Constabulary Chief of Gloucestershire, Albert Pacey, was forced to agree that officers could patrol without ties for the first time in their history, such was the exceptional nature of the weather. In Essex, the historic Mountfitchet Castle suffered the terrible humiliation of having the waxwork guard, who had stood watch of the tower for some years, completely melt.

The subsequent night in London was boiling. At St James' Park the minimum temperature was 24.0 °C,[19] a record that has yet to be broken. Saturday was a little less hot across the south. In London the haze of the day before was gone, replaced with a beautiful turquoise sky. It reached 35 °C, just one degree down on the day before. Poor old Tower Bridge fell victim to the heat that day as the fierce sun had stuck it in position. Out came the fire crews and their hoses while the traffic waited in the sizzling sun for them to cool the joints down. On the Saturday night, there wasn't a hint of a breeze. The first sign of a change came from Scandinavia, when a large low-pressure system, blocked from moving south by the hot, dry air over the rest of Europe, took its revenge by sending down a front of cold air south all the way across Britain. Sunday was another gloriously warm and sunny day, but it only reached 25 °C; the great heat was over and many people were relieved.

August remained largely sunny, and two more periods of hot weather occurred; one of them a week after the great heat, a second in the last week of the month. These heatwaves saw 29–30 °C rather than the more exotic values of the earlier event, but another glorious hot and dry month nevertheless went by, and in London rain only fell on three days, with 27 millimetres mainly falling from one thunderstorm. In fact, right across the country August was extremely dry. Fire risk remained, particularly across the north.

Overall, 1989–90 had not been so nearly as dry as 1975–76; several other dry periods were yet to come in the 1990s and the next decade, which still failed to reach the extreme levels of drought experienced then. However, it is the overall warmth and dryness of the twenty-four-month period up until the end of 1990 that was truly remarkable. Of particular note was the staggering warmth of the winter months and, of course, the record-breaking heat in August. Although 1991 was not a good summer, the winter was again dry overall. This meant that, despite a more average year in 1991, water levels were still low across much of England. It wasn't until 1992, after another unusually warm and dry spring ended in a wet summer, that water levels returned to normal and the long dry period finally came to an end.

22

The Hot, Arid Summer of 1995: A Rival to 1976?

The two very hot summers of the first decade of the twenty-first century, 2003 and 2006, were far less memorable than other golden greats such as 1976 because rain and cloud interrupted the heat and sun, sometimes for long periods. The glorious summer of 1995 suffered no such breaks, and the sunny weather persisted into the autumn, making it a genuine challenger to 1976. This renewed period of drought came only three years after the last long-term drought in Britain had finally ended in 1992. The main difference between 1995 and 1976 was that the drought was far less severe and long-lasting, although the lack of rainfall did have an impact on agriculture and the water supply, which became critically low towards the end of summer. Another, perhaps less notable, difference was that the heat set in at the end of June, while May and June 1976 were sunny, warm and dry. However, July and August were drier than in 1976.

The 1990s was a decade that had more than its fair share of fine summer weather. Both 1989 and 1990 proved very hot, dry years, and the spring of 1992 broke records for heat in most of northern Europe. The year 1993 also benefitted from a warm spring, but was followed by a dismal cold summer. The next year, however, saw hot days occur from June onwards; July was a very hot month, as was the first third of August.

Winter rains were normal in 1995, but April fell well short of the average with only 14 millimetres at Heathrow and May was similarly dry. When June also became extremely dry, with a paltry 10 millimetres at Heathrow, it was still fairly cool. However, in the last week of June and the first week of July hot, sunny weather became firmly established. This persisted without any significant break, or rainfall, until the last week of August.

The unbroken heat was more intense than during July and August 1976, even if in the longer-term the water shortfall was far less dramatic. By the end of July, both urban and the normally lush rural landscapes of Britain became completely desiccated, rivers were already running very low and many ponds and reservoirs began to drop down to critical levels. At the same time, wildfires were beginning to spread across many areas of heathland, particularly on the Yorkshire moors.

The water crisis worsened with great speed. In August, the government began to tackle it with the traditional hosepipe ban that affected wide tracts of the country. However, they also sought to alleviate some of the public anxiety by promising to tackle the issue of leaks across the pipe network, which water companies seemingly ignored, meaning millions of gallons of the supply was wasted while greater restrictions on domestic supplies were being proposed.

On 1 August, the highest temperature of the summer, 35.2 °C, was reached at Boxworth in Cambridgeshire, and 30 °C or more was reached in London on six consecutive days, from 29 July to 3 August inclusive. By this time the media was reporting a huge backlash against the water companies as increasing numbers of consumers began finding themselves at the mercy of privatised water companies cutting off domestic supplies at will. The area that suffered some of the most widespread and stringent water cuts was Yorkshire. The unusual weather pattern that developed through the summer meant fairly uniform heat for much of England and Wales; however, there was an east–west split after the spring in terms of rainfall, with the weak, westerly rain-bearing flows failing to reach beyond the Pennines, which caused a rain shadow that persisted for many months. The normally lush Dales became brown and dusty, and the natural supply held in reservoirs dropped to critical levels; many were almost empty by late August. As water company employees came to cut off local supplies, they were sometimes spat on and some even attacked; not surprisingly, they dubbed this phenomenon 'water rage'.

The National Consumer Council (NCC) spelled out clearly the fact that, as private, profit-making concerns, the water companies could not deny water supply to consumers without paying financial penalties. In 1995, it was clear the infrastructure was in a particularly dismal state; there was no compulsion for the newly privatised businesses to invest in a widespread programme of repairs that would be both time-consuming and expensive. The drought brought their recalcitrance sharply into the public eye. At the time, the increasingly unpopular Major administration looked to be very much on the side of the water companies. John Gummer, then Secretary for the Environment, said any additional spending on measures to alleviate the supply issues were quite simply not necessary. The NCC disagreed, stating in a press release on 21 August that 'any consumers without normal access to fresh water to flush their loos and for cooking and bathing, and who are paying for it in their bills, should receive compensation. Costs should not be borne by the consumer when companies are unwilling to invest in the control of leakage.'

Not surprisingly, the issue of compensation became a political hot potato right away, and the residents of Halifax were among the first to draw attention to the absurdity of the current rules on the issue. With 35 per cent of supplies cut off for lengthy periods, they were told no compensation would be forthcoming; however, a burst water main in the town, which cut off some residents for two weeks, reportedly entitled those affected to £10 back on their bills for each day of disrupted supply. Switchboards at the local water company were jammed, and people became furious that a forced denial of the water supply remained effectively their problem. Mike Hoffman, then chairman of Thames Water and vice-president of the Water Services Association, claimed that only 5 per cent of Britain's water consumers were without water during the current drought, when five years ago that could have been 100 per cent.

It was interesting to see that, at this time, the Chartered Institute of

Environmental Health was reporting to the media that the flushing of toilets accounted for 33 per cent of all domestic water consumption, while the targeted behaviours of using hosepipes to water gardens and wash cars only accounted for 3 per cent of use. They suggested that the widespread installation of low-flush toilets would be far more effective than hosepipe bans.

The experience of 1995 was, taking aside the issue of drought, an exceptionally pleasant one. The average maximum temperature in July for Heathrow was a stunning 27 °C, and the temperature reached 30 °C or more there on eleven days. In the drought-stricken county of Yorkshire, Leeds averaged 24 °C, with three days over 30 °C and only 10 millimetres of rain for the entire month of July. Gatwick received 20 millimetres in July, far below average, but the particular dryness of August was sharply brought into focus by the actual rainfall total for the whole month – a paltry 0.76 millimetres, with an average maximum of 26.1 °C. Heathrow likewise picked up less than a millimetre of rainfall in August and an average maximum of 27 °C for the second month running – and an average monthly temperature of 21.0 °C in July and 20.5 °C in August.

The weather broke at the very end of August, with some heavy showers and thunderstorms introducing a brisk westerly airflow. September started out as a rather wet month, although the motorway sidings on the M1 nevertheless showed signs of large wildfires for many weeks afterwards, and wildfires on the Yorkshire Moors still smouldered below the surface for weeks after the rain and took far longer to fully put out. The environmental damage this caused was enormous. Sun and warmth renewed the dry theme from around mid-month, with highs around the mid-20s in London. As autumn came and the colder weather arrived, rainfall levels slowly returned to normal. By summer 1996 Britain's water supplies had recovered, but the water companies and the government waited anxiously for the next drought to arrive.

23

The Record-Breaking Heat and Drought of 2003

There was little doubt that 2003 produced some extraordinary summer weather, including the hottest temperatures ever recorded in the UK. These occurred during a remarkable heatwave that affected most of Britain and large parts of Continental Europe throughout August, causing widespread rises in mortality and heat-related illnesses. However, the summer was not a classic in its own right; at least not in Britain. Periods of great heat and some long periods of sunshine alternated with dull and rainy days and disappointing temperatures. Nevertheless, it was a very sunny and often quite dry year.

Winter 2002 had been fairly mild, although heavy snow fell in January in the south-east for the first time in several years. February, however, was very sunny, very mild and unusually dry. The lack of rain really became marked after the middle of March; for example, no rain fell at all at Heathrow from 13 to 27 March, and only 10.6 millimetres of rain were collected over the entire month.

This sunny, warm and dry theme carried on through to April, which produced summer-like conditions that, on reflection, provided an early indication of the heat and dryness that was to characterise the summer months. Between 13 and 18 April, temperatures at Heathrow climbed progressively, reaching 26 °C on the 16th in the midst of a spell of temperatures that widely reached the low 20s across Britain. At Worcester this episode produced a daytime maximum of 27.3 °C, the highest temperature recorded in April since 1949. Locharron in the West Highlands peaked at an extraordinary 26.7 °C, which broke the Scottish April record in place since 1870. After a short break, above-average temperatures and sunny weather returned from 22 April and lasted until the end of the month. By mid-April heath fires were breaking out in many places, a great deal of which were sadly reported to have been started deliberately.

As mentioned above, although the summer of 2003 was exceptional in terms of warmth and sun, there were flies in the ointment that ensured the summer was not fixed in the popular imagination in the way that 1976 and 1995 were. One of these was a cloudier and sometimes damp spell of weather that characterised the first three weeks of May. However, at the end of May London saw temperatures reach 29 °C.

June was a very unusual month. Although it proved to be very warm indeed, it was often dull. This ensured that it was not especially memorable and had a moderate average temperature. The combination of overcast days, some rain and thunderstorms and a lot of humidity meant much of June was regarded in a negative light in the popular view. Nevertheless, maximum temperatures in June were above 20 °C on every day of the month bar one. The average maximum was well above average at 23.3 °C in London and daytime maxima reached levels of 26 and 27 °C on several occasions. However, rain fell on ten days and there were some heavy thunderstorms, with often hazy or cloudy skies.

July 2003 was broadly similar to that of 1990, and the heat moved up a gear. Between 8 and 24 July the weather was dry, hot and sunny. In this spell, the 30 °C barrier was breached several times in the south and 33 °C was recorded in London on 15 July. Lawns began to wilt in the sun, and sleeping at night was often troublesome in the hot, humid and still air. However, to the great surprise of most meteorologists, during the last week of July pressure dropped. While it remained warm, the weather again became cloudy and significant rain fell on several days. The first day of August was rather cold and wet, and for the first time in some weeks the temperature in London failed to reach 20 °C.

It was just a blip. The next day, Friday 2 August, dawned clear and sunny and it reached a balmy 25 °C in southern England; the following weekend was a summer classic, with temperatures surpassing the 30 °C mark widely across the country under clear, warm, blue skies. From that point in August the summer reached its zenith. From 3 to 14 August, 30 °C was reached across most of England and indeed much of the UK. Soon records began to fall. In fact, it became ferociously hot during the first week of the month.

The second weekend of August was the hottest ever measured in the UK. Saturday dawned clear and hot. At the coast in Brighton the microclimate created a thick, damp Haar (sea fog) that sat over the beach and seafront for much of the day. Meanwhile, blazing sun and clear blue skies sitting over Preston Park just a mile or so inland created a memorable, even tropical feel to the day, which saw 36 °C reached in London. Central London that night was stiflingly hot, as the heat island of the city meant it was markedly hotter than the surrounding countryside.

The next day in the early morning the temperature was already in the mid to high 20s and the sun was shining down hard. At Canary Wharf in the late morning that Sunday my car was registering 42 °C in the shade and at the Whitstable shoreline, with a slight onshore breeze, it was only slightly cooler at 38 °C.

During that afternoon, the magic 100F (37.9 °C) mark, never reached before in the instrumental era in the UK, was broken across much of southern England. The previous record of 37.1 °C, recorded at Cheltenham in 1990, fell early on and Heathrow was at 37.9 °C by early afternoon. The hottest sites were along the north Kent coast, with Gravesend reaching 38.1 °C and Brogdale, just outside Faversham, recording 38.5 °C,[20] an astonishing reading for the UK and an all-time record. Some doubt was cast on this reading by a number of observers who questioned its validity, claiming that the Brogdale site was too sheltered. However, the Met Office now cites this as the accepted all-time record, and it beat the previous record by a considerable margin.

The extreme heat continued into the following week, with 35 °C recorded in several places on the Monday, and only a very slow cooling off followed. In fact, it was only later that week that values dropped down below the 30 °C mark at all, and it stayed hot and dry until the last week in August, when cooler, more unsettled weather brought in cloud and some light rain. By that time the British countryside was parched and brown and it stayed that way until long into the autumn. My lawn was still brown in early November.

The heat in London was especially intense. Standing on a crowded tube was a dreadful experience and one came off gasping for fresh air. Warnings were posted on the tube platforms' overhead signs alerting passengers that heatstroke was a real danger to all and water should be carried at all times.

While the heat in Britain broke records, further south, in France in particular, it was estimated that this was the hottest summer since 1540, which famously lasted well into the late autumn. The heat was so extreme that 14,800 people were reported to have died as a direct result in France alone. The victims were often elderly people. In France, August is the month when most families and professional people go on holiday. This meant that the elderly were often left to look after themselves and many of them were not found until the holiday period ended. With few doctors and relatives present to help the elderly, the death toll rose at an unprecedented rate. A refrigerated morgue near Paris was used to store the large numbers of unclaimed bodies and furious arguments broke out, with many people, and the media, blaming the authorities for the lack of reaction to the crisis. The government actually blocked emergency measures to recall key medical staff from their holidays and the health minister consistently refused to cut short his own vacation and deal with the rapidly deepening crisis.

The criticism plagued the Chirac administration for a long time afterwards, and real resentment remained in some quarters. This was exacerbated when the government in turn blamed the French nation for going on holiday and abandoning elderly relatives in the heat. The conclusion drawn by experts in France was that it was specifically down to the unusual length of the heat, rather than the high temperatures themselves. On more than seven days in August maxima in excess of 40 °C were recorded quite widely. Furthermore, very high night-time temperatures brought little relief.[21]

Countries such as Belgium and the Netherlands also recorded intense heat (37 °C was reported in both countries), but these broke no records. Nevertheless, the longevity of the heat also took casualties in these countries, with forty-one heat-related deaths reported in the Netherlands. Southern Europe also had an unusually hot summer. However, with far more air conditioning and experience of high temperatures, countries such as Spain and Italy were not as impacted as France. Nevertheless, across the continent as a whole, Wikipedia reports that over 70,000 people died as a result of the heatwave in Europe.

Back in the UK, after weeks of very hot weather, the temperature dropped back to normal levels and rain fell from grey skies on 24 August.

However, while August had been yet another hot and dry month, September proved to be exceptional. Not only was it unusually warm with lots of sunshine, but an astonishingly paltry 7 millimetres of rain fell at Heathrow during the entire month. From 4 to 21 September the weather was hot, with 26–28 °C reached on many days; even at the end of month values were still reaching the 20s, with bright and sunny weather making it feel like a continuation of summer. This was the driest September since 1959, but it was not until 2014 that 1959 was convincingly beaten for dryness. During the second half of October, another dry month, temperatures gradually returned to normal. Only after this did the summer truly fade into autumn. Lawns that were not watered remained parched through October, and heathland fires occurred widely. It looked like the drought might last into the winter and store up significant problems for the following year. November, however, proved a wet month after a dry first week. Over the winter, the natural and commercial water situation slowly returned to normal.

At the time it seemed that 2003 was the inevitable result of climate change for the UK, and the record July of 2006 seemed confirm this. However, 2007 saw a major downturn, with a run of abysmal summers that continued unabated until 2013. This was a shock in many quarters. At first it was thought that the poor summer of 2007 could be a blip, but every year for the next five years added to an unbroken run of cool and often wet summers. Only 2010 bucked the trend, and then only for the first half of the season.

As the planet continues to warm, it is clear that the incredibly complex mechanics that govern day-to-day weather seem somewhat less predictable than before. Of particular interest recently was the spectacular flip in the UK from water shortages and long-term drought up until March 2012 to a sudden reversal in regime to endless rain, leading to the second-wettest year ever – despite some bone-dry early months. While 2012/13 delivered another cold winter, with lots of disruptive snowfall occurring well into April, four of the last five winters have been cold, and 2013/14 was the stormiest ever. It was almost with great relief that July 2013 was found to be dry, sunny and hot, and 2014 also provided a long, warm and rather dry summer followed by the driest recorded September.

24

Summer Month Comparisons, London

Year	June >25 °C	June >30 °C	July >25 °C	July >30 °C	August >25 °C	August >30 °C	Total >25 °C	Total >30 °C	Score
2013	2	0	22	6	10	1	34	7	48
2012	1	0	4	1	8	2	13	3	19
2011	4	1	3	0	6	1	13	2	17
2010	11	1	15	1	2	0	28	2	32
2007	4	0	0	0	5	0	9	0	9
2006	12	1	23	12	3	0	38	13	64
2003	6	0	9	2	18	9	33	11	55
1995	5	2	17	5	21	9	43	16	75
1993	6	0	4	0	3	0	13	0	13
1990	1	0	16	4	19	5	36	9	54
1989	12	1	21	7	13	0	46	8	62
1988	2	0	0	0	5	0	7	0	7
1983	2	0	26	8	17	1	44	9	62
1980	3	0	4	0	6	0	13	0	13
1978	7	0	3	0	2	0	12	0	12
1976	17	10	19	9	19	2	55	21	97
1974	4	0	1	0	1	0	6	0	6
1965	0	0	1	0	1	0	2	0	2
1962	0	0	0	0	0	0	0	0	0
1959	7	0	11	4	9	0	27	4	35
1955	0	0	14	1	15	1	29	2	33
1954	0	0	0	0	1	0	1	0	1
1949	7	1	18	3	12	1	37	5	47
1911	5	0	22	6	14	6	41	12	65
1826	19	1	20	7	20	1	59	9	77

The above table shows how some of the best and worst summers in the last century compare with one another, along with the second-hottest year in the CET, 1826. The score at the end is calculated simply by awarding one point for each day of 25 °C or higher in a month, and two points for any day over 30 °C.

This table only reflects the temperature, ignoring the sunshine and rainfall which sometimes affect people's perceptions and overall impression of what a summer was like. However, this simple points system gives a remarkably accurate view of the best, worst and most average summers we have experienced.

There are some anomalies, but these are often reflective of the facts being somewhat different from the memory of a certain summer. For example, despite a very poor August, 2006 scores 64 points, considerably higher than 2003 which only scores 55. This is because of the intensity and longevity of the heat in July. Few other hot summers can beat it in the last hundred years, bar three: 1911, 1995 and 1976. These three summers are without doubt the hottest over the period, but one can clearly see how 1976 is the outlier of the group. At 97, it beats its nearest rival, 1826, by 20 points and sits so far out ahead of the others that a return period for this score will be considerably longer than once in at least 350 years, which is the length of the record we have. It may be that the only likely challenger for 1976 is the extremely hot and long Europe-wide heat wave of 1540, giving a return period of approximately 470 years; however, with no instrumental data, this is impossible to confirm.

One figure that will surprise those who remember it is the relatively low score for 1959 of 35. The summer of 1959 was most notable for its exceptional length. The summer warmth and sun continued on through the whole of September and October with very little cloud and rainfall. In fact, 30 °C was recorded late in September and October also saw temperatures in the high 20s recorded quite consistently. However, apart from a hot spell in early July, and the prolonged sunshine and dryness, temperatures in the key summer months were quite modest. It is also worth noting that 1826 scores higher than 1995. The latter may well have been in second place were it not that the lower number of days reading 25 °C or higher in June, combined with the longevity of the heat and the very cool first three weeks of June, put the actual mean average temperature of 1995 behind that 1826. It is worth noting that it is the extraordinary number of days over 30 °C that makes 1976 so unique and, as mentioned above, unlikely to be equalled for a very long time indeed.

At the other end of the scale, it would be hard to find a more dismal summer than that of 1962, with its score of 0. June of that year was extraordinary in that, although it was often bright, sunny and quite dry, northerly airstreams brought some hard frosts at the start of the month that no doubt saw the demise of many tender plants in people's gardens. Ground frosts occurred on the first four days of June in Sevenoaks and, on the 30th, minima as low as 6 °C were still being recorded.

The equally awful summer of 1954 was cool throughout, but unlike 1962 was also very wet and at the time was derided in the press as the worst summer ever; some papers even blamed US nuclear warhead testing for the bad weather. It was cloudy, wet and cool on nearly every day in July, with an average maximum temperature of only 18.9 °C, four degrees short of the long-term average. Also, 1974 was interminably wet, and the jet stream drove depression after depression across north-west Europe with few breaks. It was no surprise to anyone that the autumn saw severe flooding in many parts of Europe as the saturated ground overflowed with the addition of heavy autumn rains. Many crops failed completely, and prices for many basic foodstuffs rose sharply in the winter of 1974/75. The year 1980 brought another dismal summer, its July the worst since the 1950s. Nevertheless, unlike 1954, 1965 and 1974, there were some hot days, particularly in August, and these raised its score somewhat higher than one might expect from such a cold summer season.

In more recent times, 2007, following on the heels of the heat and drought of 2006, came as a terrible shock and July was relentlessly cold and wet. In contrast, 2010, perceived at the time by the media – and everyone I know – as another poor summer, was in reality quite a high scorer. The second half of June and first half of July were consistently hot, but it was the subsequent wetness and coolness that people really remember. Anything under a score of 20 is fairly disappointing. The summers of 2011 and 2012 were both wet and cool in the main and do score fairly poorly, although August 2012 did see some hot and sunny conditions. Interestingly, the major heatwave of the year in 2011 took place at the end of September and resulted in the hottest-ever temperature recorded in October, 29.9 °C on 1 October. Indeed, there was a welcome break from the cold and wet summer pattern of weather when July 2013 turned out to be sunny and hot, with an exceptional average monthly temperature at Heathrow of 20.6 °C and a score of 48, leaving it not too far behind the likes of 2003.

PART III

GREAT GALES

25

The Great Tempest, November 1703

Not long before the era of reliable weather records, in November 1703, a violent gale hit a large part of England and Wales. This unprecedented event has become established as the most severe storm ever to have hit the region, killing thousands at sea as well as many on land. It caused widespread catastrophic damage to trees and property. Furthermore, losses of shipping were on such a vast scale that it would take Britain's naval and merchant fleets many years to recover.

A major study of the storm by journalist and writer Daniel Defoe provided, for the time, an unusually detailed account of the storm itself and its impact, as well the impact of earlier storms, such as a great gale that hit much of England, including London, in February 1662. This earlier storm was also described by Samuel Pepys in his diaries for that year.

Daniel Defoe had recently been released from prison following prosecution and conviction for 'seditious' political writings and was regarded as an enemy of the state. In the tense political atmosphere of the time, journalism was only just starting to find its feet, despite the obvious displeasure emanating from both monarchy and government, both still obsessed with crimes of political and religious dissent. Defoe found himself not only on the wrong side of the establishment but also unable to work and was bordering on destitution when he published his first book, *The Storm*, in 1704. This work marked the start of a series of books that were to make him famous in the years that followed, and included an early investigation into the various plague outbreaks that ravaged the capital in particular, off and on, until the Great Fire of London in 1666 greatly reduced the source and spread of the disease.

November 1703 was certainly unusually stormy and Defoe mentions that there had been strong winds for a full two weeks prior to the big storm, with havoc on both land and sea on a number of occasions.

Tiles were blown off many buildings in London and a number of ships were reported lost during this period. On the Wednesday before the storm, 24 November, the day began sunny but turned dark at around four in the afternoon. A violent squall crossed London, introducing an exceptional gale that blew down a neighbouring chimney, nearly killing Defoe. The wind continued through the entire night and would have been cited as an exceptional gale had not the great storm followed hard on its heels on the Friday.

Defoe describes a fairly windy day on Friday 26 November (this would have been 6 December in our modern calendar, which is ten days ahead) but not one that was in any regard exceptional. However, from about 10 p.m. the wind began to increase and the renewed ferocity of the gale began to pound buildings across much of the country.

One of Defoe's contributors, William Derham, similarly describes the raucous events leading up to the ravages of that fateful Friday night. Derham lived at Upminster, then a modest country town to the north of London, in the Essex countryside. On the Thursday he noted a violent squall with thunder, lightning and hail. The Friday began windy, and the strength of the wind remained 'high' all day and was still blowing hard when he went to bed. He was awoken at midnight by a howling, booming wind that gradually increased until 3 a.m., whence it blew with 'excess'. The winds, he stated, were from a south-south-west direction through Friday but veered west-south-west during the night; however, because his metal weathervane was snapped and blown off the roof during the gale, he was uncertain of the wind direction. Nevertheless, nearly all the sources agree that the wind was largely from the west, which would prove important, as Defoe observed later, in terms of where the worst damage occurred. From 7 a.m. the wind abated fairly rapidly and the barometer rose. As Saturday morning dawned, at least 8,000 people were dead, millions of trees were felled and a vast swathe of Britain saw an unprecedented trail of destruction.

When Defoe published advertisements in the press a week after the storm, asking for accounts of its effects across the country, letters flooded in. Some gave horrific accounts of people's experiences, including many near escapes from death as well as those whose fate proved less fortunate. A common feature of the storm was the terror people felt as their houses and cottages crumbled around them and chimney pots fell in, sometimes crushing those too scared to flee. However, it was a completely dark, moonless night and the world outside seemed to many an even more perilous a prospect than facing the storm from within. The streets were 'thick' with debris such as roof tiles, lead sheets, branches and bricks, driven by winds well over hurricane force, or in simpler terms above a sustained level of 74 mph, with gusts greatly in excess of that figure. Of great interest to Defoe at the time were reports that the winds were accompanied by an earthquake. It is quite possible that the impact on buildings from tornadoes may have created not only a good deal of noise but lots of shaking, as reported in the Glasgow storm of 1968. The winds were certainly accompanied by thunderstorms and widespread flashes were seen during the night, and in the absence of power lines one can only conclude that thunderstorms were commonplace. A reported house fire that broke out in Norfolk may have been the result of a lightning strike; the flames were fanned so readily by the violent winds that the family within barely escaped with their lives to describe how standing on the windward side of the fire would have proved fatal, as those present found they were unable to stay in a fixed position such was the strength of the wind, and they risked being blown into the conflagration.

The storm also coincided with a very high tide. Flooding was worst in the west, where the Somerset levels were deeply flooded and loss of life, both human and livestock, was confirmed. The storm surge that swept in at the outset of the gale – as high as 8 feet – was driven into coastal towns and estuaries, flooding vulnerable areas to a significant depth.

When the storm finally ended, on Saturday morning, Defoe describes the scene that befell all those brave enough to open their doors at first light in London: 'The streets lay so covered with tiles and slates, from the tops of the houses, especially in the out-parts, that the quantity is incredible; and the houses were so universally stript, that all the tiles in fifty miles round would be able to repair but a small part of it.' The death toll in London was officially twenty-one, but Defoe reports that in the outskirts of the city many more died or were injured.

One feature of the storm he noticed was something that I also saw clearly after the 1987 storm. The level of damage to buildings was often dictated by their orientation. Those facing a westerly or south-westerly direction would often be damaged or destroyed, while others not in the path of the wind were spared the worst.

Pressure had fallen as low as 970 mb during Friday night in the south, but further north one of Derham's friends in Lancashire measured lower pressure still, and some reports suggest at the centre of the storm was likely to have seen pressure readings as low as 950 mb. With no contemporary charts to look at and a relatively scarce set of pressure measurements across the country, it was down to a later reconstruction of the chart to indicate with accuracy that the centre of the low probably crossed Liverpool and the Mersey area early on Saturday morning. This means that the isobars to the south would have been at their tightest, and it was indeed areas to the south of the Midlands where the damage was worst. From the Midlands northwards damage was notably less severe, and increased progressively southwards but with little difference east to west. Evidence of this progressive severity southwards comes from a report from Oxfordshire, where the correspondent states that the wind 'did not do much harm', blowing down chimneys and tiles but causing no injury.

As the storm struck the West Country, a massive tidal surge tore up the Severn River, huge trees were felled across Somerset and the Bishop of Wells and his wife were both killed. Their deaths were caused by a massive chimney stack which collapsed on to their bedroom, sending them both crashing down through the floor on to the ground level below.

The financial impact on the parts of the country most affected was enormous. One letter reports that at Stowmarket the town's church spire had collapsed, causing significant collateral damage and presenting the parish with a bill for £400 (over £30,000 today) for the full repair, a fortune at the time. This type of figure would have been repeated in parishes right across the country, coupled with huge domestic bills for the substantial damage to property, nature and human life. In fact, the cost of tiles went through the roof in the weeks after the storm, rising from twenty-one shillings per hundred beforehand to £6 per hundred after the gale, while bricklayer labour shot up from less than a shilling to 5 shillings an hour. Agriculture also suffered from the effects of salt on grazing and grassland, and livestock were lost in vast numbers.

The impact on vessels at sea is hard to easily grasp, such was the vastness of death and destruction wrought on shipping. It is estimated that between 8,000 and 15,000 people were killed at sea. Such was the violence of the storm and its widespread nature that it has been impossible to pull together a conclusive figure. Britain was also rendered particularly vulnerable from these losses, both from a defensive and military perspective, during a time of heightened international tension. The Royal Navy was decimated and they alone reported fourteen men-of-war, their principal warships of the time, lost to the storm with as many as 1,500 crew and officers killed. The merchant and commercial vessels of the time, mostly far less robust, fared even worse than the warships.

The Downs area of Kent was sheltering a large number of ships that day, but as the violence of the gale began to reach its height, many of the ships lost their moorings and began to be driven onto the Goodwin Sands. Here they were pounded by the winds and the relentless, heavy seas and broken to pieces.

Many sailors survived, stranded on the sands, but far from saving them the locals from the south Kent coast actually came out the next day, circling the sands in boats, waiting for sailors to die. As they drowned one by one, the locals picked among their belongings. A total of 1,200 men died on the sands, many of whom only drowned because of the actions of the local hawkers.

The captain of one of the ships, moored with the others in the Downs, wrote to Defoe and told him of his vessel and crew's extraordinary escape from death. His crew felt the full violence of the storm from 1 a.m. onwards and began to watch other ships lose their anchor and moorings. Most of them cut down their masts in an effort to drift in a more controlled manner – only to be driven onto the sands, which we already know meant certain death. The ship's mate suggested to the captain that the mast be cut and the anchors raised so the vessel would be left to float out to sea to ride out the storm. The captain did not agree and thought this would be suicide. In the event, he later agreed the only chance the ship had was for the mast to be cut down, for want of any other course of action. The vessel was then torn from its moorings and, to the horror of all on board, driven inexorably towards the Goodwin Sands. However, by a huge stroke of luck, the ship in question missed the sands by only a few feet, avoiding numerous smashed vessels and their drowning crews. The ship's crew were helpless to save anyone as they were driven with increasing pace out into the open sea. As it happened, the ship was safely driven out into the open waters of the Channel by the fierce winds with no loss of life. By eight in the morning, as the winds abated and calmed, the exhausted, wet and frozen crew had all but given up any hope of survival when they saw they were passing the coast of southern East Anglia. From a night of doom and horror the crew began to regain hope, only for a renewed gale to set in shortly afterwards. The nightmare began all over again from Saturday afternoon, and the ship and her crew were now blown out into a fearsome and angry North Sea, passing on the way an 'open boat' full of survivors from another ship. Despite their desire to help their fellow sailors, again the vessel was being driven rapidly eastwards out of control. They were in no position to effect a rescue and watched with mutual despair as the boat and its occupants drifted away in the spray and rain, never to be heard of again. The ship rattled on through the gale with her occupants in renewed and increasing despair, expecting death to come with every passing hour. Late on Sunday the winds finally dropped, and land was sighted. Having no idea where they were, it wasn't until they reached closer to land, and help came out to them, that they realised they had made it to the southern coast of Norway.

Another great tragedy occurred when one of the great new wonders of the age, a modern, manned lighthouse, sited just 4 miles south of Plymouth on a series of nine rocks, was destroyed. The designer was one Henry Winstanley, who first built the lighthouse as a wooden structure in 1698. Although it did withstand the elements early on, Winstanley added a stone cladding to the structure and continued to strengthen the building with various additions. Winstanley had been observing the violence of the weather in the days before the storm as the bad weather had interrupted his work on the building. He was keen to finish strengthening the structure, but, due to the increasingly poor conditions and relentless gales, he was unable to reach it. As the wind dropped on Friday morning and the sun came out, Winstanley was rowed across from the shore the short distance to the lighthouse. However, before long the wind picked up again and a full gale began to blow early in the afternoon. The renewed force of the wind disabled any return journeys to land that day. Including Winstanley, there were six people manning and operating the facility on 26 November; that evening they would have watched as the increasingly mountainous, angry seas battered the structure with ever more force until the building could stand it no longer. Sometime during the night the entire lighthouse was destroyed and everybody there was either crushed to death or drowned by the raging seas.

Another desperate report came from a merchant ship heading for the West Indies. The correspondent described how, having lost its mast, the hopelessly damaged vessel was driven onto an unknown course. The captain, on observing what he saw as certain death, made an agreement with the ship's surgeon. From the captain's quarters, two shots rang out; they had made a pact to shoot each other rather than drown. In the event, the gale subsided shortly afterwards and the ship sighted land, making it into the harbour safely. While the surgeon died immediately, the captain lived long enough to witness the ship's rescue and the futility of his fatal contract.

Some of the Navy's great flagships, including the HMS *Northumberland*, HMS *Mary*, HMS *Restoration*, and HMS *Stirling Castle*, were lost and thousands of officers and men perished. These losses left the government and Navy in total shock; they must also have been reeling from what then would have then been a massive gap in the country's defensive programme. Huge investments were needed to bring the Navy back to its former strength, and the human toll was actually even worse than it immediately appears. One estimate, which calculated the population of Britain at the time as 5 million, has estimated that the loss at sea of 8,000 would equate now to 100,000 lost lives against the current population, demonstrating the incredible scale of the disaster.

Daniel Defoe's investigations have left us with a detailed and constructive account of perhaps the greatest cataclysm to have hit the UK in recorded history. However, at the time the clergy and many in the community believed quite simply that the wrath of God was the cause of the storm. Stories of earthquakes and strange vapours and lights fuelled rumours of God's anger being visited upon a morally lacking populace and abounded for years afterwards. Nevertheless, most educated observers took little notice of this and barely mention any unscientific or moral judgements when investigating the causes and effects of the storm.

Queen Anne was said to be greatly distressed by the impact of the storm and was herself affected at first hand when part of the palace suffered complete collapse at the height of the gale. The collapsing building left her entire household cowering in terror through the

1. Lake Toba in Indonesia is actually the vast crater of a 'super-volcano' that erupted 73,000 years ago, causing an almost instant ice age that reduced humanity virtually to extinction. (Lori Newman)

2. January 1677. One of the great London frost fairs that became commonplace during the period known as the Little Ice Age, which lasted from the Tudor period up until the end of the nineteenth century. (© Topham Picturepoint)

Above left: 3. The blizzard of January 1881, the worst of its kind recorded in England and Wales, caused enormous damage on land and loss of life at sea due to prolonged gales. Icing and flooding were particularly serious in London, where many were drowned by the Thames. This is the deserted Sussex town of Shoreham digging out after the snow. (Marlipins Museum)

Above right: 4. Ryde on the Isle of Wight was in the area worst hit by the blizzard conditions in January 1881. Communications both on the island and to and from the island came to a standstill for many days. (Wootton Bridge Historical)

5. The normally mild Bude on the north Cornish coast was cut off from the outside world for days by one of the worst recorded blizzards in England in March 1891. Here, residents of Landsdown Road dig themselves out of towering drifts. (Ray Boyd, http://bude-past-and-present.org.uk)

Above: 6. A train blocked in by deep snow during the severe winter of 1947 in Cheshire. The severe cold lasted from the final week of January until early March, and was immediately followed by severe and widespread flooding. (David Kitching Collection)

Right: 7. Deep snow in London on 1 January 1963 after days of heavy snow, taken by the late Marcel H. S. Heath. (Eric G Heath)

8. Skaters on the frozen River Cam in Cambridge in late December 1962. Weeks of cold and snow followed, and the river was frozen until the end of February. (Neville Newman)

9. A Hertfordshire road provides a typical rural scene in England during the winter of 1962/63, which proved to be the third harshest since 1659. (Richard Saunders)

10. Bristol docks, frozen completely for the first time since 1895, in February 1963 (Steve Selwood/R. Hill)

Above left: 11. A snapshot from 30 December 1962. Even the heart of central London was overwhelmed by snow at the start of the most severe winter since 1740. Here, two policemen struggle to bring a car back on its way at Horse Guards Parade in Whitehall. (© Topham Picturepoint)

Above right: 12. Snow on Christmas Day 1970 in Studham, Bedfordshire. Deep snow blanketed much of the country, causing great disruption right through the Christmas holidays and into the New Year. (Jackie Nobbs)

13. The Highland blizzard of January 1978 was one of Scotland's worst snowstorms of the last 200 years and took several lives in the area around Inverness. The photograph shows the severe snow depths achieved in Tomintoul, Moray, after the storm. (Royan Fettes)

14. Deep snow in Yorkshire in 1979 during Britain's coldest winter since 1963. Bitter weather lasted from New Year to March and combined with widespread industrial strife to bring down Jim Callaghan's Labour government soon after. (John Bentley)

Above: 15. The great freeze of January 1987 brought the coldest spell of weather since 1895 and some of the deepest snow since 1963 to eastern Britain. This is Gravesend during the height of the intense snowfall. (Andy Veitch)

Right: 16. Deep snow being cleared from the Surrey countryside in January 1982; during this spell, England's lowest-ever temperature, -26.1 °C, was recorded in Shropshire while Braemar in Scotland equalled the all-time UK record it set back in February 1895 of -27.2 °C. (Alan Edwards)

Bottom right: 17. Local residents of Chelsham in Surrey clamber over great snowdrifts blocking the roads after days of heavy snow and strong winds in January 1987. (Alan Edwards)

Above: 18. The Isle of Sheppey's branch line, buried under 20 feet of snow in January 1987. (Stuart Pearce)

Left: 19. A deserted town centre in Folkestone during the heavy snows of February 1991, in which daytime temperatures in the south remained below freezing for ten days. (Ian Mansfield)

Bottom left: 20. Cars buried under more than 50 centimetres of snow during the December snowfalls of 2010, which left thousands of Christmas travellers trapped at Heathrow and Gatwick on the Saturday before Christmas. (Patrick Nobbs)

21. The 1975–76 period was the driest in well over 200 years and combined with the hottest summer ever recorded to empty rivers and reservoirs, such as this one at Staines, near London, pictured on 17 August 1976. (© Topham Picturepoint)

Above left: 22. Christmas Day 2010. This was the first snowy Christmas Day since 1981 but did not qualify as officially white as no single flake of snow fell on the actual day itself. (Ian Mansfield)

Above right: 23. Drought is not uncommon in the UK; one drought occurred in 2003, which saw a parched landscape across much of the UK, such as here in Sevenoaks, Kent. (Patrick Nobbs)

24. The summer of 2003 produced drought conditions right across Britain and the rest of Europe. The reservoir at Glendevon in Scotland dropped so low that remnants of a previous village located in the valley, long since flooded, reappeared. (Barry Ferguson)

25. The tidal storm surge of 1953 killed over 300 people in England and nearly 2,000 in the Netherlands. Canvey Island, pictured here, saw fifty-three deaths as the island's sea defences were torn down and freezing seawater swept many people away in the dead of night. (© Topham Picturepoint)

Above left: 26. The great gale of 1987 is second in strength only to the storm that crossed the south on 26 November 1703 and killed over 8,000 people; most were lost at sea, but losses on land were also substantial. This picture shows devastated parkland at Hastings the day after the storm of 1987. (Andrew Popkin)

Above right: 27. Trees crushed cars and houses and eighteen people lost their lives in the October 1987 gale, ensuring scenes such as these in Southend, Essex, were common across southern England. (Colin Pickett)

28. A flash flood that washed through the centre of Lincolnshire during a severe thunderstorm in May 1920 took twenty-three lives and was one of the worst disasters of its kind. (*Grimsby Times*)

Overleaf: 29. Britain's longest-lasting tornado caused widespread damage over the east of England from Bedfordshire to Norfolk in a run of over 100 miles; the vortex is pictured here as it cut a swathe of destruction through the village of Linslade, near Leighton Buzzard in Bedfordshire. (© Press Association)

Right: 30. A policeman on his walkie-talkie stands next to a gigantic boulder, one of thousands that devastated Lynmouth in August 1952, killing thirty-four people. The high street, to his left, became a new river channel that destroyed everything in its path. (© Topham Picturepoint)

Below right: 31. Norwich, August 1912. In just twenty-four hours, 6 inches of rain fell over Norwich, causing serious flooding that cut the town off, washed away numerous bridges and proved fatal. (Norwich Millennium Library)

Bottom right: 32. Lightning over Sevenoaks during a violent storm in July 2014. One of the most violent storms ever recorded in the UK hit this area in June 1980, dropping over 100 millimetres in two hours; other very exceptional thunderstorms hit Dorset in 1955, Kent, Sussex and London in 1958 and Hampstead during the August heat wave of 1975. (Mike Harris)

Above left: 33. Guildford is submerged after several days of torrential rain that caused remarkably serious floods across much of south-east England in September 1968. (Alan Edwards)

Above right: 34. Friary Road in Guildford at the height of the September 1968 floods. South London was virtually cut of from the outside world during these floods, and river levels rose for days as upstream rain swelled them; East Molesey in Surrey was one of the towns worst affected by this phenomenon. (Alan Edwards)

35. Gigantic waves pound the coast at Porthcawl during the extraordinary gales and floods of 2013–14. (Steve Garrington)

36. Gloucester
Cathedral
surrounded by
deep floods in
January 2014.
The nearby
Somerset levels
were flooded
from December to
March. (David R.
Ward)

37. The Lewes
Avalanche in
December 1836
buried fifteen
people, eight of
whom died in
England's worst
known avalanche.
(Ian Mansfield)

38. A summer sea
fog rolls in towards
Brighton on a hot
day in September
2012. (Sam Moore)

Left: 39. The Laki fissure volcano in Iceland still visibly stretches for many miles. Its 1783 eruption created vast clouds of sulphur that resulted in death and famine across Europe for over a year. (Martin Ystenes)

Below: 40. Smog over London in December 1962. This was the last lethal smog in the city, caused by coal fires and industrial pollution, before air quality was improved dramatically. (Eric G. Heath/Marcel H. S. Heath)

rest of the night as windows smashed and the wind wrought havoc outdoors. The queen, upon hearing of the dreadful losses out to sea, ensured that those in the service of the realm who left behind families would be compensated. She also oversaw a number of charitable schemes to help those affected and initiated a programme of rebuilding in the capital.

Without doubt, were this storm to occur today there would be devastation on a massive scale, far exceeding the toll of 1987. Even though our buildings are built to a higher standard, there are still plenty of old and vulnerable structures that would certainly crumble in the face of such natural fury. Our sensitive infrastructure would be wrecked and power and delivery of goods would almost certainly come to a standstill. Out to sea the impacts would have equated to those of any major tropical hurricane, but with predictions and early warnings better than they have ever been, our modern technology would doubtless save thousands of lives.

26

The Great Modern Catastrophe: The North Sea Storm Surge and Flood Disaster, January– February 1953

The northern European tidal surge floods of 1953 constitute the worst natural catastrophe to hit the Continent in modern times. Over 2,500 people died in the raging, icy torrents that swept in from the North Sea on a Saturday night, taking most of the communities it affected almost completely by surprise. However, this event became a watershed moment in terms of the importance of flood defences and the way they are managed in the countries that were affected. An extraordinary and unfortunate set of circumstances combined to create this catastrophic flood; a high spring tide; deep low pressure pushing down the north sea; a 3-metre storm surge; little or no warning; and a tidal surge moving in under the cover of darkness.

On 28 January, a small depression formed in the mid-Atlantic several hundred miles to the west of Spain and deepened. Pressure was low over Scandinavia, high over Greenland and high to the south of the UK, bringing clement weather to north-western Europe. During 29 January the low pressure moved northwards, and by the next day it was deepening to the north of Scotland. At that point it moved westwards and the isobars were squeezed tightly together on its western flank. During Friday it moved just east of Scotland but then unexpectedly sank southwards, taking the strongest wind field straight down the North Sea coasts of Scotland and England. It finally made landfall in the coastal region of Schleswig-Holstein in northern Germany.

This produced a violent and sustained north-westerly gale that drove an already exceptionally high spring tide into a huge storm surge. The gale was so powerful from its outset that it sank a large passenger ferry. On any other night, this would have been a unique and catastrophic disaster; sadly it was just the beginning of a series of disasters that this fearful storm was to leave in its wake.

The ferry *Princess Victoria* left Stranraer heading for Belfast at about 7.45 a.m. on Saturday 31 January. As the vessel passed into the open sea it was suddenly exposed to an extreme swell and the full force of the gale gusting up to 115 mph. An hour after its departure the stern doors were smashed open and the vessel immediately began to list. A survivor noted how calm everyone was despite the horror unfolding before them: 'Before the ship foundered floats were dropped into the sea. There was no panic. I never saw a bunch of people act so coolly.' Lifeboats were quickly lowered, but two were smashed by the water. A further two were launched successfully, filled with people. At that moment, suddenly and with little warning, the ship lurched over onto its side, crushing the remaining lifeboats and making escape for those still on board impossible; the ferry then quickly sank. Once this happened the survivors were all certain that nobody aboard could have survived. A total of 138 people were confirmed drowned by Monday; forty-four passengers survived and were brought ashore.

The sea defences in eastern Scotland were quickly tested; some proved more resilient than others. Those at the fishing village of Crovie in Aberdeenshire failed. Where the shallow waters brought the surge up particularly high, water tore through the sea defences with such force that it was able to destroy whole buildings. Inland in Scotland the violent winds did tremendous damage.

Towns such as Wick and Thurso were littered with fallen trees, slate and cables the next day. Many people still lived in prefabricated homes and these were torn to pieces while their occupants cowered inside. Shipping was in great distress as well, and the Barra and South Uist lifeboats attended a gruelling rescue attempt of a fifteen-man vessel. The bitter cold, strong winds and freezing water rendered two men unconscious from exposure and exhaustion, so the rescue was abandoned. By the time the lifeboats had returned to shore, both men were dead. More than twenty people lost their lives in Scotland and it was considered the worst storm for 500 years.

During the evening the centre of the depression sank further south and the hurricane-force winds started to batter all of eastern Britain. The low pressure and winds created a dome of water which, as it approached the exposed coastlines – those from eastern Scotland right down to Kent – slowed down and bunched up, rising up into a storm surge up to 17 feet high that then combined with the high spring tide to devastating effect. The enormous surge began to tear down the sea defences of eastern England shortly after dark. At Mablethorpe, in Lincolnshire, the coastal surge came crashing through the sea wall. Shortly after, sea and river defences all the way down to Skegness gave way once the surge hit them. Water tore up rivers, creating enormous tidal bores of water upstream surging over banks and overwhelming any defences. The seawater rose to 20 feet deep in places, taking the lives of numerous residents in the low-lying farmland and drowning livestock in their thousands. Sutton-on-Hoo was completely submerged, and by Monday over forty people were known drowned and thousands had to be evacuated from the area.

As the surge bore south, so the flood defences in Norfolk and Suffolk were breached every bit as easily as those further north. At King's Lynn, the River Ouse, which had never before been recorded as doing so, burst its banks and poured into the town. So high was the surge as it funnelled into the river that it rose an unprecedented 31 feet. This in turn created a 7-foot wave that rushed into the town from the south, smashing windows as it washed through the town centre, drowning fifteen people almost immediately. The power blacked out and more than a fifth of the town was under deep water. Some one thousand people were evacuated in the first twenty-four hours after the storm, but thousands more remained and rescue workers and volunteers had to work without a break for days to ensure people got to safety.

Along the coast there was devastation on a scale unprecedented in modern times. Cromer and Hunstanton were typical of some of the familiar holiday destinations of the time, where holiday homes, caravans and bungalows were wrecked. At Hunstanton, twelve American service personnel living in flimsy bungalows along the coast were killed and others drowned in the towns and countryside nearby as the waters tore into the low-lying fields. One of their comrades, Reis Leming, showed incredible bravery which won him the George Medal when he saved twenty-seven people from a similar fate at Hunstanton. Tens of thousands of livestock were swept away and lost and the cost to agriculture in these areas is incalculable. Much of the farmland in areas badly flooded was polluted because the saltwater soaked deep into the ground and contaminated the groundwater and the soil took months to recover. More immediately, drinking water in all the areas affected was contaminated and tankers had to be brought in. Felixstowe was also badly affected because the River Orwell burst its banks and bore down on yet another post-war prefab housing estate, sweeping thirty-eight people to their deaths and imprisoning 300 more. Harwich was also swept by a 7-foot tidal surge.

Next the surge pushed down into Essex, and the coastlines there began to crumble under the pressure of the pounding seas. By now it was later at night and few people were aware of what was happening until they were awoken by family members, neighbours or the water itself. As the unchecked sea burst across the dockyards at Sheerness, a submarine in dry dock was tossed onto its side as the floodwater cascaded. The gales and floods came on a powerful northerly airflow that not only brought strong winds but also delivered freezing temperatures. Snow fell in a number of places that night, with night-time temperatures close to freezing. The severe wind caused many people to perish from exposure and hypothermia alongside those that drowned. Essex, much of which is low-lying and coastal, was badly affected by the 17-foot surge. Southend, Jaywick and Clacton were badly flooded and wind and sea damage ran in to tens of thousands of pounds. Thirty-seven people died in these towns.

The Thames Estuary was next to be hit. Here the tidal surge had become yet more powerful as it gathered pace on its journey south and it raced towards the low-lying island of Canvey. The entire island of Canvey flooded to a depth of many feet, freezing and filthy water reaching the upper storeys of some houses. More than 3,000 people were eventually evacuated from their homes but fifty-eight people died on Canvey and thousands were made homeless. The losses suffered by this community were truly terrible. The rescue took some days. On the Sunday the troops that came in to organise the rescue fell foul of the next spring tide, which washed in with great speed and was almost as high as the previous one. Rescue vehicles were submerged in a new torrent of icy seawater. One seventeen-year-old naval cadet was critically injured trying to save a baby he saw floating by on a door. Diving into the flood to get to it, he was struck on the back by swirling debris but he survived. The baby, alas, was later found drowned.[1]

The water now began to surge up the Thames, with no barrier to stop it, causing floods all the way up to Putney. Belvedere and Erith were badly flooded and many homes had to be evacuated. The power station at Dartford had to close because it became isolated by the floodwater and could not be manned; it was only when troops were brought in to run a ferry service from nearby higher ground to the power station that staff could get to work and operations began again. Much of east London's dockland areas were flooded, including Silvertown, where 1,000 families had to be evacuated and even the tidal basin at West Ham (now the Olympic Park) was badly flooded. The water even pushed back up the Grand Surrey Canal, causing it to overflow and burst unexpectedly into Peckham, where a lot of damage was done. Floodwater surged over at Blackwall, causing severe flooding in the tunnel, which was closed for days, and low-lying Greenwich and Woolwich nearby were also affected.

Now into the early hours Kent towns to the east and north of the county were badly affected. Whitstable, which was then a modest fishing hamlet, saw the tidal surge burst from the east in the early hours, inundating the lower parts of the town to extraordinary depths. The golf club was completely submerged and only the tops of cars were visible in the town car park the next day. Margate had a lighthouse jutting out from the promenade at that time and the force of the waves destroyed it completely.[2] The pier was left cut into three sections and seawater surged into the centre of town as many buildings along the promenade were smashed to pieces by the fierce waves. Ramsgate and Herne Bay suffered similar ravages, and in this part of the country the strong winds blew right through into Sunday, continuing the havoc brought on by the high spring tides.

In Britain it was estimated that over 1,600 km² of coastline was damaged and 1,000 km² flooded by the sea and overflowing rivers. Some 30,000 people had to be evacuated, with over 24,000 homes damaged or destroyed. At a time when there was already a housing crisis left over from wartime bombing, this was a major headache for the government. The queen toured many of the affected counties quite extensively, which helped raise morale after the terrible experiences so many had to endure. In relative terms, the death toll – 307 people in Britain – was enormous and no other single natural disaster since has claimed such a massive loss of life.

The Netherlands suffered even more terrible consequences that still resound loudly to this day. The country has always been at war with the sea, and only after many battles have the low-lying lands been slowly reclaimed and rendered habitable, if not cultivable, over centuries. Early in the morning of 1 February, the Dutch coast, which sits directly facing the oncoming direction of the surge, felt its full force. The area of Zeeland to the south-west seems to have been affected worst. The isobars on the weather chart that morning were packed most closely together here, giving stronger winds and higher surges than further north, allowing the sea to move in with greater force.

The sea tore into Zeeland, Noord Brabant and other low-lying areas, which were quickly overrun and deeply flooded. The high Schieland dyke, which is a massive structure, ruptured at the Groenendijk at around 5.30 a.m. and water began to surge into the Hollandse Ijssel, where about 3 million people then lived. This dyke was the only source of protection from the sea at the time, and the breach was a catastrophe. The mayor of the nearby town of Nieuwkerke, in a moment of sheer panic, came up with a plan. He persuaded the captain of a local ship to ram it into the gap in the dyke before an unprecedented catastrophe could occur. This was a tremendous risk as the ship could easily have done more damage to the dyke, and one cannot be sure how calculated it was, but the plan worked. The Groenendijk was temporarily shored up using a ship. It is agreed that this ingenious act of desperation may well have saved hundreds if not thousands of lives.[3]

Nevertheless, dykes and sea walls did give out across much of the coastal south-west and the floods came without any warning at all, as all communications and electricity supplies were already severed. In the early hours, the icy seawater smashed through the polders and into towns and villages at great speed, giving little time for those affected to escape. The beautiful towns of Middelberg and Veere were badly flooded and the people swept into the water did not survive the bitter cold for long. North Beveland and Walcheren were almost totally flooded, and thousands of people were stranded in freezing conditions on roofs, others congregating in whatever parts of towns and villages the floodwater was unable to reach. A typical example is the small town of 's-Gravendeel in South Holland; isolated for days from the outside world, nearly sixty in the village were killed and the remaining 600 people had to crowd into the second floor of the town's secondary school. At The Hague, both the port and beach at Scheveningen were devastated. The dykes near Rotterdam failed in many places, and the city was badly flooded.

Troops from several countries were mobilised to the Netherlands to give relief to the stricken country. The Prime Minister, Dr Drees, put out a plea to all neighbouring countries to send relief in the form of blankets, tools, workclothes and any other provisions that they could spare – this was still a time of rationing in the UK. Nevertheless, help flooded in quickly. Sadly, with over a fifth of the entire country underwater, there was very little communication coming out of the isolated areas. Sometimes entire families were drowned, and nobody was left to report them missing. All in all, 1,836 people were killed that day, 37,000 in livestock were lost and nearly 50,000 buildings damaged, around a fifth of which had to be knocked down.

In Belgium, Ostend was badly inundated and the sea defences crushed while the tidal river, the Scheldt, which weaves down into Antwerp, felt the full force of the surge and the river burst over, flooding the city itself and various points north of it.

So why were so many people blissfully unaware of what was coming, despite the fact that the winds blowing in Scotland were clearly moving south-eastwards and several hours' warning could have been given? The truth is that our modern world has changed in so many ways since 1953 that we might not be able to easily grasp the answer. Very few people had televisions, and those that did tended to be wealthier people. For the great majority of people, the radio was still considered the primary form of entertainment for all of the family. Gale warnings were broadcast widely on the radio on the Saturday, but, as one newspaper said at the time, 'which land lubber jumps up at the mention of a gale warning to shipping?' Additionally, the path the storm took was quite unusual. As the depression formed it looked like it would follow its predecessor and track westwards into Scandinavia. The fact that it began to barrel south that night, moved very fast and arrived after many people were in bed, or had turned off their radios, meant that was no real warning available. In the Netherlands the KNMI did have an early-warning service, but the gales and floods took out the power quickly before the worst of the effects of the water had arrived in any given town. Of critical importance to the outcome of the disaster was the inadequacy of the sea and river defences.

So, with 2,551 lives lost, what lessons were learned? In Britain the response was robust and sea defences right across the eastern coasts that had been wiped away so easily in 1953 were rebuilt to resist another equally violent storm. Canvey Island, which now has a vast sea wall that stretches above the roofs of nearby houses, has gone from a sparsely populated backwater to a highly populated residential zone. The confidence in the current defences is therefore such that people do not feel insecure and even these robust new defences were rendered yet more secure after being rebuilt to an even higher standard in 1998. The Thames Barrier that was completed in 1984, after ten years of construction, was a direct result of a report drafted by Sir Herman Bondi in the immediate aftermath of the 1953 disaster. Construction was begun in 1974 and it soon became a high-profile project. I remember taking a tourist trip on a boat with my dad and grandparents to see the construction site from the river in June 1977, but it was not until 1983 that it was first used operationally. Interestingly, between 1983 and 1993 the floodgates were closed eleven times to prevent tidal floods. Between 1994 and 2004, however, that number rose to forty-three. The cause of this is unclear; however, the investment in the world's second-biggest moving flood-defence system has without doubt already paid off and saved lives – unbeknownst to those protected by it.

In the Netherlands, the impact of the storm saw the beginning of the vast Delta Works project. This was begun in the 1950s and was borne of the desire to never see a natural disaster exact another death toll like that of 1953 again. With the Delta Works, the fight against the sea became more serious than ever. The project was designed so that moveable sea barriers were built across all the major deltas in the country, bar two; these have been left open so shipping can navigate the Scheldt and Rhine easily, and have been mitigated by other defensive structures. The project was declared complete in 1997.

Had the 1953 storm not struck when and how it did, it is possible that the resources and will to undertake such vast projects may never have arisen. It is thus a sad fact that it took such death and destruction over such a wide area to show the vulnerability of all low-lying coastal communities and put in place the protection from the forces of nature they very much need.

27

The Sheffield Gale, February 1962

A remarkable set of circumstances, never before experienced, combined to create a violent, localised gale that hit the town of Sheffield early in the morning of 16 February 1962. Such was the strength of the wind that over half the homes in the town were damaged and many destroyed completely, leaving hundreds of families homeless.

So what uniqueness enabled this storm in Sheffield to cause such widespread damage? The sustained hurricane-force winds that were achieved during this storm, blowing across an urban area, were in themselves an extraordinary occurrence in the UK. However, what was even more remarkable was that, while the same storm was battering places such as Manchester, Birmingham, Leeds and Rotherham, the sustained wind speeds were more in the region of 45 mph. Very strong indeed, yet almost half the speed of those of Sheffield – the town was a massive outlier in terms of wind speed.

Unusually strong winds were already in evidence by midnight and increased steadily from then. A man taking a bus home from a late shift in the early hours of 16 February found himself in a surreal adventure. The wind was so strong that he and a policeman were forced to shelter in the broken display window of a fur shop while waiting for the last bus. When the man, who was in his early twenties, got off at his stop he was blown like a ragdoll across the pavement and lay pinned to a garden hedge, unable to get up. To get home, only a few yards away, he had to crawl on all fours against a formidable force of nature. This was at about 2 a.m. and was only the start of the extraordinary Sheffield gale.

By 4 a.m. the wind was blowing so hard trees bent, roofs and tiles rattled and many dislodged. However, this was nothing compared to what was about to happen. From 6 a.m. the wind rose to the incredible sustained level of 70–80 mph and Sheffield was thrown into chaos. Winds gusting close to or even over 100 mph were by then in evidence and a 96 mph gust had already been officially logged. Whole rows of houses facing the wind had their entire facades torn off, others collapsed completely with their occupants inside. This included one entire family who, too terrified to sleep, were cowering together in their front room when suddenly the entire house blew down, leaving one remaining wall standing and them open to the elements. They were luckier than others; this storm took ten lives. In Sheffield, three people were killed. One fifty-nine-year-old woman fell victim to a falling chimney, and her husband was seriously hurt. Two others were lost in the same way, one of them a seventeen-year-old. When the fire brigade came to rescue the trapped lad, the top floor collapsed and came crashing down, trapping the rescuers and the family. Across Yorkshire, seven more people were killed by falling chimneys and masonry as the gale pounded the north. In Scotland a gust of 177 mph was recorded at Uist in the Western Isles of Scotland.

The next morning the gale kept going across the town and any children that got to school were soon sent home. Some 100 out of the 250 schools had been damaged or wrecked. By midday, a total of 100,000 homes were damaged to varying degrees; 100 were destroyed completely and 6,000 were rendered uninhabitable. A total of 250 families were made homeless; whole streets were blocked by piles of rubble, cars were crushed and one of the 150-foot floodlights at the Bramall Lane football ground was lying twisted and contorted on the ground. The higher parts of the town had to be evacuated completely, and a 100-foot crane raised to refurbish the local technical college was brought crashing down, badly damaging the building. The city went into a state of shock. The post-war prefabricated housing stock suffered extensive damage, many of them totally ruined. One eyewitness remembers waking up as a young child and being baffled as to why their neighbours' furniture was strewn across the street the next day.

By the evening of 16 February, the town hall had become the main reception centre for the thousands of local people badly affected by the storm.[4] In the aftermath, the building trade pulled together and worked with a wide range of other skilled labour forces (unusual for the 1960s) to begin the huge task of clearing up and then rebuilding the devastated town. Teams from as far afield as Birmingham and Coventry joined this body of workers in the following days, during which insurance claims piled up and reached the £3 million mark – more than £60 million today.

So why was Sheffield struck with such incredible winds when towns only a few miles away found themselves with far less damage, some even with none at all? The synoptic charts gave no clue – the storm showed uniform isobars across the areas both to the south and north consistent with the wind speeds that affected them. At first most meteorologists scratched their heads, and attention turned immediately to the Pennines, the hills and mountains that lie to the west of town. The immediate answer given, and one that many papers and radio reports featured in the coming days, was the 'lee effect' of the mountains. In essence, when the wind is blowing over the tops of the mountains at a certain speed it is lifted upwards; however, as the topography flattens quickly on the lee side of high ground, the wind begins to drop downwards and achieves a faster rate than the atmospheric and synoptic markers would suggest. However, modelled wind speeds accounting for this effect still fell far short of the actual numbers reached on the day.

The answer when it came was not a straightforward one. However, it demonstrates how complex topographical and synoptic factors can prove critical when it comes to surface winds. Researchers began by looking into the causes of this abnormal event by examining the temperature profile of the airstream on the day.

In essence, the strong westerly airstream consisted of two unusually contrasting layers of air. A deep layer of warm air had sat on top of a shallower layer of much colder air. As this blew across the mountains, the heavier, colder air sank below the warmer layer. In theory, this would have made it difficult for the cold layer to push upwards to create the aforementioned lee effect. However, in practice, as the cold air reached the Pennines and bounced quickly upwards, it was then knocked back with great force by the warm layer aloft. The cold air bounced back downwards with great force and created a series of exaggerated waves. Because of its weight, the colder layer was propelled along progressively faster. As it headed downwards, the second wave pushed out towards Sheffield at furious speed.

The set of circumstances necessary to create this scenario relied on the specific height of the inversion, meaning the reversal caused when cold air is trapped under warmer air, plus the precise topography and temperature. The most violent winds were squeezed into a narrow band that became progressively wider and less powerful as it spread outwards after hitting Sheffield, rather like an avalanche losing energy as it spreads out into a valley. It is perhaps interesting to note that this phenomenon had not been recorded in Sheffield before this event – and in the fifty years since it happened, it has not occurred again.

28

The Deadly Glasgow Storm, January 1968

January 1968 began on a cold note. There had been heavy snow in England and Scotland, with the situation in the south of England described as the worst since 1963. However, the weather soon took a far more stormy turn. On Sunday 14 January, pressure was high to the south of Britain, with fine, warm weather over Spain and France. The bitter cold of the previous days in the UK had retreated to the east of Europe and sat over Poland and Germany. To the north, however, a large low pressure was centred near Iceland. The contrast of the warm air to the south created a notable pressure and temperature gradient that meant a lot of energy was circulating in the convergence zone of the air masses – namely the northern British Isles.

When a small depression formed in the mid-Atlantic and blew quickly westwards, it added further energy to the potent depression sitting to the north-west of Scotland. As it began to push east, the pressure rose across the western flank of this now complex low. This rise of pressure squeezed the isobars to the south of the low's centre incredibly tight, creating a fierce zone of violent winds. Early in the morning of 15 January this intense wind field began to move inexorably towards the west coast of Scotland. By the early hours, while Scotland was sleeping, the storm made landfall.

The early hours of Monday 15 January proved to be terrifying for people right across Scotland, but nowhere was worse hit than the west and south. In fact, the winds broke records right across this area and the north of England as well. An extraordinary gust of 134 mph was recorded in the Lake District. Nevertheless, it was the more built-up parts of south-west Scotland that saw the worst damage.

As soon as the powerful winds tore up the Clyde into Clyde Bank, one of the large cranes collapsed into the dry docks and a 7,000-ton dredger was pulled away from its moorings, bashing up against adjacent vessels as the winds drove it further out of control. As it smashed into a variety of larger vessels, one of them sank. This was largest to go down that night, the vast Greek bulk carrier *Ocean Pegasus*, weighing 24,000 tons. All in all, in and around the Clyde, seven vessels sank that night and three men were drowned in the melee. A further non-commercial vessel, a small passenger ferry, also sank into the river. Other forms of transport also suffered at the hands of the brutal winds. Several passenger planes were thrown about on the tarmac at Abbotsinch Airport, many of which were badly damaged, while the railways saw widespread disruption because of lines blocked by fallen trees and other debris.

A major urban danger in the UK from gales is falling chimneys, and as the 100 mph winds hit Glasgow the towering tenement buildings that were such a major feature of the city then proved lethal. Many were badly damaged, and in one of these blocks a chimney crashed through several floors, killing two mothers and two children. In this case it was the stack of the adjacent building that had collapsed down onto the neighbouring block, smashing through floor after floor until it hit the ground. One of those who had been in the block next door recently recounted how she was best friends with one of the girls that was killed. They had been playing together the evening before and she asked her parents if she could stay over at her young friend's flat. Her own parents weren't keen and wanted their daughter to spend the night at home; unknowingly, with this decision they saved her life.

There were hundreds of other narrow escapes. A huge construction crane was twisted and buckled by the wind before it smashed into a tenement below, tearing off its facade before plummeting to the ground. It was a miracle no one was hurt here. Chimneys and rubble crashed down everywhere, bursting into the streets and crushing cars; many people were injured in their beds. The gale raged across Scotland for many hours, tearing down trees and power lines, and by the end of the morning twenty people were dead. Nine of the dead were from the Glasgow area alone. It was estimated that 3,000 telephone lines were down, leaving people unable to call 999 at the height of the storm. Even so, 1,000 calls did get through. The impact of the unfolding disaster across Glasgow became starkly apparent during the day when it was calculated that 70,000 council houses, almost half the total stock, were damaged.[5] The council were expected to pay for this kind of damage with no central funds to fall back on, and money was woefully short. The army were brought in to manage some of the aftermath and their role in a civilian, urban crisis sparked a debate over whether this was appropriate in peace time. The army secured damaged buildings and property in the first instance and helped the local council in assessing the gigantic task ahead of rebuilding some of the devastated areas in both public and private control. This action was most controversial with the local unions who panicked, thinking that precious work was being stolen from them. Nevertheless, when they were shown the gargantuan size of the task by army planners, these fears evaporated. The task would take years and, even with army help, would certainly overwhelm the available resources for some time to come.

Clinics, schools and numerous civic buildings were quickly formed into reception centres housing the homeless who numbered about 800 immediately after the storm given that as many as 250 homes had been permanently destroyed.

Meteorologist Ingrid Holford commented that on the day the storm struck Glasgow that 'nature really went to town with disasters' on Tuesday 16 January. A canal in Shrewsbury had burst its banks along a 50-metre section and hundreds of thousands of cubic metres of water poured into the surrounding countryside and soon flooded the town. In England several people were also killed by the violent winds, and both regions saw widespread structural damage.

In the Netherlands, the violent winds breached dykes and sank several ships, including a large Russian trawler. Out in the North Sea a giant oil rig, Sea Quest, broke from its moorings and was set adrift into the open water, resurrecting bitter memories of the fate of the crew of the Sea Gem, which also broke loose from its base and floated free in December 1965. On that occasion the rig then collapsed, killing many of the crew.

The biggest headline of the day was a huge earthquake that struck the west of Sicily – that morning most papers and the radio news were saying at least 430 people had died and the UK was sending aid and a naval vessel into the Mediterranean to help with the clear-up and rescue effort. Unfortunately this also served to put the gales in Scotland further back in the headlines, despite the huge death toll, perhaps explaining why this is not as well remembered by the British public as one would have expected.

One aspect of this storm that was not immediately known, but subsequently proven, was that some of the most severe damage was attributable to tornadoes. Eyewitnesses from the higher elevations around the city said there were several distinct episodes of steadily increasing winds that sounded like 'freight trains' and built into a crescendo, eventually setting the buildings and everything around them shaking violently until they gradually moved away. There is little doubt that this is a description of tornadic activity.

With a vast trail of destruction behind it, the depression that caused so much damage was not exceptional in any aspect until it hit Glasgow. Interestingly, a similar storm hit exactly the same place exactly forty-one years before, in January 1927, with the city again experiencing far more damage than any other location in Scotland. In this storm fifteen people were killed in the tenement blocks and over 100 injured across the city in a strikingly similar sequence of events. It is thought that part of the explanation for the localised ferociousness of the winds on the city can be explained by its unique location; fairly mountainous on either side and upriver of the Clyde, Glasgow proper begins where the terrain opens out into a bowl shape. The snaking shape of the Clyde and other topographical features from the west seem to have created a series of funnels for the wind, which burst out into the basin of the city with violent force.

In conclusion, even today it would in many ways be quite hard to forecast the severity of the wind on Glasgow without the knowledge of how the wind is going to act across a particular set of features. Computer simulations, satellites and a more detailed view of the complex upper-air situation should all help today's forecasters understand when severe winds like this are likely to strike again. What they cannot predict is where tornadoes will strike, or if indeed they will appear at all.

29

The Great October Storm of 1987

There can be few people, if any, that have lived through a winter in our islands without experiencing a gale. However, depending on *where* you live, the amount and strength of wind will usually vary greatly. The great shock that the deadly gale of October 1987 delivered was that steadily increasing wind speeds that would not be uncommon in the Western Isles, Highlands or Shetlands hit one of the most densely populated parts of Europe. One of the other great shocks was that, at a time of increased computer power and sophisticated data modelling, the storm came with little or no warning.

In fact, warnings of severe gales did go out but they were after most people had gone to bed and came at too short notice for the public to act, although they did help shipping. The now infamous Michael Fish broadcast, where he joked about how a woman had phoned the BBC and asked if there was a 'hurricane' coming, did in fact include advice to batten down the hatches as it was going to 'get very windy'; even so, the forecast pointed to the tightest isobars remaining well to the south of Britain.

This storm killed eighteen people and caused many millions of pounds worth of damage, including an extraordinary amount of structural damage, even in central London. The truly heart-breaking aspect of this storm was the loss of untold millions of trees, many ancient and loved by generations. It is also a fact that if the storm had happened during the day the numbers killed would have been far higher.

For those of us who watched the *Countryfile* 'weather for the week ahead' on Sunday lunchtime somewhat religiously, as I did in 1987, there was in fact already a concern about an unusually severe depression developing in the Atlantic during the coming week. Sure enough, a very deep low was shown for the 15 October, with enough isobars around it to make a dartboard. This would certainly be powerful enough to bring severe gales somewhere to the UK the following week, if not a risk of structural damage, were it to hit. Although the UK had some of the most powerful weather data computers in the world at that time, what it lacked was sufficient observational stations out to sea to feed into them. This was almost certainly one of the reasons why a rapidly deepening depression over Biscay during the middle of the week became rather lost to the computer models; insufficient surface data at sea was not recording its somewhat explosive progress out from Biscay towards Britain.

The weeks immediately before the storm had been extremely wet and disturbed. In London, early October had brought us some severe thunderstorms more akin to those of summer in nature. The weekend before the storm, the Sussex countryside, for example, I saw numerous rivers with broken banks and a wide area flooded. I had also just witnessed 16 inches of rain fall in two days at my parent's villa on the Costa Brava, creating floods that killed at least sixteen people, and it has been suggested that unusually high sea temperatures put the weather into an extremely disturbed and boisterous mood that autumn across much of Europe.

My experience of this storm is probably typical for those living in the suburbs of London at the time. By bedtime it had begun raining and the trees were moving a bit, but it still felt like a normal night; nevertheless, the strong gusty wind did seem to be gaining strength outside. In the early hours there was a terrific crash and I woke with a start. There was a lot of noise, something like a train going past. I looked out the window and saw that the roof of our utility room behind the kitchen and directly below me had blown off, hitting my window as it went. It clung there for a few seconds before it blew away into the darkness. I have no idea what time it was but I was suddenly quite awake. Out in the garden the scene was wild. Clouds raced past the moon at breakneck speed and the wind did not drop for a second; it only boomed and howled around the roof, and the booming, thundering chaos lasted all night. The next day the power was out and we relied on a transistor radio to tell us that the storm had affected everywhere in the south and that most other people were without power as well.

Indeed, London awoke to a scene of devastation. Roof tiles, bricks, glass and debris were strewn everywhere; branches of trees were torn down and great boughs were tipped over, fully leaved, some even torn out of the ground, as if great, strong arms had twisted and turned them each and every way until they snapped. Wrecked and crushed cars and fallen trees were visible in every direction, and great walls were blown down, leaving piles of rubble where they had once stood and crushing many cars. The loss of power to the rail network meant signs in many stations were posted saying, 'No trains today, Power down.' On the main road into Greenwich some houses had entire corners ripped off; some were completely open to the elements, their facades gone, others partially or even totally collapsed. Beds, cupboards and the occupants' everyday items and furniture were open for all the world to see, material flapping in the wind and the rain soaking it all. Many streets seemed to have been affected by the orientation of the building – south- and west-facing buildings appeared to fare worst. The gigantic oak and plane trees that lined Greenwich Park in front of the maritime museum all came down. A deep mourning began for the ravaged trees; all around London's parks, twisted, writhing roots, boughs and branches were piled high, while the sound of chainsaws rang out for weeks. A number of volunteer groups helped clear up local areas in what was often depressing work.

So exactly what had happened? A couple of days before, a large area of low pressure sat over the mid-Atlantic with unusually sharp temperature gradients attributable, at least in part, to the unseasonable warm sea temperatures. On 14 October, a secondary depression developed quickly at the base of the depression, deepened and travelled north-east across the UK. Next, another depression formed in a similar area north of Biscay on the 15th and deepened even more quickly, fed by the contrast of two increasingly cold and very warm airstreams. By midnight the disturbance began strengthening explosively, shooting up from Brittany to become centred over Cornwall late on Thursday, deepening by then to 970 mb. The most intense winds formed to the south-east of the centre along some very tight isobars indeed. As the storm moved north-east across the country, these ingredients created what is sometimes known as a 'bomb' – an unusually deep and violent depression. The strongest winds were squeezed along the southern flank, covering all of southern England by early Friday morning while the centre deepened below 960 mb. Temperatures in the warm sector early in the morning rose to 17 °C but, as the back edge of the storm passed, cold air quickly became established and they dropped back rapidly to 8 or 9 °C. This cold back edge of the depression has been postulated as a likely cause of the most explosive winds in this, and other, similar storms. The phenomenon has been called a 'sting jet'; the theory is that as this portion of the storm evaporates it drags the jet stream above sharply downwards, coiling around the cyclonic formation and causing hugely powerful winds as it dissipates below.

The areas that bore the brunt of the storm were those along the south coast most exposed to the gales. Portsmouth and the Isle of Wight, Southampton, Brighton, Folkestone and Dover all saw unprecedented destruction on a scale not seen in the south of England since 1703. The damage was so extensive across south-east England that it would be almost impossible to write about it all in any detail – but every part of the south-east lost precious trees, roofs were blown off, chimneys collapsed and whole holiday parks flattened. The government stated that this was the greatest night of civil disruption since 1945, and the scale of the loss of trees on the evening news was hard to believe. In Sevenoaks the roaring, thundering wind was bending huge old trees right over until many of them toppled or snapped and collapsed on to the ground below. Six of the large oaks planted in Victorian times were blown down. As in much of the UK, most trees were still in full leaf at this time and weeks of torrential rain meant the wind was toppling them from wet, muddy root bases with relative ease. Large swathes of woodland were literally swept down across Kent, Sussex and Hampshire. Five people died in Kent, two of whom were sailors swept out to sea. Others were killed by falling trees, chimney stacks or masonry and many more were injured. Winds at Portsmouth and Eastbourne measured well in excess of 100 mph before the measuring equipment broke. In Norfolk a gust over 110 mph was recorded, and these wind speeds are representative of what Hampshire, Surrey, Sussex, Kent, Essex and parts of East Anglia experienced that night. The highest official gust was 115 mph, recorded in Shoreham, Sussex, just next to Brighton,[6] and indeed near Quimper in Brittany an amazing gust of 137 mph[7] was confirmed. In London 90 mph was reached, but again equipment broke or failed before speeds could be confirmed. Even more destructive, however, were the sustained wind speeds of 80 mph that affected these same areas. This explains the terrible noise that seemed never to abate the previous night. If one considers that the definition of a hurricane-force wind is for there to be sustained wind speed of 74 mph, many in southern Britain now knew what the experience of winds from such a tropical storm might be like. Much was made by the media about the fact that this was, in their view, a hurricane – even though the gale shared few characteristics of one. It seems that this debate around terminology was used as a tool to discredit the weather forecasters, whose lack of warning and subsequent refusal to accept that this had indeed been a tropical latitude hurricane ensured the nation's fury was squarely focused on them.

Tropical hurricanes are destructive in completely different ways, and the level of destruction they can wreak can easily be shown by the effects of Katrina on New Orleans, with sustained winds of over 140 mph, gusts nearer 180 mph, tornadoes, storm surges, and rain measured in feet, not inches, causing a death toll of thousands. Nevertheless, people felt, and still feel, that the adjectives, 'gale' or 'storm' do not do this event justice and so many still refer to it just as the hurricane. It was also interesting to note that the papers never mentioned the fact that Scotland and some parts of northern England endured wind speeds of this force probably in most winters. They must have looked on and wondered why there was so much fuss. However, built-up areas not used to such storms are very vulnerable and had the highest winds occurred in daylight the death and injury toll would have been far higher.

On the coast at Folkestone, stories of great destruction began to emerge that were representative of every town along the southern and eastern shores. Close friends bore witness to it; one of them experienced the horror of having his entire family home on the cliffs of Capel-le-Ferne being destroyed in one fell swoop while inside it. Another extraordinary sight also greeted local people in Folkestone that morning -- a huge cross-channel ferry that had drifted at the mercy of the sea the night before was beached below the cliffs at the Warren in Folkestone. Such a sight will hopefully not be repeated anytime soon. Fortunately, the crew who were aboard that night all survived uninjured and were rescued. An eyewitness, then at university in Brighton, was coming back from a party and walked through the centre of town at the storm's height: 'As I struggled against the wind it was hard to breathe at times and spray stung my eyes. As I crossed the parkland outside the Pavilion I saw the first tree fall. It stunned me and then I saw more trees fall, great huge trees crashing down. They made a terrible noise as they fell. It was an unforgettable sight.' In fact, one of the great minarets on the Pavilion itself crashed through the roof of this historically important but seemingly vulnerable building, causing terrible damage inside. According to the local paper, the town was covered in salt for days from sea spray blown inland.

Along with the 15 million trees that were destroyed that night in the UK, it is estimated that approximately £2 billion (over £5 billion today) worth of damage was done. The Association of Insurers said in the aftermath of the storm their members received in the region of over 50,000 claims a day,[8] and a total of £350 million (just under £0.9 billion today) worth of claims was reported.[9]

There is also little doubt that the cessation of trading in London on 16 October contributed to the 10.8 per cent fall in global markets the following Monday, widely known as 'black Monday'. Apparently, as soon as the London market opened on 19 October, selling began in earnest based on fears of a possible timber surplus. This pushed certain sectors of commodities stocks right down, in a short space of time. The apparent drop in market confidence began a selling frenzy that soon escalated into a full-blown panic based on a number of other complex factors. Nevertheless, this storm's impact on London is still considered a contributory factor, if not a catalyst, for the panic which resulted in billions of dollars wiped off the equities markets.

Even as billions fell off the stock markets around the world, this seemed to pale into insignificance when compared to the permanently altered and scarred landscape of southern England. Toys Hill, Emmets Garden, Bedgebury, the Ashdown Forest, Pettworth, Chartwell, Knole Park; these historic locations saw millions of trees blown down in just one night.

Twenty-six years on, many of these places are once again full of beautiful trees and the terrible scars have been healed. At the time it seemed as if it the countryside would never be the same again. At Toys Hill in Kent, an experiment has been run to examine the natural response to the hurricane damage. A small, isolated area of woodland has been left totally to nature to see how it would recover; it has done so wonderfully. While a lot of natural debris remains, the woodland character has altered significantly from the other 'managed' parts of the forest, with lush, bright woodland far more open to the sky than the surrounding areas.

And what of the Met Office and the poor forecast? Looking at it logically, the forecasters were just visualising and describing what the computer models showed them. It is absurd to think they are personally to blame for the storm and for the level of accuracy of the computer data. It was unfortunate that, despite forecasts for days warning of strong winds, that one segment by Michael Fish, in which he reassured a woman who phoned the BBC to ask whether an existing tropical hurricane she had heard about would hit the UK, obscured his actual forecast. The part where he warns the public of an approaching gale and to 'batten down the hatches because it is going to get very windy indeed', is always carefully edited out.

The Met Office undertook an enquiry into the failures of the 1987 forecast and made many changes. They began to implement investments in technology upgrades early on and now use a far greater number of automated weather buoys out in the ocean that can more closely monitor sudden changes in current and sea temperature. Forecasters are also now highly trained, and with investments in satellite technology these many changes have facilitated a constantly evolving and improving scenario in terms of weather prediction at short to medium range. In the last three decades, computer power has also scaled up to levels unimaginable in 1987. At that time the Met Office computers could only resolve 200 million calculations per second; now this figure is over 1 trillion per second. Forecasts are now complied four times a day, as this level of resolution has enabled a revolution in meteorology as well as advances in climatology all over the world.

One further result has been the ability to make medium-range forecasts largely used by the public and private sector organisations for planning across a wide range of activities. The public is still far from ready for any kind of long-range forecasts, largely because they expect accuracy; the horizon of accurate forecasts still remains around five to seven days. Longer-range outlooks are normally based on percentages calculated using computer and data modelling. These show trends, not details.

A good example of where this has gone wrong was a 2009 summer forecast of a 'BBQ Summer'. This widely quoted and broadcast headline, coined by the Met Office (or perhaps their PR agency), was used to describe a 65 per cent chance of above-average conditions.

While in the south-east it was at least an average summer, in the north and west of the UK, 2009 was a poor summer by any measure.

The Dutch weather service successfully issues ten- to fifteen-day forecasts that simply reflect the percentage likelihood of a given outcome. For example, 'there is a 70 per cent chance of unsettled weather with average temperatures; there is also a [30 per cent] chance of temperatures being above average later in the period'. The audience can decide what it thinks will happen, to some degree, and sees how chances of a given outcome rise and fall with the waxing and waning of the models. This kind of change in tactic might help the media interpret the actual data itself in a balanced way. It would also make a mockery of some of the more desperate tabloids that paint random 'Day After Tomorrow' doomsday scenarios based on the ramblings of literally anybody calling themselves a 'weather expert'.

Events such as the 1987 storm have clearly shown the Met Office learnt that it needed to invest in computer power and up its game in terms of training and its own structure. These changes will certainly ensure that we are better prepared if such a storm should hit us again. Based on the 1703 storm, on balance it should have been a 300-year return period before another such destructive gale hit the south of the country – but nature knows no such rules, and it was only two and a half years, in January 1990, before a similar storm struck again and proved every bit as deadly and destructive.

30

The Burns' Day Storm, January 1990

It seemed almost impossible to believe. Less than three years after the extremely powerful gale of October 1987 was marked down as a 1-in-300-year event, a yet more deadly storm hit Britain on a wider scale. It is estimated by the BBC that this storm killed ninety-seven people, forty-seven of them in Britain, and the scale of damage was extensive.

Although the storm was not quite as violent in terms of wind strength as the 1987 storm, it covered a much wider area. Eight people died in Ireland and many more in the Netherlands, Belgium and Germany. The highest winds also occurred during the afternoon, with ferocious winds crossing Britain when the day was at its most busy.

The Met Office, having learnt a good deal of lessons after the 1987 storm, had invested heavily in increasingly sophisticated computer technology as well as its network of live data and reporting points in the open ocean. They began forecasting strong winds from Tuesday 23 January. However, a Russian ship in path of the rapidly lowering pressure of a deepening depression began to return numbers that showed the Met Office that a potentially dangerous storm was moving in from the south-west. By Wednesday 24 it looked as if the depression was going to move across Scotland early on Thursday 25, with the strongest winds to the south. The predictions proved correct, but despite the warnings of very severe gales few people changed their routine to accommodate them. There may have been some slight underestimation of the strength of the winds that were coming until they actually reached the south-west coast, according to newspaper reports at the time, but in general the warnings and the forecast progress of the storm were very accurate. On this occasion it was the whole of the south of England, much of South Wales, the Midlands and East Anglia that were hit.[10]

During the morning the storm swept into the south-west of England, immediately causing tremendous disruption and taking many lives. Soon it became exceptionally windy across most of the south and damaging gusts quickly began to cause more widespread damage. The lights began flickering in London in the late morning, and the gale was audible in well-insulated office buildings. At about 1 p.m., people were literally being thrown about by the wind and a powerful gust picked up a parked motorbike with incredible force, launching it into the door of the Barclays branch of Russell Square with a horrific bang, showering the floor with glass. Out of town, trees that had been damaged by the 1987 gale toppled and fell in their thousands and once again gardens across the country saw fence panels blown down, while large debris swirled around the streets, causing death and injury. It was a wild and frightening day on the coasts and hills of the south, which again saw much devastation, and widespread structural damage. Many thousands of trees collapsed, lorries and cars were blown around like rag dolls and both electricity and telephone supplies were disrupted as power lines blew down for the second time in three years. Nevertheless, there was somewhat less damage than 1987, especially in terms of trees, largely because they were bare of leaves. Nevertheless, the moist and waterlogged soil also rendered them very unstable and many fell.

Among the passengers trapped on board a passenger ferry travelling from France to Dover with 130 or so other passengers and crew were my aunt and uncle, who spent much of the day, and indeed some of the following evening, on a fretful journey as the engines failed. The RAF began to organise rescue efforts and lifeboats were despatched; however, the crew managed to restart the engines at dusk and the rescue operations were recalled. Across the country the rail services began to be interrupted, and British Rail's London Midland service was shut down and all London stations, bar Victoria, were closed down at rush hour, leaving thousands of commuters stranded. Much of this was due to fallen trees blocking lines and interruptions to power. On the roads, the M1 was shut and a reported sixteen HGVs were blown over while other determined drivers kept going, with police describing them as 'lunatic' and reporting having observed several of them continuing along on two wheels – at speed – as the wind tried its best to tip them over. In the West Country, forty-five A-roads were closed by overturned lorries, with one section of the M27 blocked by four such incidents along one small stretch. Manchester, out of the path of the worst of the storm, still suffered similar travel disruption and power cuts that stopped rail and road traffic, while floods and overflowing rivers affected parts of Yorkshire. Gatwick Airport had to close in the afternoon as 80 mph winds began blowing grounded planes from their moorings, some planes suffering damage as they spun around. By mid-afternoon people from Cornwall to London and into the Midlands were reported killed, many of them by falling trees. One woman in Croydon was crushed by a falling wall while waiting for the bus and died. In Bristol a schoolgirl was killed when a conservatory collapsed on to her whole class at school, with several other pupils badly injured, one critically. By the end of the day, forty-seven[11] people were reported to have died and countless others were injured in a melee of disasters far too numerous to report. Large numbers of roads in towns and cities in the south remained closed into the weekend as buildings or construction sites were damaged and made unsafe by the powerful winds. Many people were hurt on the streets as debris from such sites blew wildly into the path of traffic and pedestrians throughout the afternoon.

In Scotland, cold air was dragged down into the depression as it crossed the country, bringing about easterly or north-easterly winds that resulted in blizzard conditions, and many areas were cut off by heavy snow and gale-force winds.

As soon as the winds left England, so they began to impact the Netherlands, where eleven people were killed by falling trees and loose, fast-blowing debris. One man was killed by the gears of a windmill that ran out of control that afternoon, causing a fire. The coastguard there reported that they feared a Russian vessel carrying up to sixty crew had foundered off the coast, and a rescue had to be organised. In France at least six people were killed and disruption to shipping and ferry services, as we saw earlier, was severe. The northern coasts saw high tides drive seawater in across many vulnerable coastal towns despite the robust sea defences put in place since the tidal surge of 1953. In Germany the River Elbe began to flow increasingly out of control, and both Frankfurt and Hamburg, well inland, suffered both structural damage and river flooding.

The aftermath of the Burns' Day Storm (25 January is the birthday of poet Robert Burns), as it immediately became known, was not as financially severe as that of 1987, yet the death toll was extremely high for the reasons given above. It is worth noting that in the period 1987–93 there was a relatively high frequency of severe gales in England. However, after that period, no storm on a par with the most severe storms of those years struck southern England until October 2013. The political world soon began looking for explanations for the storm in terms of global warming, and climatologists had already identified a possible 'greenhouse effect', driven by vast increases in CO_2 levels, that could result in both hotter summers and more potent winter storms in north-west Europe.

However, at the time the Met Office, when questioned on this aspect of the event, repeatedly refused to be drawn. As they pointed out, this storm was nothing unusual; numerous equally or more powerful ones hit Britain every year, only this one had taken a somewhat more southerly track and had hit the most populated areas of England.

Despite the early warnings, it was debated in Parliament whether these warnings had been effective enough in reaching the public. While the emergency and armed services were briefed on 24 January, some MPs argued that the public would not always interpret existing warnings as severe and would vastly underestimate the impact on them. An American-style system, used for hurricanes, was suggested. This system advises the public to take action when a threat is imminent and warnings are accompanied by key safety advice. This was put forward as a possible solution. It is interesting to note that today's red warnings from the Met Office do just this but are only a relatively recent phenomenon.

As the storm unfolded on 25 January, the spectre of a major impact on the insurance industry, which had been so dramatically affected by the 1987 storm, soon reared its head. A major drop in share prices for the city's key insurers began almost immediately. Early calculations estimated that the overall cost of claims for the storm would reach £2 billion in the coming months and the insurers were likely to pick up about half of that bill. In 1987, claims reached £1.2 billion and this shocked the government into introducing a new Bill, dubbed the 'Bellwin Scheme', under which the government would pick up 75 per cent of the costs of the storm that the insurers did not cover. However, there had been several other major disasters since 1987 that had also dented Lloyds and other insurers at a global level. These included the Piper Alpha disaster, which saw fire destroy an oil rig out in the North Sea with great loss of life, and Hurricane Hugo, a full-strength hurricane that hit the Caribbean and parts of the USA, both in 1988. The vast sums involved in the clear-up from this storm would come to impact everyone. As a consequence, there was a stark warning to both government and the public that the costs of premiums would be on the rise as the industry absorbed the impact of outstanding claims. Local councils were also faced with a huge bill, with London alone looking at a £21 million alone, and it was here the Bellwin Scheme was to have most impact. Despite this help, Labour MP Margaret Hodge, who is now head of the highly respected Public Accounts Committee, calculated that the average poll tax bill, a previous incarnation of the current council tax system, would rise by £4 per person and highlighted the fact that there was still no strategic management plan for public emergencies in London. As such, there could be no coordinated response to any similar future disaster to hit the capital that would ensure better outcomes for public transport and the use of the emergency services as well as a more efficient prioritisation of public resources.

Soon after this storm there followed a radical and long-lasting change in the weather. The next seven months were exceptionally sunny, dry and calm and there followed a beautiful spring that began in February. The May Day bank holiday was one of the hottest on record and 3 August saw the then all-time temperature record of 37.1 °C established at Cheltenham.

PART IV
TORNADOES

31

The Great London Tornado, 1091

The first fatal tornado to have been documented in Britain struck central London on Friday 23 October 1091 (by the modern calendar) and is also likely to have been one of the most violent. Given that nearly a millennium has passed since the event, it is made all the more remarkable that such a local disaster is so well attested to; nevertheless the facts are not that numerous.

In context, 1091 was twenty-five years into the rather brutal and repressive Norman regime that began with William the Conqueror in 1066. His son William Rufus had been causing a great deal of controversy at the time by sequestering church funds in large amounts to use for his own purposes. Londoners would have been fully aware of this, and it is no surprise that the heavily oppressed native English of the time saw the tornado as divine retribution against Rufus' crimes against God and the Church.

The twister bore down on the great church of St Mary Le Bow and tore the old building to pieces. TORRO, the British severe weather and tornado research body, estimates that this was a powerful T8 tornado because the gigantic beams from the rafters of St Mary's, each of which would have weighed several tons, were tossed in the air. Measuring 26 feet, they were found embedded into the ground nearby with only 4 feet protruding. It has therefore been calculated that this is the equivalent of an F4 tornado, which would have created wind speeds around the funnel of between 200 and 240 mph at its zenith.

The tornado next smashed into the densely packed residential streets of present-day Southwark, destroying a reported 600 homes and numerous sturdy churches. Two men were killed in the melee and the tornado then moved over the Thames and took out the then wooden London Bridge, destroying it completely.

Luckily for Rufus, when the tornado struck he was on a military campaign in Scotland against Malcolm Canmore, eventually proving victorious. The destruction of London Bridge would have paralysed traffic and hampered trade in the city for some time. When he returned to London, Rufus went on to build a far more solid brick bridge,

PART IV
TORNADOES

restoring this critical route over the Thames. This would no doubt have further asserted Norman power over London, and one could speculate may even have become a symbol of it for some. Whether he paid for this new, more solid bridge through his dubiously acquired Church funds is, however, not known.

32

Britain's Most Deadly Tornado, South Wales, October 1913

On the evening of 27 October 1913 a violent thunderstorm descended on the Taff Valley north of Cardiff. As the storm progressed up the valley, a tornado touched down and ploughed through the tightly packed terraces of several of the valley's mining communities, effecting widespread damage along its path. Six people were killed and many others injured. This remains the most deadly tornado ever recorded in the UK.

On the morning of the 27th, a deep low-pressure system sat to the south-west of Cornwall and began to intensify during the day. The south-west airstream that accompanied the low was extremely active and produced some heavy showers and strong winds. It was a mild day generally across much of the south of the UK, including South Wales; temperatures rose to around 15 or 16 °C during the day despite it being fairly windy.

The first appearance of the violent thunderstorm was at Exeter shortly after 4 p.m. The winds began to strengthen, a steady rain began to fall and flashes of lightning appeared to the south. This continued for some minutes before all hell broke loose. The shower suddenly turned into a torrential deluge only to be joined by a terrific fall of hail accompanied by vivid lightning and loud peals of thunder. This storm soon passed through to the north and left Exeter, moving across Devon into Somerset. Its intensity was increasing continuously as it moved northwards, and sometime after 5 p.m. it reached the coastline and began to absorb additional energy from the waters of the Bristol Channel. It passed east of the wild north Devon coast, leaving England just east of Watchet. It made landfall in Wales just to the east of Barry. It appears that the tornado formed somewhere in the vicinity east of Esail Isaf, near to where the A470 moves up into the Taff Valley towards Pontypridd. In its initial stages it was only strong enough to provoke light damage to outbuildings and trees, but, with the rising topography of the valley, the storm intensified and the tornado gained more energy.

As it passed through Pontypridd buildings began to be damaged and the width of the tornado expanded from 50 to over 200 yards by the time it had reached Clifnydd. Here Mr B. Evans, a Fellow of the Meteorological Society, was one of the few official observers to witness the storm. He described intense blue flashes of lightning from the oncoming clouds, accompanied by little thunder but, with each flash, he saw 'three or four interweaving flashes, all of a deep blue. And, what was strange were the waves of blue fire that seemed to be rolling on the ground'.[1]

Shortly afterwards the funnel approached. Mr Evans continued,

A few seconds before 5.50 p.m. we heard a noise resembling the hissing of an express locomotive. The sound grew rapidly in volume, at last resembling the rushing speed of many road lorries racing along. We endeavoured to move out of the room to the passage for greater safety because a hurried remark was made that the engines of these supposed passing loaded steam lorries had collided before the house, and were about to burst, when the panes of our windows were broken by stones, tiles, slates, dried cement, and splintered timber. The missiles broke the Venetian blinds and struck the opposite walls. We made for the rear of the house, but all the windows were being bombarded by small material and corrugated iron sheets. We could distinctly hear the chimney-pots fall on the roof, and the material sliding off, being dashed on the pavement and doorstep. We could see the kitchen clock from the hall passage. It had stopped at 5.51 p.m. It was not struck by any object. It is the largest clock in the house. Two smaller clocks in other rooms were not affected.

As the immediate effects of these tornadic winds moved off, torrential rain battered the house and lightning set fire to the newly laid tar outside.[2]

Now the vortex began to flex its muscles. A 60-foot-high ash tree was ripped from the ground and sucked into the funnel. It was thrown down a full 2½ miles away. The tornado ripped roofs of houses damaged churches and smashed in thousands of windows. One man was blown 30 or so feet into the Glamorgan Canal but escaped with his life. Another man, who was unfortunate enough to be caught outside at Clifnydd, was picked up by the funnel and thrown some 400 yards into a field with such violence he was killed. Two men from the local football club were also caught in the storm. Mr A. Woolford was hurled against a wall and killed instantly while the trainer, Walter Breeze, escaped with relatively minor injuries.

As the tornado moved away north, still almost in a straight line, it next hit Abercynon. There a row of sixty tightly packed cottages all had their roofs torn off, and many others were very badly damaged. The vortex had approached the village in the direction in which the houses were all laid out, and it tore right along them. A teenager helping her mother in the local chapel was seriously injured by falling debris, as was the son of the local postmaster.

One eyewitness, a collier, had just got into the bath after work when the tornado hit. The house began to collapse and the man and his wife got out just in time. To their horror, however, the collapsing house still contained their baby daughter, asleep upstairs. After the storm passed, he then had the awful task of getting through the rubble upstairs and was greeted by a scene of total devastation. It must have been a miraculous moment for him to find that a solid beam had dropped down at such an angle as to protect the baby from all the debris. He found her still in her bed, fast asleep and totally unaware of her ordeal.[3]

The tornado next hit Edwardsville, where hundreds more buildings were damaged and more people were buried in the rubble, some losing their lives to the devastating storm. The tornado bore down on the local school, tearing off its roof, smashing all the windows and scattering vast amounts of rubble and metal all around it. The school was completely wrecked and the children had to be accommodated for schooling at the local church while repairs were made. Even as the tornado tore into to the more mountainous regions north of the Taff Valley, it kept on going. By approximately 8 p.m. the storm moved across from Wales into Cheshire, where it touched down and began to do damage again. Peckforton Castle had the greenhouses in its grounds completely destroyed and numerous livestock were killed. At Runcorn another man was picked up off his feet and blown into a nearby wall but luckily survived to tell the tale.

When the tornado was over, about 100 people were injured and the damage was estimated to have been in the region of £30,000–£50,000. In today's money this would be the equivalent of £3 to 5 million.

This was a remarkably electrical storm, and there were confirmed instances of sightings of ball lightning. Few tornadoes in Britain have since taken such a long journey through a relatively populated area as this one, and none have taken as many lives. However, 2005 and 2006 both saw incidences of a tornado touching down in centres of high population, in Birmingham and London respectively, causing great damage and some injury, but luckily taking no lives.

33

The Record-Breaking Leighton Buzzard Tornado, May 1950

The weekend of 20–21 May 1950 had a summer feel to it across the south of England, and Sunday 21 promised to be a warm and sultry day. Pressure was low to the south-west of Ireland, which brought up with it very warm air from the south of Europe. However, coiled around the low pressure was a much colder air mass with a marked cold front that lay from Bristol down through Brittany and into north-east Spain. Lying across the top of the low pressure, the front was occluded and slow-moving. As it pushed north towards London, it lay in a line from Bristol across the country into Surrey and Kent. The air in the vicinity of the front became deeply unstable and, with the warmth of the day – around 22 °C in the afternoon – cumulonimbus clouds began to form early on. By early afternoon some severe thunderstorms broke out across much of the Midlands, the south-east, East Anglia and the London area.

Not only was this a spectacular and relatively rare event, the tornado was a record-breaker. It travelled from the area between

Great Missenden and Wendover all the way to the coast of Norfolk, where it finally fizzled out – a total of 100 miles. The tornado itself was accompanied by a terrific thunderstorm of exceptional violence. Lightning struck a number of people, killing four of them, and the torrential rain caused substantial floods, while large hail and strong gusts blew down thousands of trees.

The line of storms from which the tornado was generated passed right across London and Surrey earlier in the day and was described as producing 'vivid flashes of lightning and loud peals of thunder'. These were accompanied by pounding, torrential rain. Lightning hit Hammersmith Bridge, rupturing a gas main under it, which burst into flames and took some time for fire crews to bring under control.

At about four in the afternoon dark clouds pushed across the Berkshire countryside and at the head of the clouds a large funnel was seen coming from the south-south-west along a valley towards the town of Wendover. As the tornado hit the town it tore the roofs off two pubs and damaged every building in the high street, with debris flying about in every direction. As the tornado travelled on north-eastwards it tore down hundreds of large, mature trees and almost immediately the rain broke out accompanied by large hail. The downpour caused severe flooding, quickly inundating the interiors of houses newly opened to the elements after losing their roofs.

As it continued towards the RAF base at Halton, the men there looked on as the twisting, swirling column tore down trees in its path and debris flew around it. Sparks flew as it destroyed the electricity substation at Halton Camp and then moved inexorably towards the larger town of Leighton Buzzard. As it happened, the tornado did not score a direct hit on Leighton Buzzard's town centre, instead passing over the station and descending on the village of Linslade just to the east. Here, lightning and strong winds caused chaos in the village, flooding it so badly that the next day it was still completely cut off. At Linslade the tornado bore down on the village with renewed vigour, announcing its arrival by picking up adjacent parked cars and tossing them around as if they were small debris. Some 300 houses were badly damaged, hundreds of mature trees torn down, slates were torn off roofs, windows and doors crushed in their frames. A witness described the increasing darkness and a screeching, howling wind as the storm approached: 'I went out to take the dog from the kennel and as I did, so the storm broke. It was almost pitch dark but I could see trees, chimneys and slates all being sucked hundreds of feet in the air.'

The tornado was powerful enough to buckle steel seats at the local park and, as it destroyed a nearby sack factory, steel girders were hurled at several trees and split them cleanly in half. As is the case with many tornadoes, the damage was kept to a relatively narrow band, mostly affecting two residential streets at Linslade, but the accompanying storm went on to wreak far more damage of its own in Leighton Buzzard and then more widely. Lightning also hit numerous buildings.

Arriving in Bedford an hour later, the vortex was still strong enough to wreck gardens and blow open solid doors. A group of men running for shelter from the storm on a golf course were hit by lightning and two of them were killed. The tornado weakened somewhat thereafter and veered between funnel cloud and vortex. Later research found that the local topography influenced where it touched down; the lee of high ground, in particular, caused sudden alterations of wind direction that drove renewed vigour into the system.

In its last stand, the tornado drifted out into the great flatlands of the fens, bobbing up and down as it went. Finally, after four hours and more than 100 miles, it finally dissipated over the cool North Sea near Blakeney on the Norfolk coast.[4]

Flooding in Bedford, Hitchin and towns on the Ouse was severe. The river burst its banks, stranding motorists and householders alike. The next day, traffic was still marooned on the main roads in the area and towns were isolated. The damage caused by this extraordinarily long-lived tornado ran into tens of thousands of pounds; in today's money this would have been several millions. Yet, apart from the deaths caused by lightning, it seems that the tornado itself was not recorded as injuring anyone and no animals were killed, although one cat was carried, terrified, for some distance while a number of chickens, whose coup was sucked up and tossed into a nearby field, were found totally nude nearby – stripped bare of their feathers. The Air Ministry itself was a victim of the storm. Its central office in Dunstable was hit by lightning and several windows exploded. Others were blown in, leaving the offices exposed to torrents of torrential rain and the one-and-a-half-inch hail that accompanied the storm, badly flooding the building.

There is no record in Britain of any tornado that has lasted longer or of one having travelled further than this tornado. In Europe the longest known track of a tornado is actually 400 km, recorded in September 1669. Thought to have begun as a waterspout on the Atlantic coastline, the tornado moved onto land at La Rochelle and made it all the way to Paris.

34

The Kensal Rise Tornado, December 2006

On 7 December 2006, the morning began bright and sunny, if a bit chilly. A sudden storm moved quickly across south-west London and an intense burst of hail roared across windows and streets accompanied by constant lightning and almost continuous thunder. The wind gusted violently and it was almost completely dark for several minutes. It was over very quickly and the sun came out shortly after; however, in Kensal Rise, in west London, the storm left a more lasting impression and became national news.

As the storm approached this busy residential part of London, residents noticed a swirling vortex approaching that went from a funnel cloud to a fully blown tornado in a matter of seconds. As soon as the tornado touched down it began to cause widespread damage and, as one eyewitness described it, 'excitement turned into terror' as the 20-metre-wide funnel began tearing a path up the road. Within a couple of minutes more than 100 homes were damaged, twenty of which were rendered uninhabitable, and millions of pounds of damage was done. Six people were injured, two seriously, and at its height eyewitnesses in their houses experienced the sound of a 'freight train' roaring towards them. Roofs were lifted off, windows blown out and walls caved in. At least fifty cars were damaged and one house had its roof completely torn off according to the fire service that attended the scene. Another house had its sides torn down, leaving the building inside exposed and the structure hanging by a thread. One eyewitness described the experience thus: 'I was in my living room …

as I went to the window I heard a sound which was like a jetliner. I could see a huge cloud rolling up the street making this tremendous sound. I went to try to take a picture of it but a shower of debris smashed all the windows in my house.' This was the most serious tornado to hit the capital since December 1954, when six people were injured and the roof of Gunnersbury station was lifted off.

As the tornado moved quickly away, the immediate area of the storm's path presented an extraordinary sight. Terrified residents were quickly led out of damaged homes to safety by the emergency services. Some people coming home from work that night were unaware of what had happened and were greeted by chaotic scenes. That night Brent Council set up an emergency relief centre and in the following days it became clear that a number of families would have to be rehoused while repairs were made.

In terms of synoptics, the day itself saw nothing terribly special about the meteorological charts. A deep, mobile depression was moving swiftly west to east just to the north of Scotland and frontal rain was followed, in the early morning, by bright weather and showers. The west-north-west airstream over London was, however, cold and deeply unstable thus the resulting shower activity arrived with a strong 'vorticity' potential. This means that the forces and conditions that create thunderstorms, and the downdrafts within them, were in a particularly heightened state of activity.

It is not uncommon for far less violent storms to create funnel clouds in the UK, and sometimes these can touch down and become tornadoes. It is estimated by the Met Office in the UK that over thirty tornadoes touch down on average in any given year, although on days of widespread storm activity, numerous touchdowns can be reported, creating what are known as 'swarms'. October and November 1981 saw more than one such outbreak in the UK during a very wet and stormy spell of weather, and this pushed up the annual total of reported touchdowns that year to 150. However, it is fairly rare for tornadoes to touch down in urban areas. Nevertheless, two remarkable occurrences – the Kensal Rise example and a tornado in Birmingham in July 2005 – were reported within eighteen months of each other. As mobile phones and video cameras have become more common, so have these storms become more visible, and awareness of their frequency in the UK has grown in recent years. The Kensal Rise storm is calculated to have been an F2 on the Fujita scale or a T4 on the TORRO scale and, despite the destruction it caused, pales in comparison to the F4 and F5 monsters that on rare occasions touch down in populated parts of the US and can kill hundreds of people in a relatively short space of time while causing huge financial and psychological damage to whole local populations.

PART V
THUNDERSTORMS AND HAIL

35

The Derby Day Storm, May 1911

The summer of 1911 was one of the hottest and sunniest of the twentieth century, and the heat and sun continued on right into September before breaking. The hot weather began in May and the Epsom Derby was in full swing towards the end of the first heatwave of the year when an extremely severe thunderstorm killed seventeen across the UK,[1] many of them at Epsom and in the nearby south London area.

The weather had been superb for some days at the end of May. London reached 26 °C on 28 May and it continued fine and warm into June. However, on the 30th a shallow depression over Normandy began to extend northwards, provoking several thunderstorms along the south coast. The depression continued to move north, increasing instability over the south of England. When combined with the humid warm air over the region, thunderstorms looked likely. Forecasters predicted that 'fine and dry weather at first' would become 'unsettled later with thunder showers'.

The day dawned warm and sunny at Epsom and the rest of London, as forecast, but during the afternoon everyone at the Derby felt a noticeable increase in humidity and noted how oppressive the air became as the afternoon wore on. By 5 p.m. the sky had turned cloudy. The vast crowds probably barely noticed this change.

The Derby was, and still is, a very popular attraction. While 130,000 attend on an annual basis today, back then it was closer to 400,000 and it was regarded almost as a public holiday for many, with fairground attractions, good food and racing. On the day in question, an even greater draw was the attendance of the king and queen. The royal couple were a great attraction at the time as the king was shortly to be crowned. Preparations for the coronation were being made in central London and the press and members of the public called this the 'Coronation Derby'. Amid the great excitement produced by the coronation, the crowds swarmed onto Epsom Downs that day, all in the hope of catching at least a glimpse of the royal carriage.

The final race of the Derby was run at about 5 p.m. and the *Times* correspondent reported that he was overwhelmed by the day, praising the quality of the racing as marvellous and the diverse crowds, even including 'humble sheep shearing folk from our overseas Dominions'. He concluded that 'we shall never see a greater Derby day'. It was in this convivial atmosphere that the great crowds began to empty from the ground as the sky above darkened dramatically.

Just after 7 p.m., the first thunder was heard. Soon after, rain began to fall hard and 'fierce, vivid lightning' streaked across the sky accompanied by 'crashing thunder that shook the houses'. The rain became ever harder and more intense, lashing down in sheets across the downs with remarkable ferocity under the now ink black skies, punctuated only by the loud cracks and booms of thunder and constant lightning. In just a few minutes, most streets were awash and torrents of water poured down the lanes from the Downs into Epsom. Several bales of hay that lay underneath the railway bridge at Epsom station were struck by lightning and caught fire; soon enough the fire brigade was present dousing the flames, but by now it was barely possible to walk through the torrents raging through the streets.

In a horse-drawn van parked near the racecourse, a huge flash and bang was observed and a horse and boy, aged only sixteen, were killed instantly.[2] Meanwhile, a group of thirty people that were all returning home from the Derby had reached nearby Banstead Common when the storm broke. They all found shelter under a large wall that housed the Sutton District Reservoir. A bolt of lightning hit the wall and an immense explosion rang out. Two of the men fell dead where they stood, and six others were badly injured. One of the dead men had actually been standing between two friends from Plaistow that both survived, such was the seemingly random nature of the injuries. Among the injured was also a local policeman from Sutton who was taken back to the station in a state of severe shock; he had lost the use of his limbs down one side and had terrible burns. Another was a Sutton postman named William Tedder who had just dismounted from his bicycle and suggested to his companions that they shelter with the others when the bolt struck him down. Luckily he survived. In a tent, eight job masters were hit by lightning and one was left unconscious, and a man leaning on the rails of the racecourse was electrocuted but survived.

The storm moved up across much of the south-east of England, stretching from Kent, Surrey and Sussex, right across London and then on into the Home Counties. It made slow northwards progress. Wimbledon in south-west London was badly flooded and the fire station was struck by lightning and set alight. Local fire crews had to race back from another call to put it out. Early evening saw central London also hit by the storm. The area around St Paul's was quickly inundated with water midway up the wheels of carriages, and a torrent of floodwater poured from there out towards the embankment.[3] The Victoria embankment itself became deeply flooded by the run off from the slightly higher ground of the Strand, but not before the Strand was itself turned into 'a raging torrent', flooding many of the cellars of the shops and hotels along it, including those of the Savoy. The Royal Exchange was struck and set on fire and it took some while before this fire was brought under control. To the east of London there was serious flooding in a number of places from Limehouse to Poplar, and several lightning strikes started fires across east London as well.

The storms continued well into the evening. A policeman at Mitcham who had gone out on his bicycle to undertake his duties was later found dead, with burns and injuries suggesting another death by lightning strike. Yet another policeman was killed not far away at Morden, struck by lightning while sheltering under some trees. Acton and Ealing were especially badly hit. The station at Acton soon acquired several feet of water, completely swamping the tube station platforms and halting all trains on the main rail line. Nearby, the wife of a gravedigger, a woman by the name of Hester, was taking the fellow his tea when she was caught in the storm and sheltered under a large wall. The wall was struck by lightning and collapsed, killing her instantly.

Rail travel was generally badly disrupted right across the south-east of England. Two landslips paralysed the lines at Merstham, south of London, and at Park Royal, on the line to Birmingham, this taking some days to clear. The floods at Acton and Ealing also took a couple of days to clear up before the lines were open again, and central London and the surrounding areas spent much of the first days of June mopping up in time for the coronation celebrations.

As the intense storm progressed further into the Home Counties, an incident of ball lightning was reported from Clifton in Bedfordshire. A large ball of fire was seen descending onto a series of farm buildings, setting them on fire and killing or badly burning a number of farm animals. Henley and Reading were both flooded and suffered several lightning strikes, and a similar situation was reported at Enfield. In Hertfordshire, the police station at Hitchin was struck by lightning and the force of the strike blew the gas mains, causing an explosion that then set the building on fire.

On the same day, the north of the country was also hit by a deadly thunderstorm at Durham. A miner who had come out of the pit and was on his way home in the heavy rain was hit by lightning and killed. His two companions were barely injured. In Scarborough, the Great Church there was struck by lightning and damaged in yet another violent storm.

The remarkable Epsom storm, and the additional storm cells that developed that day, were caused by severe instability brought about by warm, moist air meeting with cooler air aloft in a zone of slack pressure. This is not unusual in late spring, a time of year during which several memorable tornadoes and storms have formed in the past. Nevertheless, such a death toll from lightning from a single storm is very rare. All the deaths had one thing in common, however; those killed were all out in the open, sheltering under trees or walls, or fully exposed to the elements. Nobody indoors was harmed, although a lot of houses and buildings were struck, no doubt creating shock and panic for their occupants.

36

London's Deadly Sunday Thunderstorm, 14 June 1914

A warm summer's day in the middle of June 1914 unexpectedly turned into a day of tragedy in the London area as a result of a particularly violent thunderstorm that hit the south of the city early on a Sunday afternoon. The storm killed seven people, including four children, and badly injured several others, as well as causing widespread flooding. Coming only three years after the disastrous Epsom Derby day storm of May 1911, this was the second lethal storm to hit the area in just three years.

The hot weather, which had begun some days before, was the prelude to what is often described as the 'last great summer' of the pre-war era. Tensions were already beginning to mount across Europe and it was only two weeks later, on 28 June, that Archduke Ferdinand of the Austro-Hungarian Empire was assassinated in Sarajevo by a group of Serb nationalists who wanted the empire ended and nations such as theirs to become independent. This assassination proved to be the final catalyst for the all-out conflict that practically wiped out a generation of young men a century ago.

Sunday 14 August dawned sunny and warm over most of England and Wales and it looked set to be a fine and warm day. Humidity, however, was higher than on the previous day, and there was without doubt a rather oppressive atmosphere in the morning. From research carried out after the storm, and an analysis of the rainfall data, the storm seems to have begun on the south coast during the morning and a series of extremely severe storm cells began moving up, in a north-westerly direction, towards London. Looking at reports for resorts on the south coast, the area from Portsmouth to Bournemouth received nearly an inch of rain. These storm cells then seem to have rapidly developed as they moved north-east across the country, and the first storms reached the low-lying parts of south and south-west London at noon, where they soon reached their peak intensity.

Shortly after midday the storm hit south and west of London. Many households would have been on the verge of Sunday lunch, but the warm weather meant that a lot of children and young people were amusing themselves outside in the remaining time before the family meal. Intense thunder and frequent lightning strikes, described by eyewitnesses as 'blood red' and 'vivid', broke with staggering speed and intensity, catching most people by surprise. This was no ordinary British summer thunderstorm, and the rain was of rare intensity. At Richmond Park, close to the most intense activity, 45 millimetres of rain fell in the first forty-five minutes alone. At Clapham an intense hailstorm, also reported at Wandsworth, began at 1.30 p.m., just after the storm unleashed its full force. Around this time a group of five children were sheltering under a large tree on Wandsworth Common. A policeman heard them singing to try to stave off the fright this immensely violent storm must have caused them. Lightning and explosive thunder were now constant, and the hail rained down on everyone who had been caught outside. The youngest child, Walter Hilliard, was only three years old. After a sudden blinding flash, an explosive thunderbolt rang out and the singing stopped. All five children lay on the ground, three of them badly burnt and paralysed but still alive. The policeman raised the alarm and bystanders ran for an ambulance while others tried to deal with the distress and horror before them. Three of the children – aged just three, four and five years old – died of their injuries. After an hour at Bolingbroke Hospital, the others were released without serious injury but in terrible shock.[4]

Seconds after this first deadly bolt, a second strike hit another tree yards away, where several more people were sheltering. Three people lay dead, killed instantly; their bodies were badly burnt. Among the injured was a man holding on to his small child. The child was killed instantly, as was the man's young daughter, her face buried in his coat; another woman lay yards away, also dead, while her fiancé was found badly burnt and paralysed but still alive nearby. A small baby who was in a pram next to the group was found screaming but uninjured. A man passing in his car saw the tragedy happen and took the injured man, and another badly injured victim – the mother of the baby found in the pram – in his car to hospital, where they were treated for burns and shock. Another man was hit by lightning and set on fire but survived, while an elderly gentleman terrified by the intense storm was found collapsed and in shock; he also later died. Another man at Windsor was hit by lightning but survived. In total, seven people were killed and eleven struck by lightning in the immediate area of Wandsworth common; the large plane tree the latter group had been sheltering under was reportedly split 'from top to bottom'.

The storms lasted some time and only after 3 p.m. was it reported that they abated significantly. However, after a further ninety minutes, the severe thunder, lightning, rain and hail returned. Flooding became increasingly serious as the torrential rain continued. The District line at Wimbledon was completely flooded and lay underwater. A power outage across most of this part of the network ensued just as effluent from an overflowing sewer added to the chaos. Further in to town, the normally unheard of River Wandle turned into a torrent, sending floodwater pouring into neighbouring roads to a depth of anything from 2 to 5 feet deep. Tram, rail and trolley services were suspended for much of the afternoon and evening, and road traffic was hampered by the rapidly flowing water and flooded streets.

It was a tragic weekend overall, and this immense storm remains very unusual in terms of both the death toll and intense rainfall. Richmond Park's weather station recorded an astonishing overall total of 92 millimetres in less than four hours. The area of most intense rainfall stretched in a narrow band from the area where Heathrow is now, across to the southern suburbs of Streatham, Wandsworth, Clapham, Balham and Dulwich. To the south, Kingston, Wimbledon and the surrounding areas were all badly affected up to Lewisham. However, Greenwich, slightly north and east, was just outside the worst-affected area. To the north of London, places such as Hampstead saw little or no rain at all.

The most intense band of rainfall saw 75 millimetres or more fall during the storm. The outer band, an area roughly triangulated from Croydon to the south-east, Windsor and Chertsey in the south-west and West Ham in the east, only had 12 millimetres. Other storms did occur across a number of southern areas that day, most notably at Folkestone, but none of them came close to the London storm in terms of intensity of rainfall, duration and number of lightning strikes.

37

The Louth Disaster, 29 May 1920

When one of the most significant storms to have hit the British Isles in the last century struck the Lincolnshire town of Louth in May 1920, it became notorious as one of the most tragic of British weather disasters. An extremely violent thunderstorm provoked a devastating flash flood that, in a short space of time, killed twenty-three people.

Saturday 29 May dawned clear and sunny. A by-election was being held in the district and a number of visiting dignitaries had arrived that morning; an air of excitement hung over the town.

Meanwhile, up above, a shallow trough lay in a sausage shape over the middle of the UK. Its centre was close to North Wales and it stretched out eastwards over the North Sea. Louth, about 16 kilometres from the east coast in Lincolnshire, was situated at the top part of this trough and the flow of air was easterly. To the south of it, however, there was a very warm and moist westerly flow over the south of Britain and the near Continent. The newspapers all warned of thunderstorms that morning in East Anglia and, as the morning wore on, the air grew somewhat more oppressive and it began to cloud over. At about 2 p.m. it went almost completely dark. Lightning lit up the dark sky and thunder reverberated around the town. Rain soon began to lash down and people found themselves sheltering indoors for the afternoon, away from the lashing rain.[5]

Outside of town, a delivery van encountered the first of the rain. The driver reported that it was so intense that the van was completely unable to move due to the sheer lack of visibility, with torrential rain and spray blowing around. This was not a normal summer thunderstorm. Quite often a summer storm may deliver just a few minutes of heavy rain and thunder before it moves away. On this occasion, after a full hour, the extreme rainfall, thunder and lightning were all still battering Louth and the surrounding area. The streets began to fill with great puddles of water and flooding appeared as gutters and streams all around became utterly overwhelmed. Of great significance at this stage was the fact that the storm was quite widespread and vast volumes of water were cascading down over a wide catchment area. Millions of gallons of water were all trying to flow somewhere and one of the main channels of escape was the local river, the River Lud. This river flows right through Louth and on, out into the North Sea.

As the storm raged, the Lud began to rise at a spectacular rate and, at one point, was seen to rise as much as 2 metres in the space of ten minutes. Outside of the town great tracts of land were torn up by fast-moving water flows that came from nowhere but turned into furious torrents, leaving deep ditches in the earth still visible long after the storm was over. What people could not have known was that, out to the west, at a place called Little Welton, a footbridge overlooking the river had begun to get blocked up by debris and soon started damming up further with rocks, dead animals and trees. In the space of a couple of hours, the impact of this damming saw the local valley flooded to an extraordinary depth of 10 metres.[6]

Just after 4 p.m. this dam burst. A wall of water more than 5 metres high surged into the town at nearly 40 mph. The first bridge to meet the water was smashed into pieces, the torrent taking vast lumps of concrete into the raging waters and sweeping further into town. Hearing the great crashing of water and debris, many people instinctively knew what was coming and rushed upstairs as the flood burst through doors and smashed windows. Those outside were not so lucky. A mother and her daughter out on bicycles were immediately swept away and killed, while a man who had just reached his top window watched helplessly as his neighbour who had responded less quickly drowned in the street outside. As this was a Saturday afternoon, albeit a wet one, many people were out walking. A disabled woman was drowned, as was the daughter who would not leave her side. The power of this vast wall of mud, water and boulders continued to smash into houses, many being demolished by it. Husbands watched as their wives drowned, wives their husbands, parents their children and children their parents. One young man who managed to climb into a tree clung to his mother and father as they fought the surging water, but both parents were swept away and died. Upstairs in one house a midwife and doctor were seeing to a young woman about to deliver her child when the flood burst into the floor below. Soon the doctor and the woman's husband were busy trying to help those around them.[7]

The death toll grew by the minute. The Berry family, living at Engine Gate, were almost all killed. Home alone with her four young children, the mother and her children were suddenly overwhelmed as the flood broke down the doors and tore through the house. As the waters rose the family were forced into the kitchen, where the young mother managed to hold onto her one-year-old, Edith, and push her other two youngest children to safety on top of a kitchen dresser, while she stood on a table. However, the water kept rising relentlessly as the terrified children held onto each other. In the gloom, four-year-old Jack slipped under the water and was lost. In an effort to grab him the mother lost hold of her baby, who was in turn lost in the raging waters and began to drown. As she tried to find either one of the children, another, Hubert who was five, also fell in. The oldest, Mary, who was ten, managed to pull out Hubert and his mother was able to hang him on a butcher's hook on the wall – but his clothes ripped and he fell in again and this time drowned. The mother could only watch as three of her children drowned in their own home. Then the gas mains burst and the remaining two could soon barely breathe. As they banged on a window to try to break it and get air to breathe, the pair were spotted by a young boy who worked in the shop owned by the family and he managed to pull them safety.[8]

The rain had stopped by 4.30 p.m. but the scene of devastation, in a town that only a few hours before was unscathed, was almost impossible to take in. The flood left the town cut in two as the bridges had been destroyed, 800 people were homeless and fifty houses had been completely destroyed by the flood.

A total of twenty-three people died – they included numerous children aged between one and fifteen, but there were victims of every age group. The huge death toll and tragedy of the day touched the country deeply and a big national response was mobilised. One of the worst moments took place the following Wednesday, when a mass funeral was held for all the victims. The three leading coffins were those of the Berry children; a heartbreaking day for the town and indeed for the rest of the country, which had taken the story very much to heart. It was a long time before the town recovered, the bridges rebuilt and houses repaired. Many people were forced to live in a canvas city of donated tents for months while they waited to see when they could return home.

At the time, the flatness of the surrounding region generated confusion as to just how the area flooded so quickly; the rainfall had been incredibly intense, but this alone did not explain how such a disaster had occurred. A total of 115 millimetres fell in the storm, but it was only at the inquest that it became apparent how the damming of water outside the town had most likely been responsible for the instantaneous nature of the inundation. However, this explanation raised further questions as to whether the river being directed through the narrow streets of the town had exacerbated the speed and depth of the water. Nevertheless, the evidence supporting the damming theory was fairly overwhelming, and it was this that caused the initial surge; regardless of how the water moved afterwards, the effects would still have been catastrophic. Thankfully no comparable storm has occurred since, but the terrible consequences of this extreme event are still well remembered in the area.

38

All-Night Havoc in London, 9 July 1923

On a sweltering July night in 1923, one of the most active and widespread thunderstorms recorded in the British Isles moved northwards over Britain, delivering over fifty lightning strikes a minute in London. The storm raged for over seven hours. Numerous houses and buildings were damaged or destroyed by lightning, rain and hail delivered huge rainfall totals and floods affected many areas.

Between 5 and 16 July of that year, a potent heatwave saw temperatures pass 30 °C on a number of days in London, reaching 33 °C at its highest – the hottest day since 1911 – while on the near Continent 35 °C or more was recorded on four successive days in parts of the Netherlands and Belgium. At Andover, the temperature just missed 35 °C by a whisker. On 9 July, it was still a steamy 29 °C in London and high humidity made it feel particularly uncomfortable as the skies darkened to the south late in the evening. An extremely potent series of storms had developed in Normandy during the late afternoon as humid air in slack low pressure to the south-east of Britain met cooler, drier air to the west and north, being driven down by a high pressure sitting over Scandinavia. The storm pushed in over Brighton and Eastbourne in a relatively narrow band towards 10 p.m. and moved more or less due north.

Areas to the east of Maidstone saw no rain at all – nor did eastern East Anglia – while, a few miles away from the edge of the band, towns such as Tunbridge Wells and Croydon received between 25 and 50 millimetres. To the west of Reading there was also little or no rain. However, this band stretched right up to Yorkshire and at its centre more than 51 millimetres of rain was recorded overall. Hampstead recorded 65 millimetres of rainfall, and lower areas of the capital such as Kew recorded 52 millimetres, with Westminster seeing 51 millimetres and, to the south, Croydon recording 40 millimetres.[9] Flooding was widespread and unpredictable; in some parts of the country bridges were washed away and small rivers quickly became torrents. The newspapers the next day were in awe of the intensity of the storm and pictures of burnt-out houses and homeless families shared space with the extensive floods.

The lightning statistics from this storm are, however, the easiest way to describe its intensity and its longevity. Over six hours, just under 7,000 flashes of lightning were recorded in London; in some cases, nearly 1,500 were recorded in one hour. At one point, forty-seven flashes a minute were measured; it is not hard to imagine why so many houses were hit. Many people were reported to have been terrified by 'thunderbolts' – this is when lightning strikes in the immediate vicinity and an instant deafening rapport or explosion rings out. Storms of this intensity are rare in the UK, but can occasionally affect wide areas. A very violent storm hit southern England in June 1981, with lightning almost continuous and torrential rains lasting the entire night. Such storms are often 'imported' from the near Continent, where they build in the baking continental heat and then move north; such was the case in July 1923.

The widespread nature and violence of the 1923 storm was also demonstrated by the vast number of calls to the Fire Brigade received from a wide variety of locations. Houses were hit and set on fire in locations that included Dulwich, Putney, Peckham, Harrow, Poplar and Stoke Newington. Indeed, there were many others, from the east and south of the city in particular. The fire brigade attended at least forty major fires, the majority taking place between three and five in the morning. Nobody in London slept that night, and a new and alarming discovery was made; wireless sets were found to be an efficient conductor of electricity into people's front rooms, and several exploded as the currents from lightning strikes found them.

The telephone network in London, which was at that time managed by an operator service, was badly affected. More than 3,000 lines went down and all the twenty-three foreign lines, including those to Paris and Brussels, also failed. It was pointed out that, unlike the domestic lines, the foreign access lines were not buried; it was actually on the Continent, where lightning had hit the various junction boxes and cut off international calls, where the problem lay.[10]

As the storms began moving further northwards, so the chaos spread. The most intense storm cell snaked up through the middle of England, badly affecting Bedford, Nottingham and Leicester, only fading north of Sheffield. At Bedford, lightning was as intense as in the city and a row of four cottages was hit repeatedly and all of them set alight. A plaiting factory was struck and set on fire, and a bullock was killed at Ravensden. Even as far north as Hull, there were reports of fearsome lightning strikes. It was extraordinary that no one was killed in any of these incidents, but there were some lucky escapes. At Ilford in Essex, lightning hit a chimney and forked down in to the bedroom of two sleeping toddlers. The charge blew a huge hole in their wall, but both youngsters escaped unharmed.

A column in *The Times* eloquently described the approaching storm from Sydenham near Crystal Palace in south London, as it approached from the south-west:

> The centre of the storm seemed to climb higher as it came nearer and while it flickered on the cloud it was stabbed through with falling spears of jagged fire and sometimes instead of the horrid stab of molten fire there was a pouring stream of liquid light. It was not long before the rain came, it fell in driven lines, distinguishable in the recurrent glare. As the lightning came nearer with simultaneous thunder claps the rain turned to hail. Children woke and lights appeared ... downstairs lights to mitigate, if not conceal the grand terrors of the night.

The next morning was a Tuesday. Commuters to the capital from surrounding areas, along with a great many Londoners, trudged wearily into work, hot and exhausted. The heatwave had some way to go yet before it gradually pulled away, and there were several more sweltering days and nights to come.

For many men who were survivors of the First World War, the stormy night brought back terrible memories. Many adult men at the time would have experienced trench warfare and the endless artillery fire, day and night, sometimes for years. The trauma was still very real for many of them and it must have added an unpleasant, and in some cases frightening, dimension to this long storm. Women also recounted the night bringing back memories of the terror of Zeppelin attacks over London, how the flashing searchlights and sound of bombs and gunfire was immediately conjured by the intense lightning.[11] This was a country still suffering from a huge collective loss in which millions of people had died, and it is alarming to think how a violent thunderstorm such as this could bring back the nightmare of the First World War so vividly to so many.

39

The Great Lynmouth Flood Disaster, August 1952

Possibly one of the most dramatic weather disasters to have visited the British Isles in recent history took place only a few months before the 1953 tidal surge; while the east coast floods were certainly the most cataclysmic in terms of scale, the Lynmouth disaster deeply affected the country and became international news. Torrential rain and storms brought a deadly wall of water, vast boulders and lethal debris crashing into the town, pulverising everything in their wake and killing thirty-four people, including a number of children camped out near the town.

The topography of this area is in itself quite dramatic. The descent into, and ascent from, Lynmouth is remarkably steep. There are two exit routes; the first, the A39, runs at an incline of 1:4 into the main street; this is Countisbury Hill. The second, Lynton Hill, is ever so slightly less steep and climbs up out of the lower part of Lynmouth towards to the town of Lynton, which overlooks it from the heights to the west. This very scenic route then continues up towards Parracombe and Barnstaple. Exmoor itself, far above both towns, contains a series of very deep valleys that break out into cliffs along the coastline. The River Lyn, which runs out to sea here, was once a single entity but gradually cut a course into the valley below Lynton and split into two, creating the East and West Lyn rivers. Over time, debris collecting in the rivers created an ever-shorter, steeper path to the sea and flooding became more common.

Numerous floods happened here before 1952, bringing down vast boulders and rocks into the valley to leave their mark. The last of these was in 1769. A significant decline in the management of local riverbanks between the wars resulted in a large build-up of natural debris and movement of soil and rock. By the early 1950s, this meant that serious flooding had become an increasing risk.

Of course, it was the weather that played the leading role in creating this disaster. The weather in June and July 1952 had been dry and often hot across much of England. In fact, by the second half of July drought conditions struck many areas in the south. However, August immediately saw the weather patterns shift and depressions moved over, or close to, the UK for much of the month.

On 14 August, a mid-Atlantic depression pushed north-east and mixed with a warm, thundery airstream over France and damp, unstable air over England. This ignited a number of storms across the south of England and pushed exceptionally heavy rain across the south-western peninsula. As the low slipped slowly eastwards across the channel, so all these elements combined to create the fourth-greatest twenty-four-hour rainfall total ever measured in the UK and set the disaster in motion.

Those holidaying in Lynmouth and Lynton on 15 August 1952 saw a day of torrential rain. Locals initially took it in their stride – they had seen floods and torrential rain before, and this was nothing too exceptional. However, as the day wore on, the high street became a small river and later a raging torrent in the space of just a couple of hours. The rain got heavier still. After 5.30 p.m. it became exceptional. Rain beat down and thundered onto the roofs of houses and cottages.[12] The Lyn rose on both sides at an alarming rate, and by 7 p.m. lightning was flashing and thunder booming across the valley.[13] Heavy black clouds hung down low over the hills. Suddenly, the West Lyn burst its banks. Even worse, however, was what could not be seen from below; vast amounts of floodwater had become dammed in channels and culverts by trees, rocks, mud, clay and massive boulders, some 15 feet in diameter in the upper reaches of the high moorland.

Twenty-one boy scouts, who had come down from Manchester, were camping out near the River Bray. In one of many tragic stories in a disaster in which whole families were wiped out, the boys, some of them no more than eleven, endured the deluge in their tents for hours. As thunder roared and lightning flashed above them in the darkness of that dismal evening, the river suddenly burst its banks and debris-laden floodwater swamped the camp. Several boys were dragged by the surging water towards some trees in the adjacent Bremridge Woods, where they clung on for dear life in abject terror.

Their survival was down to the bravery of one man, twenty-eight year-old scoutmaster Reverend Whelan, who kept his head. Hearing the screams of the boys who were being dragged away, he managed to swim out across the water to the trees and rescue each of them. He carried them, many over his shoulder, to a nearby bungalow.[14] It was only when the roll was called that the horrible realisation that three were missing became apparent. This was the first of many harrowing events that took place that night. Thirty-one more lives were soon to be lost.

Back in Lynmouth, the West Lyn burst its banks and immediately submerged the high street, soon becoming a particularly fierce torrent. The electricity was cut off in most of the town, on an evening that was already unusually dark for high summer. Many people were now aware they were in danger, but, as the streets flooded and torrents of debris piled down, there was nowhere they could flee to.

At 9 p.m. much of the debris that had been building up above the town came crashing down, carried on a 'wall of water' 10 feet high. The surging flood was a terrible combination of fast-moving water, mud, rocks, trees and huge boulders brought down from the moors. The West Lyn now split in two, with a new channel punching its way directly through the centre of the town. In the darkness it was hard for people to make out what was happening, but ground-floor levels of buildings in the lower town were quickly flooded. Hotel guests and residents alike were soon reaching the highest points of the buildings as huge boulders pounded them and water surged inwards and upwards. It was these boulders that many of the terrified survivors described thudding and pounding against the walls all night, shaking buildings with every onslaught, and bringing many crashing down. An eyewitness who was on holiday from London described the build-up of the flood:

The trouble started at about 7 p.m. last night when the West Lyn broke its banks, divided and made another channel right through the centre of the town before joining with the East Lyn river. Within half an hour the thirty to thirty-five guests had evacuated the ground floor. In another ten minutes the second floor was covered, and then we made for the top floor, where we spent the night. There were times when we thought the whole building was coming down, and we saw by this morning's light that about half of it had disappeared. The force of the floodwater was so strong that all the cars in our hotel garage – about fifteen to twenty of them – were washed straight out into the Lyn and from there they were carried out to sea. Mine was among them.

Another survivor who had been nearby said, 'Some of the residents and I, where I was staying, were looking out the window last night when we saw three people being washed out to sea. We managed to get hold of them and brought them through the window. By this morning boulders were piled 20 feet high outside the same window.'

By midnight the terrifying ordeal for the people of Lynmouth was at its peak. Many of the large hotels at the front were being pounded by boulders and debris brought by the vast amounts of fast-surging floodwater. Lynmouth Bridge was piled high with cars, one of which was resting on the parapet. The bridge held out until daybreak but then collapsed when one of the supports on the Lynton side gave way, and the walls of the Lyndale hotel then collapsed under the pressure of the released water. A honeymooning couple from Lancashire said, 'The floods rose in about an hour and we saw three cottages opposite our hotel just crumble and disappear. We could not see any sign of the occupants.' Further up in the town, at Barbrook, a row of several cottages was destroyed entirely by the flood and almost everybody killed. One survivor, a town councillor, lost most of his family, including his son, grandchildren, wife and daughter. Another survivor, a local man from Lynmouth, was winched to safety by the fire brigade along with his wife and stepdaughter; at this time the torrent was flowing 10 feet deep into his house. The chef at the Lyndale Hotel had evacuated his children to a neighbour's across the road early in the evening as the signs of immediate danger increased. However, at 3 a.m. the householder was in trouble and crying out across the water for help. Firemen in the vicinity managed to bring everyone back across to safety. 'At that moment,' the chef recounted, 'in another house, I saw a man turn his light on. The house collapsed immediately, as if he had switched on a bomb and he, his wife and their two children were swept away. All of them I knew well.'[15] The chef's family all survived and were speaking from the safety of nearby Minehead, where a lady had taken the whole family in.

Many of those who died were in caravans or more temporary

structures such as mobile homes. However, the great surge also undermined many long-standing stone and brick buildings by washing away their foundations and tearing out the base. Lower down the town towards the harbour, a well-known landmark, the Beach Café, was destroyed, as were four adjacent cottages. By the early hours of the morning an apocalyptic and chaotic scene was laid out before the survivors. For the first time they saw the utter devastation the flood had wrought. All four of the main road bridges in the town had been destroyed, 130 cars had been swept out to sea and dozens were missing. The famous cottage in the town associated with the poet Shelley was completely destroyed. The lighthouse in the harbour, which survived the night, collapsed early the next morning, as did the ancient Rhenish tower that was a major tourist attraction in Lynmouth.

An estimated 200,000 tons[16] of boulders had smashed into the town. Houses torn to shreds hung precariously over raging torrents; cars, smashed to a pulp, littered the beach. Many of the bodies of the dead had been carried some distance. In nearby Parracombe, the local postman was swept away by the floods.

Destruction on this scale is a rare event in Britain, but in the aftermath both the local authorities and the armed forces acted swiftly to bring aid and relief to the stricken town. Not far away, at Fremington, Army forces stationed at the 'Amphibious Warfare Centre' were well placed to be the first on the scene. They entered the town early in the morning and began the rescue effort. With the water treatment and sewerage works destroyed and all power out, the first task was to evacuate the remaining residents to avoid disease and further danger, as well as finding the homeless temporary accommodation. With 130 homes destroyed, hundreds damaged and over 400 people made homeless by the flooding, the authorities had to billet families in the much larger town of Minehead to the east. With an overwhelming sense of goodwill, the townsfolk opened their homes to the devastated families of Lynmouth and the surrounding area, many of whom were totally destitute.

More than 1,000 people were evacuated on Saturday and taken to safety. Hundreds more visitors, some with belongings, some without, began to reach London by train late in the day and began talking to the press. That Saturday night, several survivors were interviewed and their stories broadcast over national radio.

By Sunday, awareness of what had happened was spreading across the globe. Aid, both financial and practical, including clothes for the homeless and even extending to a set of caravans, immediately began to arrive. This was largely in response to a national appeal that was launched for the victims in the press and on the radio. The response was so vast it soon became overwhelming, and a halt had to be called to any further non-financial aid. It was also not long before the newspapermen and photographers arrived on the scene and witnessed the devastation at first hand from the Sunday morning.

To the people of Lynmouth, the future must have seemed bleak at first, and the trauma overwhelming. However, this massive effort soon paid dividends and progress was made on all fronts, bringing a renewed sense of hope for the people and town of Lynmouth. On 2 September, residents were once again allowed to return. They found an extraordinary change, and the town even declared it could once again admit visitors. The queen, Winston Churchill and Harold McMillan were among those to travel to the town in its most desperate hour, and soon attention turned to how to rebuild the town in the longer term.

One of the key realisations in the aftermath had been that recent narrowing and culverting of the rivers, to increase the amount of living and retail space, was responsible for choking the debris and floodwater and increasing the height and power of the flood. Both rivers were widened by some margin and the riverbanks rebuilt over these increased stretches. The Lyndale Hotel was demolished and a wall built between the new river outflow and the harbour, which was completely levelled by the flood in August 1952 and had all of its vessels wrecked. This was rebuilt to separate any future surging floodwater from it. A new road was also constructed and soon it was agreed that the riverbanks should be widened, smoothed and rounded to help the water flow far better. This work can still clearly be seen today in the rebuilt town.

Just how exceptional was the rain? At the nearest measuring station, Longstone Barrow, a total of 225 millimetres of rain fell from 9 a.m. on the 15th over twenty-four hours.[17]. The geography of Exmoor caused the moisture-laden air mass to rise across the high ground as it approached, releasing huge volumes of rainfall across the moor and into the valleys of the coastal strip. Cooler air that had collected over the Bristol Channel added yet further fuel to the unstable atmosphere, provoking an intense and long-lived rainfall pattern; so began an extraordinary day. A reconstruction of the rainfall pattern of the event suggests that heavy rain began falling in the area from Ilfracombe to Barnstaple to the east of the south-western peninsula at about 11.30 a.m. on 15 August. It fell torrentially off and on through the day, with some breaks, but slowly intensified, with the weather reaching its most violent and exceptional phase from about 5.30 p.m. onwards that Friday evening. High above the town, in the area known as the Chains, debris-laden channels and culverts soon became raging torrents. It is hard to say if the disaster would – or even could – reoccur, given the major reconstruction of the town, but huge lessons were learnt and if 225 millimetres of rain were to fall again in one day again, Lynmouth would be far better prepared than it was on that terrible night in 1952.

40

The South-East Supercell Storm, September 1958

A quite remarkable storm wreaked havoc over south-east England on the evening of 5 September 1958. The storm was in the form of a single-cell system; in other words, it was large enough and strong enough to be self-perpetuating in nature, much like those often found in the plains of the American Midwest. More common in Britain are convective storms driven by unstable cold air coming into contact with warmer currents rising up from a landmass heated by the sun.

The weather in the summer of 1958 had been very disappointing and followed the wet and dismal pattern of many summer seasons in the 1950s. However, by September the weather had warmed up considerably. High pressure squeezed up to the east of the UK and low pressure was pushing up from the Bay of Biscay towards the south-west of the country. A 'plume' of very warm air pushed up from the south and by the 5th it was warm and close.

On the day in question, 27 °C was reached widely across the

south-east and the morning and early afternoon brought sun, haze and humidity.

Later in the afternoon, however, an area of intense instability created a thunderstorm over the Isle of Wight that soon began to take on an exceptionally violent set of characteristics. This storm moved up over West Sussex, increasing in intensity as it moved, and by 7 p.m. was heading towards Horsham and Gatwick. The dark sky to the south appeared black and dark grey as the storm approached,[18] and one eyewitness described the clouds as having a 'greenish hue'. Viewed from afar, there was constant flickering lightning and, as it became darker, a distant cannonade of deep, booming thunder became audible. Soon, in almost complete darkness, glaring flashes of lightning lit up a still countryside and thunder began to crash and boom with terrifying frequency, shaking houses and terrifying adults and children alike.

When the storm was unleashed, in locations such as Gatwick, late that afternoon, it was with extraordinary ferocity. Torrential rain and sheets of giant hail tore across the land, driven by a furious wind, reaching speeds up to 80 mph and taking visibility down to almost nil. These first gusts tore off the tops of trees and flung them around crazily as increasingly huge hailstones began to fall. Lightning became almost constant and several tornadoes touched down, at least three of which were reported in this vicinity alone, causing a great deal of damage. One tornado hit Horsham. The Gatwick terminal building shook with the force of an accompanying 'whirlwind' that lifted off an entire hangar roof and blew numerous windows in as the storm, and in particular the large hail, struck the airport.

By 7.30 p.m. the storm had covered much of Kent and had reached the southern suburbs of London. The hailstones that fell were of scary dimensions, weighing between 140 and 191 grams. These are among the largest hailstones ever recorded in Britain. Sevenoaks, Tonbridge and Tunbridge Wells were all hit directly by the storm, and flash flooding began creating serious damage, shutting down rail, road and the airport at Gatwick in a relatively short space of time. The principal rail routes to Portsmouth, Southend, Dover and Brighton were halted as landslides and flash floods damaged track or blocked the way. The rain was so intense that in two hours the storm deposited 125 millimetres at Sevenoaks. Across an area extending

w tore into basements with such force and depth residents
d time to escape, and the force of the water knocked out
s supporting walls, causing several buildings catastrophic
A recent report on the storm, the Haycock report, confirms
man was drowned in his basement flat at Kilburn by this
oding.

lice, responding to a sudden onslaught of pleas for help, took
our to arrive from nearby Islington as the deep, fast-moving
wed against their cars as they drove uphill. The Mayor of
at the time, Dr Georgina Burnett, saw the damage at first
d pointed out how much worse the death toll would have
the flood come at night; many families only just managed to
daylight. In this relatively small area, sixty families had to
sed temporarily, twenty of whom later found their properties
beyond repair. In all, 250 people were affected and found
s living in emergency shelters set up for them in Kentish
ile more permanent solutions could be found.

ospitals in the area – Manor House, at Golders Green, and
l Free in Hampstead – were badly affected, with patient
t disrupted and accident and emergency services suspended
en hours. The fire brigade was swamped with calls – 2,000
n that one evening – and were operating on an eight-hour
evening time.

e might imagine, local rainfall totals were incredible,
when accounting for the fact that the storm was over by
. Just over 170 millimetres was measured closest to the
the storm. Below are other measurements from some of
y locations most affected. While this illustrates the storm's
atchment area, it likewise shows the incredible intensity of

d climatological station	170.8
Hill Park	131.3
	106.7
th Park, Waterlow Park	102.1
t Hill	101.7
d Garden Suburb	99.1
od, Farm Avenue	86.4

up to south Essex there was at least 60 millimetres of rain, causing widespread flooding.

One of the most memorable features of the storm was apparently the lightning. This was due not only due to its incredible frequency but also to its intensity. Vast leader strokes lasting up to five seconds were splitting into sometimes 'hundreds' of connected bolts that lit up the entire horizon from end to end with barely a break. An astonishing 3,000 lightning strikes were recorded that afternoon by the meteorological station at Harrow. Then a research station for thunderstorms, the centre was able to pinpoint the most violent part of the storm, which clearly showed that up to 2,000 strikes, or two-thirds of the total number, occurred in the first hour.

As the storm hit the southern suburbs of London, many people reported feeling genuine terror as the darkness fell and the full intensity of the storm enveloped them. Lightning strikes were so frequent that a great number of houses were struck and many across south London set on fire. In the Medway area of Kent, two huge oil storage barrels were hit by lightning and exploded. Fire tore into the sky and the embattled fire brigade had to prioritise this over the vast number of flooded citizens hoping for assistance. In another part of the county one woman barely escaped with her life when a flash flood broke down her garden wall and burst through her kitchen window, rising immediately up to her shoulders. Covered in mud and exhausted, she managed to escape out the front door and take refuge with neighbours.

Places such as Sidcup, Bromley and Orpington were badly hit as floods swept into crowded cinemas (it was a Friday evening) and flooded shops, destroying weekend meat supplies, clothing stocks and other goods. As the storm began to move north, it also spread eastwards into Dartford and the Medway towns of Chatham, Rochester and Sittingbourne, which were all struck by the storm in its most violent form and badly flooded. Southend in Essex, and the surrounding area, was almost cut off by landslides (there are steep cliffs running along much of the coastline leading up to the town) that blocked road and rail access to the town, and numerous houses were hit by lightning and flooded out.

East London had 'the worst storm anyone could remember', one local paper reported the next day, and, as in many other areas, pubs, hospitals and cinemas were inundated. One such place was the

Coronation Cinema at Manor Park, where floodwater swirled into the auditorium. The fire brigade arrived swiftly and set to battling to pump out the filthy muddy water. Despite all the commotion and the flood itself, the audience were determined to get their money's worth – the film showing was *Wonderful Things*,[19] one of the top-grossing films of the year – and everyone stayed put. Frankie Vaughan starred as a Gibraltar fisherman who falls in love with an English girl, Jean Dawnay, in this hit musical – in fact, the theme song was a big chart hit. As the storm moved away, the weather cleared and the storm moved out into the North Sea. Evening fell and people stared in disbelief at the extraordinary trail of flooding and chaos this exceptional storm left behind.

41
The Hampstead Supercell Storm, August 1975

An enormous thunderstorm that broke over north-west London during the hot August of 1975 was one of the most violent single thunderstorms ever recorded in the UK. The storm proved fatal to one man and injured several others, while the rainfall recorded over its short duration is among the most intense of the last 150 years.

August 1975 was a classic summer month. Hot sunshine and high temperatures were experienced on all but two days, and the average maximum temperature at Heathrow was 25.8 °C. In fact, the afternoon temperature exceeded 25 °C on eighteen days that month and 30 °C on four. The highest temperature of the summer, 33 °C, was reached on 4 August. The hot weather had in fact begun in June, and I remember my father telling me early that month that a weather expert on the BBC had said there was going to be sunny, warm weather for the next thirty days. I remember thinking that nobody could know that, but in general much of June and July consisted of warm or hot sunny weather, with only a few interruptions. The first two weeks were particularly hot, dry and sunny. I remember Richmond Park being tinder dry and brown on a visit there early in

August. Rain did fall from a couple of co[...] two weeks, but not in any great amount[...] rainfall was not the case everywhere, as we [...] in question – Thursday 14 August – Hea[...] bone dry, as was Kew, and the temperatu[...] across London. This emphasises one of [...] facts about the Hampstead storm, in this [...] convective storm remained practically sta[...] cycle.

At 9 a.m. on 14 August, temperature[...] in central London. During the afternoo[...] built quickly into a large thundercloud [...] visible from some distance. While the c[...] under almost clear blue skies, over Parlia[...] darken gradually and by mid-afternoon [...] threatening.[20] Lightning began to flicker [...] rumbled above sometime after 4 p.m. At [...] to the ground like heavy, wet sponges b[...] Soon after, initial loud peals of thunder [...] much louder and more frequent bursts.

At approximately a quarter past the h[...] rain suddenly burst down over Hampste[...] It was described by one local as a 'wa[...] out of the sky'. Thunder cannonaded an[...] the ground with exceptional frequency. [...] the heath at this time were hit by lightn[...] receiving burns and partial paralysis. [...] wave of floodwater came pouring into [...] streets; Hampstead tube station was [...] as early as 4.20 p.m. This extremely r[...] area demonstrates the truly exceptional [...] storm.[21]

Next, huge hailstones began to accomp[...] flooding spread more widely. Kilburn, [...] Garden Village and Gospel Oak were a[...] Under a black sky, crashing, pealing [...] hail lashed down. The fast-flowing wate[...] streets, parks and ponds, and turning [...] and basement into a raging pool or riv[...]

water [...]
barely [...]
nume[...]
damag[...]
that o[...]
rapid [...]

The [...]
over a[...]
water [...]
Camde[...]
hand a[...]
been ha[...]
escape [...]
be reho[...]
damage[...]
themse[...]
Town [...]

Two [...]
the Ro[...]
treatme[...]
for fou[...]
of them[...]
delay b[...]

As o[...]
especia[...]
6.30 p.[...]
centre [...]
the near[...]
limited [...]
the rain [...]

Hampst[...]
Golders [...]
Highgat[...]
Dartmo[...]
Parliame[...]
Hampst[...]
Cricklew[...]

These figures proved all the more exceptional when it came to light that the majority of the precipitation fell in the form of hail and that some of it was either too large to sit in the rain gauges, or fell with such velocity it bounced out again or partially split. Mr Robert Tyssen-Gee of the Hampstead Scientific Society tested this hypothesis with a tin box and ice similar in size to the hail. He clearly demonstrated how much of the hail would have bounced out of the rain gauges and calculated the real total to be closer to 200 millimetres – nearly 10 inches – and one has to further consider that Hampstead climatological station's rain gauge was unlikely to have coincided with the heaviest precipitation.

In the days after the storm, many people turned on the borough council, pointing out that poor, often blocked drainage had caused the floods. Indeed, there were major improvements made to drainage in the area after the event and lessons were learned. Nevertheless, no such system in the UK or elsewhere would have coped with what amounted to more than a quarter of London's annual rainfall total falling in two and a half hours. It was reported that this was the highest rainfall total ever recorded in the capital, with 117 millimetres falling in June 1917 for second place.[22]

At 6 p.m. the storm reached its zenith. Rain was totally replaced by sheets of large hailstones, often 10–20 millimetres in diameter; the frequent thunder and lightning intensified and the floods swept ever further and deeper across the areas affected. The storm never moved throughout its entire duration, most likely held in place by the elevated ground of Hampstead to the north, where the rain was heaviest, and the dry, hot air sitting over London.[23]

As quickly as the most intense phase began, suddenly the storm began to wane and by 6.30 p.m. that evening it had lost its ferocity. First the rain's intensity greatly declined and then stopped altogether, then thunder and lightning petered out. Floodwater, however, had poured onto the tube lines and the railway infrastructure, severely disrupting rail travel across much of London. Trains could not leave St Pancras or Euston and the stations had to be closed during rush hour on a busy Thursday evening.

The following days brought to light vast amounts of damage. Soaked furniture and ruined belongings sat out to dry in the leafy streets that had so recently been raging rivers of muddy water, and the rubble and structural debris began to be cleared.

Haycock describes the storm as moving slowly from the north-east while ground winds drove sheets of rain and hail from the south-west. His 2011 report set out to measure the impact of a 1-in-10,000-year rainfall event over an urban landscape to show how London would be impacted by such a storm today. From a hydrology perspective, the storm had no known precedent. The characteristics of this storm are described as being indicative of an 'up-draft, down-draft mesoscale thunderstorm'. In this case, the rising warm air being generated by the London heat island encountered a sudden rise in topography at Hampstead, creating significant uplift, while cooler air aloft began to be drawn down, creating a powerful single-cell storm along a line of convergence.

Despite its extraordinary violence, the total area affected is only estimated at 111 km², explaining why much of London stayed dry. The next day, all the newspapers reported widely on the impact of this unusual event. However, without doubt, one of their favourite stories at the time was that concerning a renowned BBC Symphony Orchestra flautist, Christine Messiter, who kept the audience in the Albert Hall waiting for half an hour as she fought her way through the storm. She was due to perform Mendelsohn's *Midsummer Night's Dream*, in which the role of the flute is of the greatest importance. Evidently unclear as to the reasons for her late appearance, and spurred on by the uncomfortable heat of the auditorium, as she walked breathlessly on to the stage a member of the audience shouted out, 'Nice to see you!'

42

The Boscastle Flash Flood, 2004

After the terrible events at Lynmouth in 1952, the country hoped it would never again see such a huge death toll from a dramatic flash flood. Nevertheless, at the height of the summer holidays in August 2004, it looked to the world as if history might well be repeating itself. That evening, images of a terrifying flash flood dominated the evening news and many feared the worst.

Following a dramatic series of airlifts, to the relief of everyone, only one person was injured and no lives were lost. However, the damage to the town was catastrophic and it has taken some years to restore several of the buildings and the infrastructure of the town. The nearby town of Crackington Haven, where I spent Easter 1981 and the summer of 1976, was also badly flooded in this storm.

For those that do not know the northern coastlines of Devon, Somerset and Cornwall, the topography consists of high moorland, field and forest and small towns and villages nestling in tight valleys or coves with steep approaches to the sea, whose harbours and beaches provide protection from westerly storms. On numerous occasions, heavy rain or violent storms have seen flash floods or landslides affect these areas, often without much warning and causing much damage destruction, and even death. Boscastle itself has recorded some notable floods, for example in 1770, 1827 and latterly 1950, when a particularly violent flood hit the town. It was Boscastle that suffered the first great thaw flood during the winter of 1963 (see chapter 5), when the deep snows turned to slush on higher ground and heavy rain caused a rapid build-up of floodwater that poured through the town. This part of south-west England also seems particularly prone to acute rainfall events; in fact, the second-highest rainfall total recorded in the UK happened in July 1955, when 279 millimetres fell at Martinstown near Dorchester; also, the famous 1952 storm at Lynmouth was the result of over 200 millimetres falling onto saturated ground.

At around midday on Monday 16 August 2004, a series of large cumulonimbus clouds began to form over the high ground above Boscastle and Camelford. The accompanying storms did not immediately affect Boscastle itself, but thunder, lightning and heavy rain fell in the form of showers over the high ground nearby. In fact, it was not until 3 p.m. that the really heavy rain set in over the town. The power was soon cut by lightning strikes, and, with the intense rainfall and the saturated ground above the town expelling many tons of water, the level of the river running through the centre of the town began to rise rapidly. In the following half-hour, 25 millimetres fell at the nearby rain gauge in Lesnewth. By 3.30 p.m., the local river, the Valency, began to burst its banks. As the river began to flood the village, from high above a surge of floodwater some 3 feet deep came crashing down into Boscastle and overwhelmed it in one fell swoop. Escape from any part of the village had now become impossible, and visitors and residents alike were faced with the prospect of being trapped where they stood. Everybody now had to move from ground level to higher floors. At the local visitor centre, twelve people clambered to safety in the crawlspace above the roof as the crashing water began to crush the foundations and wear away at the infrastructure of the building. The authorities were now fully aware of the unravelling disaster in the village; however, it was also equally apparent that accessing the area by road was going to be impossible, and local fire crews would not be in a position to free those trapped.

At 5 p.m. the torrent cascading through Boscastle looked cataclysmic. Cars and caravans spun out of control, taken up from the NCP car park and tossed out towards the sea like small toys. Fire crews on the scene were now themselves victims of the ever rising and furious floodwater. The next step was to mobilise the RAF. Seven helicopters began the desperate rescue of over 100 people clinging to rooftops as the floods raged below and buildings began to crumble. This was to prove to be one of the greatest peacetime rescues in British history, and by 8 p.m. everyone had been moved to safety and the worst of the flood was over.

The aftermath, however, was dreadful. At first light on Tuesday it appeared that as many as sixteen people were unaccounted for, and many thought that such a death roll would not have been surprising. Miraculously, by the end of Tuesday, it became apparent that no one had been killed at all and everyone presumed missing was alive and well.

In terms of rainfall, the rain gauge at Lesnewth measured 181 millimetres of rain in just five hours, and some even larger totals were recorded nearby, such as the 200 millimetres at Ottershaw. The shape of the Valency valley – steep and increasingly narrow before it widens out to the sea – funnelled the intensely fast-moving water to the exaggerated depths witnessed on the day. After the water had gone, it left behind £2 million worth of damage, and it was estimated that forty-eight buildings were affected, four were destroyed and 115 cars were washed out to sea, thirty-two never to be seen again. The town has been able to build itself back up again over time, a national appeal raising funds to help with the task. Given the local topography there seems little doubt that the area will see more such floods in the future, but one can only wonder at the fact that nobody was seriously hurt or killed on this occasion. With any luck, the lessons of Boscastle and the detailed rainfall forecasts now available will help ensure, should such an event occur again, that no lives are lost.

PART VI
FLOODS AND DELUGES

43

The Bristol Channel Flood, January 1607

No ordinary flood, the Bristol Channel flood of 1607 is perhaps the most destructive flood ever to have occurred in the recorded history of Britain. By modern estimates it left in the region of 1,000 people dead, killed hundreds of thousands of livestock, washed away whole communities and created an inland sea of more than 200 square miles that took weeks to drain. In fact over, 450 kilometres of coastline were affected by this event, along both sides of the Bristol Channel. Had it happened in modern times, the death toll would have been – for our small island, at least – quite unimaginable. Yet its cause has been disputed.

The Bristol Channel is famous for its tides and has the third-highest range in the world at 49 feet; the Severn Bore, a spectacular tidal-driven wave that pushes up the channel several times a month, is a celebrated phenomenon generated by this range, which in turn is explained by the geography and shape of the Severn estuary, which empties into the channel. However, the progressive narrowing of the channel causes water to rise as it pushes ahead, exaggerating its height and power. It is this effect that seems likely to have pushed a vast storm surge upriver, devastating the low-lying communities and farmland on both sides of the channel, sweeping inland with an extraordinarily violent impact and no warning.

Evidence shows that in January 1607 an extremely high spring tide, combined with gale-force winds, created a tidal flood 2 to 4 metres deep that undermined and collapsed the timber-framed cottages and houses in its path, drowned livestock and swept hundreds of people to their deaths in an age when very few people knew how to swim.

Controversy arose around the cause of this flood following a study by two geologists, Ted Bryant and Simon Haslett, who put the case forward for a tsunami as the cause of the disaster in a BBC documentary. Their hypothesis – that the speed of the wave and the supposed fine weather on its arrival point to a tsunami

– was compelling. They also presented geological evidence for their assumptions, which formed the backbone of the argument in the documentary the BBC broadcast. However, a large amount of contemporary documentary evidence was published in pamphlet form in the immediate aftermath of the flood, giving first-hand accounts of the terrifying day the floodwaters struck. Only one of these implies there may have been fine weather on the day of the flood (a notion on which a great deal of the tsunami hypothesis was based); all the others describe a day of raging wind driving a 'tempestuous' rise of the sea that flowed in with an extremely high tide. That same day, a storm surge also struck the east coast of England, a fact it would be impossible to attribute to a geologically generated wave. I shall come back to possible causes of the event in due course. Firstly, though, let's look at what actually happened.

30 January 1607 (20 January 1606 in the old Julian calendar; their New Year began on 25 March) was a day much like any other. All but one source describes it as a windy day. This was a busy agricultural society that would have followed very fixed routines. Despite many local communities being relatively prosperous for the time, the demands on them in terms of work would have been great and life would have changed little over the generations. Religion played a fundamental role in peoples' lives, and, after the chaos of the Reformation, the protestant religion remained dominant in England, despite the fact that a Scottish Catholic king was on the throne. The great queen, Elizabeth I, had been dead some four years but the Age of Discovery had led to the first American colony at Jamsetown. Pocahontas saved Captain Smith that year and Shakespeare was still writing. In forty years' time the country would be at war with itself, the king beheaded in public and the monarchy abolished. However, the country folk of both sides of the Bristol Channel were probably unlikely to have been close to the political and regal machinations of the time.

The first areas reached by the floods were Barnstaple to the south of the channel and Swansea to the north. In Barnstaple, the local parish register recorded a night of bad weather and strong winds, stating that 'the storm begane at 3 o'clock of the morning and lasted until 12'. At around 9 a.m. Barnstaple, at the base of high ground and facing west, saw the floodwater burst over the sea defences and rise up several feet, flooding all the low-lying areas and much of the town. Bolted doors were forced open and over £2,000 (the modern equivalent of just under £400,000) worth of goods and property were lost. A man named James Frost was in his house when the inundation broke down a wall, killing him and two of his children. The flood defences along the Bristol Channel were fairly basic at the time, in fact, many of them actually dated back to Roman times and had thus withstood many floods. However, this was an exceptional event, and it is likely that the water sped up as it raced past the high ground of Minehead. After crashing along the rocky coastline of North Devon, it next reached the low-lying areas that line the way up the Bristol Channel on the southern side to Gloucester – the Somerset levels. The 'levels' were completely inundated by about 2 to 4 metres of water, and it was here that the loss of life, cattle and land began to mount fast. As the floodwater ripped through the old defences, the ease with which they were broken down is described in this disturbing account: 'The sea, as a flowing water, meeting with Land-floudes, strove so violently together, that bearing downe all thinges yt were builded to withstand and hinder the force of them, the bankes were eaten through and a rupture made into Somerset-shire.' Once this had happened and the water had broken through, there was nothing to hinder its progress.

No sooner was this furious invader entred, but he got up hie into the Land, and encountring with the river Severn, they both boild in such pride that many Miles, [to the quantity of 20 in length, and 4 or 5 at least in breadth] were in a short time swalowd up in this torrent. This Inundation began in the morning, & within few houres after, covered the face of ye earth thereabouts [that lay within the distance before named] to the depths of 11 or 12 foot in some places, in others more.

In a few hours the water had covered up to 200 square miles of the Somerset Levels, running as far as Glastonbury, 14 miles inland. Another description says that the water reached its height after five hours, by which time it had laid waste to everything in sight.

The contemporary pamphlets of the time, unsurprisingly, account for the disaster as the wrath of God. Nevertheless, they give detailed accounts of some of what happened and provide various individual stories. They make grim reading. In an area centred on the low-lying town of Burnham-on-Sea, some thirty villages were flooded and the death toll in each of them was high. At Hunsfielde (modern-day Huntspill), for example, three people were reported to have perished. In general, depths of floodwater were quoted as between 3 to 8 feet, depending on location and topography. The flood continued on up the River Avon and began to submerge Bristol, where cellars were flooded and much damage to goods and property was recorded. It was noted that travel by boat was the sole means of transport for residents for some days after. The waves had just as much power as they moved up towards Gloucester, and all the river bridges were swept away while the low-lying land was again submerged. At the village of Almondsbury, some way inland, a local, the Reverend John Paul, lamented, 'In Saltmarsh many howses overthrowne. In Hobbes house syx foote hyghe. In Ellenhurst at Wades howse the sea rose neere 7 foote and in some howses there yt ran yn at one wyndow and out at an other.'

Soon the Welsh side was overrun and as many as twenty deaths were recorded at Arlingham and Chepstow. As the Gwent Lowlands were overrun, a wealthy householder, the Mistress Van, was reported to have seen the waters coming in from the sea. Before she had time to escape, the inundation spilled in so fast that she was drowned. This low-lying floodplain was well populated but always very vulnerable. According to one pamphlet that talks about Monmouthshire, this area, very popular because of its suitability for grazing livestock, saw twenty-six communities overrun. Newport, Cowbridge and Cardiff were also overrun. The church of St Mary in Cardiff was one of the few destroyed completely by the River Taff, which, just as the Avon had done in Bristol, served as a conduit for transporting the flood further inland. An estimated £100,000 (£20 million today) of damage was done in Cardiff itself and an estimated £40,000 of worth of land was lost in low-lying Monmouthshire. In all, around 500 people were believed to have died in this area alone and untold numbers of their precious cattle washed away with them.

Across the desolated, flooded lands, families were wiped out. One Somerset man, on seeing the floodwaters, had time to stash the deeds and bonds of his land in a case which he strung to the rafters. The flood roared in and crept up and up, soon removing the stability of the house, which came crashing down, sweeping the man and his family away. When he got himself to safety, after clinging to some debris, he was washed on to a bank. There in front of him lay the bodies of his wife and children, and in despair all he could do was sit on the mud and 'let all his teares pour out'.

There were also stories of some surprising escapes, such as the toddler who clung on to an escaping chicken that kept her warm and safe until help came. Another baby floated to shore in a cradle and two farmworkers clinging to a tree managed to set sail in a bath tub, in which they safely reached dry land.

Suffice to say, the sense of loss and tragedy was enormous. Of course, to the God-fearing people of the time it must have looked like an apocalyptic judgment from on high, but many with a knowledge of tides and experiences of storms and flooding knew exactly why it had happened. The economy of the area suffered for many years after, and in many cases the cost for survivors would have been ruinous.

So why has the tsunami theory evolved? The initial inquiry was based on a theory that was first developed when looking at the following description of the arrival of the flood:

> ... then they might see & perceive a far of as it were in the Element, huge and mighty Hilles of water, tumbling one over another, in such sort as if the greatest mountaines in the world, has over-whelmed the lowe Valeys or Earthy grounds. Sometimes it so dazled the eyes of many of the Spectators, that they immagined it had bin some fogge or miste, comming with great swiftnes towards them: and with such a smoke, as if Mountaynes were all on fire: and to the view of some, it seemed as if Myliyons of thousandes of Arrowes had bin shot forth at one time, which came in such swiftnes, as it was verily thought, that the fowles of the ayre could scarcely fly so fast, such was the threatning furyes thereof.

Two things struck them; firstly, there was no mention of a storm. Secondly, the description closely matches those given by observers and evident in footage of the Boxing Day tsunami of 2004. The documentary on this topic aired in 2005, while such visions were still fresh in everybody's mind. A hypothesis was then formed based on a variety of studies of vast rock shifts, unusual layers of sand in the areas affected and a supposition that no mention is made of a storm in this passage. When the size of boulders postulated is taken into account, at first it seems that only the force of nature, such as in a tsunami, could have carried them.

However, other specialists have disputed their calculations about the amount of water a storm surge would involve and point out that it is very difficult to confirm if the proposed movement of these rocks they studied is the work of a tidal wave, or even when they were moved. The above quote is also the only pamphlet commissioned by the Church, and is written in the fevered language of the Puritan's 'fire and brimstone' that would have been familiar to all who heard or read it. The eight other key sources all mention storms and tempests prior to, or during, the flood. One chronicler describes how a gale rose in the south-west and lasted three days before the flood, as does the parish record at Barnstaple. A further source mentions a blind man who was dislodged from his bed that evening at Glamorgan, right at the very end of the flood's path, and clung to a rafter to save himself, while enduring a strong 'easternly gale'. This is yet another clue as to the weather that day. If the storm surge hit Norfolk that night and drove a flood on a north-easterly gale, and the south-western storm before this flood had turned east, then a depression must have moved from the south-west and crossed the country on a north-easterly track, explaining both the winds and the surge. It is also not uncommon for the sun to shine in places – as the religious pamphlet states happened that morning – as depressions, especially after rain bands have passed, can bring bright weather. I clearly remember seeing a pale moon in a clearing sky at the height of the 1987 gale.

Another argument for a tsunami is based on the speed of the inundation, said, by one source, to have come in 'faster than a grey hound'. Anyone who watched the Japanese tsunami in 2011 would have seen the unimaginable scale and power with which it destroyed entire modern cities, and it took just minutes. Yet in our contemporary notes, even the fire-and-brimstone description is clear that it took 'five hours' for the water to move its full course. As we know, a north-easterly surge hit East Anglia in 1953, driven by high spring tides and a gale-force wind. The tide for the Bristol Channel that day is correspondingly described as an 'extreme high tide', the highest, in fact, in a cycle of several years. When combined with a series of gales, widely described at the time, the resulting surge would have been devastating.

There is also one further key piece of evidence concerning the generation of a tsunami that still remains to be answered. If there was a tsunami, what caused it? At first it was believed that a large underwater landslip was the likely cause, as this would have displaced large volumes of water, enough to drive in such a huge wave. This has certainly happened before. Ultrasound scanning off the coast of Norway has revealed the site of a vast landslip about 7,000 years ago that sent a tsunami, 70 feet high, onto the coast of Scotland and eastern England. However, no such event occurred to the south-west of Britain in 1607, and the only other possible cause is an earthquake. Nobody reported an earthquake that day anywhere in Europe, and it is estimated that it would have taken an earthquake of 7.5 on the Richter scale to generate such a wave. Such a quake would have caused vast damage and would have had to be felt right across northern Europe. The catastrophic 1755 earthquake that destroyed Lisbon was felt over a large part of Europe and the subsequent tsunami that engulfed Portugal did impact the coasts further north, including that of south-west Britain. In fact, when it reached the Cornish coast, it was 9 feet high and some damage was caused. However, only Britain was affected by the 1607 wave.

Everyone should perhaps make up their own mind on this one, but it was clear to those familiar with the Bristol Channel at the time that the highest possible tide, combining with a storm, provided the reason for this natural disaster. In my view, this gives the strongest possible evidence that this was not a geological event.

The vicar of Almondsbury, who witnessed the flood at first hand, seems to confirm that this flood was driven by tide and wind: 'By the yeere 1606, the fourth of King James, the ryver of Severn rose upon a sodeyn Tuesday mornyng the 20 of January beyng the full pryme day and hyghest tyde after the change of the moone by reason of a myghty strong western wynde.' Another important witness in this regard is the poet John Stradling, who was caught up in the disaster. Stradling was crossing the bridge over the Severn at Ault, close to Bristol, when the water suddenly rose up and began to flood the area. Shortly afterward, he wrote in a poem to a friend that 'if you crave to understand the Severn's unwonted floods, what causes they have, and the source of this madness, the common people attribute it to the moon and the driving winds, they rise their mind no higher'.

In fact, the tide in the Bristol Channel that day was estimated at approximately 7.7 metres at the point where the Avon meets the

Severn, putting it at its highest for years. A vigorous depression that would have caused a south-west storm surge early in the day would fully explain the east coast flooding later on, as the winds to its back edge would have been from the north or north-east. Writer William Camden's 1607 edition of *Britannia* provides strong evidence of the prevailing weather and outlines the fact that the day of the flood was the third day of strong winds, poor weather and high tides: 'After a spring-tide, being driven back by a southwest-wind (which continued for three days without intermission) and then again repuls'd by a very forcible sea-wind, it raged with such a tide.'

Nevertheless, the thought of a tsunami hitting Britain is not as outrageous as it sounds, and part of the evidence Haslett and Bryant have based their views on is the fact that there is a fault line running down past the west coast of Ireland that has caused quakes before. Perhaps an even greater threat lies on the Canary Islands. The views of several experts suggest that a volcano on the island of La Palma, Cumbre Vieja, is highly unstable and that the next eruption to happen there could displace a vast amount of volcanic material into the Atlantic. Were this to happen as predicted, the water displacement would be enough to generate a wave that would ravage the coastlines of Spain, Portugal, north-west Africa, the UK and Ireland, and in particular the eastern seaboard of the USA. Simulations estimate the wave would be 10 metres high by the time it reached the south coast of Britain. Although it would take six hours for the wave to reach us, the consequences would be devastating. Of course, this is just a hypothesis, and at least one university in the Netherlands strongly disputes the instability of the volcano in question. Fingers crossed that they are right and that any threat from a devastating tsunami remains just a hypothesis.

44

The Deluge Summer of 1912

So far, this book has shown us plenty of evidence for the fickle nature of the British summer. Blazing heat and violent thunderstorms, drought and long, sunny days at the beach are all possible features of any July or August, but we are just as likely to encounter those familiar wet, grey and cool days of summer that happen even in the best of seasons. Sometimes, however, it can all go horribly wrong. Summer can bring torrential, persistent rain, unusually low temperatures and floods. Such was the case in 1912, the coldest August of the twentieth century. This relentlessly cold and unsettled month brought an early autumn to the British Isles, along with exceptional rainfall and some atrocious flooding.

July 1912 started pleasantly enough and, after the first week, high pressure dominated much of the country. Sunny skies and rising temperatures were a feature of the second week, culminating in temperatures up to, or exceeding, 30 °C in the south on 16 July. At that point it must have seemed like the incredible weather that was such a feature of the hot, dry summer of 1911 would once again define the season. Warm, fine weather in the east continued for much of July, but to the west pressure over the Bay of Biscay was falling and cloudier, wetter conditions began to push gradually westwards into the West Country and Wales. On Sunday 28 July, a depression that had been lurking for some days to the south-west suddenly deepened dramatically and cloud, wind and rain spread right across the country.

By 4 August, after some days of generalised heavy rain, the worst of the rain stayed mostly to the west but temperatures everywhere stayed low. During the second week, rain affected the west and north far more than the east and south, but on occasion the east, too, fell foul of the persistent rain and showers. Mid-month, however, low pressure settled to the east of Britain. Along with heavy rain and showers, this brought particularly low temperatures on persistent easterly or north-easterly winds. After two bright days, by which time about a third of the crops due to come in had been ruined by rot or were submerged in floodwater, the farmers hoped the dry weather would last. Sadly, the relief they sought never came.

On Sunday 25 August, a series of depressions that had formed in the Atlantic began to cross the country, and the first of these moved over all regions, making for a wet weekend. The second, however, moved to the east of Britain but became slow-moving and then virtually stationary over the coastal parts of Kent, Essex and East Anglia. It was these parts of the country that saw severe weather begin on Monday, lasting right into Tuesday. Norwich was worst affected by these rains, with over 144 millimetres of rain falling in just twenty-four hours.

This rain began falling heavily at Norwich around 6 a.m. on Monday 26 August. Local people described the rain as so hard that one could barely walk against it, and the city was shrouded in a mist, caused by the pounding rain's spray blowing in the hard east wind. By lunchtime many of the streets had become torrents and the river was overflowing. The town became deserted as the waters raged through it, and as the river burst its banks and fast-moving floodwater surged into the streets some buildings were torn down by the force of it. By 6 p.m. over 6 inches of rain had fallen; yet it continued on, though less heavily, through the night. By the next morning, up to 186 millimetres had fallen in the area.

Floods affected large parts of the town, and those that suffered most were the poor whose homes were flooded out and possessions lost. By Tuesday, 15,000 people were homeless in the area. Electricity failed, transport stopped and the telegraph and phone systems were wrecked. Worse still, with the strong winds, many trees, still in full leaf and with roots in sodden or flooded ground, fell onto roads and railways. The nearby towns such as Sheringham and Cromer became unreachable, and the city was cut off. Many major bridges were destroyed and other familiar river crossings were all impassable as they had either partially collapsed or had been washed away.

At least four people died during this event. One of them was a labourer, George Brodie, who became a local hero. He worked throughout the day to save numerous lives and helped large numbers of vulnerable people to safety. After all this effort, he was overcome by an attack of asthma and exhaustion late in the day and was later found drowned. Another fatality was a baby that was tragically lost during a rescue, and one young girl died after swallowing a great deal of water after being dropped by a rescuer; although she survived being in the water, the girl quickly became critically ill and died, possibly from cholera. Another death occurred when an elderly woman died during her rescue from natural causes. The consequences of the flood were felt for months and even years after, as many houses were left uninhabitable by the filthy water or from structural damage caused by the force of the surging water.

Outside of Norwich, much of the east of England was affected by this potent depression anchored over the south-east of the country and the southern North Sea. Many railway lines had track washed away and services from Ipswich to Corby in the Midlands were halted. Leicester was badly flooded from the deluge, and water poured through the main street to a depth of 2 feet, flooding basements and causing people to be evacuated. Cambridge also saw sudden flooding and plenty of damage. In terms of crops, reports from the east of England had not been unfavourable up until that weekend. In contrast, Cumberland, for example, had seen wheat, barley and root vegetable crops underwater and badly damaged for several days before. Ireland joined in the gloom, with warnings that this was the worst harvest across much of the British Isles since 1879. Across the border in Scotland, however, it was not far off a normal year. August had seen a period of dry, fine weather as the jet stream was far south enough to leave Scotland north of the track of the endless procession of low-pressure systems. Although plenty of rain fell, the crops were due in later and were undamaged. September brought precious little relief. Although there was less rain, it remained unusually cold and frosts began early on and remained frequent, especially across the north and in Scotland.

August was, in fact, the coldest ever and beat all of the dreadful months of the Little Ice Age, coming in at 12.9 °C on the CET. During the storms at the end of the month, most places were seeing night-time lows of 4–6 °C in the north and under 10 °C widely across Britain. Daytime maxima were generally in the 14–18 °C range, and any hot, sunny weather was a distant memory. In the EWP rainfall series, dating back to 1766, August 1912 comes out as the wettest August month in the record with 192.9 millimetres of rain. The combination of cold, damp and endless rainfall must make this one of the most unpleasant summer months Britain has experienced since 1659.

45

The March Thaw Floods, 1947

When the Second World War ended in 1945, much of the world breathed a sigh of relief. In Britain, the transition from total disruption to normal life took many years. Those lost were mourned, and those still in service and posted all over the world slowly filtered back; prisoners were released and the Cold War began. By the end of 1946, however, despite harsh rationing and endless economic difficulties, Britain was beginning to find its feet again. The Labour government were sowing the seeds of the National Health Service, and it seemed as though the road to recovery was real. It was at this moment that one of the worst winters of the last 300 years began. For much of the population, conditions became so hard that it was almost like a return to the siege mentality of the war years, only with nature as the enemy.

However, not even a bad winter lasts forever, and in the middle of March 1947 the snows began to melt. Snow that had lasted six weeks in some places and which lay in piles 20 feet deep across great tracts of the country was then rained upon – rained upon a great deal, in fact – and it wasn't long before any joy at seeing the snow finally vanish was replaced by the horror of facing the worst floods to hit Britain for 200 years. In essence, over a long winter, the snow that builds up is just water stored in a solid form that will soon turn again to liquid. With large areas of Britain under 2 metres of compacted snow at the start of March, the authorities were already worried what was going to happen to it all when it thawed. Snow will melt at the rate of about 65 millimetres a day on its own when the temperature climbs to around 7–10 °C in dull weather. In bright sunshine, this rises dramatically to 175 millimetres a day; add rain to the thaw and you will get a whopping 250 millimetres of meltwater a day, as well as the rainwater on top. Add to this deeply frozen ground that will absorb no water, and acts rather like concrete, and you have pretty much a perfect recipe for flooding.

The authorities were soon proved fully justified in their concern. As early as 11 March, a rapid thaw, which had already turned the landscape from Somerset to Kent into a series of vast lakes, moved north. By 12 March the rain had reached Wales and most of the north of England, and within hours meltwater from the mountainous areas was cascading into the valleys and rivers; one by one, they burst their banks.

The Medway in Kent had already overflowed to the tune of 2–3 metres in Tonbridge, the Avon overflowed at Salisbury and then Bath, and great expanses of the countryside were once again cut off, this time not by snow but by floodwater. Boats were suddenly needed to take supplies out to isolated communities, and those that could not stay in their homes had to be removed to emergency shelters. It was another costly emergency for which the fragile economy was not adequately prepared. Nevertheless, by 15 March the situation was more or less under control. Across the flat lands of East Anglia, where the waters had been rising for days, a flood plan had been enacted that consolidated the resources of local farmers to sandbag vulnerable points and keep dykes and dams secure, in order to ensure that valuable agricultural land remained free from the floodwater.

Then disaster struck. On Sunday 16 March, a deep depression swung in from the Atlantic and moved across the whole of the country, bringing an intense south-westerly gale across the south and the Midlands. Rainfall was also intense, and by Sunday night winds in the low-lying Fenland of East Anglia were gusting over 90 mph and getting close to the 100 mph mark. Trees came crashing down, collapsing telegraph poles right across the east and south-east of the country. In London, roofs were torn off; two houses were reportedly completely destroyed, such was the violence of the wind. In the eastern counties, where gangs of men continued working to the flood plan by shoring up the rivers, the wind began to whip up large waves that ran up the swollen rivers, overwhelming the work that had been done. As they stood helpless, the defences that had been sturdy earlier in the day crumbled around them and rivers such as the Ouse burst their banks. The floodwater, once free, hurtled at great speed towards the towns and villages that had so far been spared the floods. There were also no lines of communication due to the widespread damage to telegraph poles and electricity the gale had caused, and so the water arrived without warning. This time it caused widespread damage, and those not already evacuated had to flee as fast as they could.

Areas further north now began to see some of the more severe effects of the flooding. With the heavy rain over the weekend, Monday saw the River Trent burst its banks. As soon as this happened the water went out of control and spread rapidly across the flat ground of the Trent Valley inexorably towards Nottingham. It was noted at the time that the rapid expansion of Nottingham to accommodate the workers of the Industrial Revolution had unfortunately largely spread into the natural floodplain of the river. Early on 18 March, the suburb of West Bridgford in Nottingham was inundated. The depth of the water was quite extraordinary; the river was soon 12 feet above normal and often passed the second-floor windows of terraced houses, leading to a major evacuation having to take place at some speed. It was reported that 28 miles of streets in Nottingham were underwater by 20 March. The water moved out to sea, flooding the whole valley until it met the Humber, at which point spring tides pushed it even higher. The towns of Gainsborough and Norton saw water up to the eaves of houses, and this time the damage was significant.

By now the situation across England was critical. All the major cities except London had seen floods, including Leeds, where there was severe flooding by 20 March as the River Aire burst its banks. The River Don broke its banks and severely flooded both Rotherham and Doncaster just as the Aire, Derwent and Wharfe all went the same way, with huge numbers of people now housed in temporary shelters, being fed and looked after by a combination of the state, the armed services and volunteers.

As the flooding expanded across the north of England, several days without heavy rain followed and in the west and south the situation gradually began to ease. Unfortunately, on 23 March very high spring tides brought renewed flooding to Yorkshire and Selby was particularly badly hit, with up to 70 per cent of the houses submerged. Almost the whole population of Selby had to be crammed into the relatively small market square, where they were fed in temporary kitchens run by the military and volunteers. The centre of town was apparently the only part of Selby that was high enough to be spared.

As the situation in much of the south and west began to ease, the waters to the east, especially in the Fens, were still on the rise. Ever larger tracts of valuable farmland were submerged, in many places as far as the eye could see. Even the dividing banks and trees began to vanish underwater. Looking at films recorded at the time, it seems as if a gigantic new sea had been formed, with large waves splashing threateningly against dry land in such a way that it seemed they would soon take over altogether. It must have seemed hopeless, and even those that could remember other floods far back could not remember such a vast inundation. Now the armed forces moved in. After 24 March the worst of the weather was over and the rain let up enough for man to try to win back the Fens. The Royal Engineers, helped by the large numbers of prisoners of war, began to repair the breaches as fast as they could while vast pumping mechanisms, loaned from private companies, local authorities and even other countries, were set up. Slowly the land was drained and, with immense physical effort, the breaches in dykes and flood defence networks were rebuilt.

From the end of March, the rest of the country saw an easing of the flooding. At Nottingham it took over a week before people were able to re-enter their flooded homes and begin to salvage what they could. It is hard to imagine that this was an age without general insurance for people's homes and those affected had to rely on disaster funds to get back on their feet. However, parts of the Fens remained waterlogged for months and the fields unusable in a time of great food shortages. Luckily, May saw the start of a very hot summer, which helped the continued drainage of the fields, but despite the heat of the summer and the fact that little seawater had polluted the ground, it was not until the autumn that life returned to normal. And it must have been with great relief to everyone that 1948 proved to be a completely normal year – for the weather, at least.

46

The Devastating Floods of September 1968

The widespread floods of September 1968 were the worst many parts of the south-east had seen since 1947. Several people were killed and numerous town and city centres vanished underwater following a weekend of torrential rain and long-lasting thunderstorms. These floods were unique in that they provided the only known occasion on which parts of London were virtually cut off from the outside world because of flooding.

In a decade of rather disappointing summers, 1968 stands out as particularly poor. There had already been some major floods in Somerset in July that stemmed from a severe thunderstorm linked to low pressure in the south-west. An astounding amount of damage was caused by the fast-moving waters, and resentment still boiled in the West Country because of the miserly donation – £175,000 – provided by the government to offset a total of £2 million in uninsured losses – practically a drop in the ocean. However, on Friday

13 September 1968, a more widespread flooding crisis was brewing close to southern England, in the form of an intense, slow-moving depression.[1]

The start of September 1968 could be described as seasonal. Calm, sunny and even warm days made a welcome change from the cold, grey days of August, with a respectable 24 °C reached on 10 September at Heathrow. However, a shallow depression moving slowly towards the south from the English Channel showed signs of deepening rapidly. With a warm air mass to the south of this disturbance, the potential for some heavy rain became apparent. The Met Office warned of rain and potential thunder on Saturday morning, but no mention that anything exceptional might occur was issued.

Cloud and rain spread in from the west on Saturday morning, as forecast, and some heavy rain and thunderstorms broke out across much of southern Britain. Very heavy rain and lightning dampened spirits at the annual Biggin Hill Air Show in Kent in the early afternoon. The torrential rain fell from a particularly dark sky, and for a time it looked like it was going to be a dreadful day for spectators. However, the rain stopped mid-afternoon and the clouds broke over the North Downs, allowing the sun to come out. At Epsom my parents drove through torrential rain into south London on their return from a sunny week in Wales. The rain stopped, however, and as the conditions improved no more was said about the bad weather. It was only later that the significance of those Saturday storms became apparent to the people of the south-east.

During the night, pulses of even heavier rain accompanied by several severe thunderstorms and squalls spread across the area, affecting counties to the east and south of London at first, but then much of the south-eastern quadrant. Vivid lightning flashed across the early morning skies, followed by loud, crashing thunder, waking households across the region. The rain was still cascading down at breakfast time on Sunday, and continued on into the afternoon.

As the centre of the depression sank into the Bay of Biscay, more bands of rain pushed north into the south-east of England, and with higher pressure to the north, the front came to a halt just south of London. Where this front stalled – in a band across Surrey, Sussex, Essex and Kent – rainfall totals were the highest and the relentless rain beat down throughout the day. Many people quickly realised that rainfall on such a scale was going to lead to floods; nevertheless, with no warnings out, nor any advice to stay indoors, most went about their Sunday in the normal way. By late afternoon, streets everywhere were flooded from London, Surrey, Sussex and Essex down to Kent. A tornado touched down on the Hoo peninsula, tearing off branches and causing some damage to the local area. This in itself is only significant in terms of illustrating the sheer instability of the atmosphere. In fact, it was unlikely to have been the only one that day. Streets in Bromley and Lewisham were badly flooded by early evening. The River Quaggy in Lewisham, barely 6 inches deep on a good day, swelled up incredibly into a 15-foot torrent, submerging cars and breaking windows with its newfound power as it swept violently though the town. In Surrey, the River Mole began to rise extremely fast and soon burst its banks upstream as the levels rose. Leatherhead was badly flooded almost immediately, and it was impossible to cross the town north to south. The city of Guildford saw the River Wey burst its banks in the afternoon, and floodwater swamped the low-lying streets to a depth of 6 feet or more. Lightning hit numerous homes during this deluge, causing fires and structural damage at a number of locations, and by evening the south of London was cut off from the outside world. As many as 120 stations were closed in the city and in the surrounding areas. Surrey was impossible to cross by car, and three people had been drowned by the end of the day. The rain continued into the evening and night. By 6 p.m., 140 millimetres had fallen at Canvey Island, 100 millimetres at Kew and 75 millimetres over a large swathe of the south-eastern quadrant.[2]

In Kent, deemed to be the worst-affected area, at the towns of Maidstone and Tonbridge the Medway overflowed and flooded adjacent streets. At Edenbridge, a diverted train sat at the station as the River Eden poured through the high street and floodwater reached 5 feet. As the water swamped the platforms, the 150 passengers were left stranded with no help in sight and no immediate means of rescue. By Monday morning, all rail contact between Kent, Surrey, Sussex and London was severed and many lines to the south of the capital were underwater. The main London stations, such as Victoria and Waterloo, saw thousands of travellers stranded on Sunday night and a vast number of commuters were forced to stay home on Monday, many of them battling to save their homes and possessions.

Back at Epsom, floodwater had swept the high street and some roads were underwater to a depth of 6 feet. At Kingston, East Molesey and

Sunbury there were severe floods as the millions of gallons of water that had emptied in to the rivers Mole and Thames upstream began to raise levels downstream throughout Monday. Floodwaters continued to rise, despite a drier spell, reaching 9 feet or more in places such as Tonbridge and Edenbridge. Guildford town centre remained deeply flooded and most of London's southern suburbs were flooded to some degree. Tens of thousands of people were trapped in their homes, and the government was forced to draft in troops to relieve the exhausted and overstretched police and fire services that had worked tirelessly for twenty-four hours or more. In fact, it was only when the RAF were scrambled and took a helicopter to the scene that the 150 trapped passengers at Edenbridge were taken off the stranded train after more than twelve hours. Nearby, the beautiful medieval Hever Castle, once the home of Anne Boleyn and her family, was swamped by floodwater. A mad dash by the estate to save priceless exhibits and possessions was soon underway but many precious items were damaged. In the same area, an elderly couple were being rescued by dinghy when the first floor of their house began to crumble and then collapsed, overturning the rescue craft and flinging them, and the rescuers, into the torrent beneath and requiring the rescuers to be saved themselves.

Even the small stream that runs below street level near the football ground at Plough Lane in Wimbledon became a torrent, flooding the low-lying areas below the 'Village' and causing much damage. It was also immediately apparent that crops such as potatoes and corn were likely to be damaged by the filthy, stinking water that was causing such havoc and rendering most things it touched unusable.

Such severe floods almost inevitably caused loss of life. All sorts of livestock were swept away and killed or drowned where they stood in the rapidly deepening floodwater. Tragically, three people were confirmed drowned by Monday. In one case, a family were crossing a bridge by car when it collapsed into the swollen river below. A middle-aged couple sitting in front managed to get out, but the mother of one of them was trapped in the car and, despite the couple managing to keep her afloat for a time, was eventually washed away by the strong current. Another woman, travelling with her thirteen-year-old daughter, at Billingshurst Green in Sussex was swept away and later found dead. Her daughter, however, was rescued. A man in his sixties from Wallington in Surrey died from a heart attack as the floodwater ravaged the area he was visiting near Dorking. By Monday night, heavy rain was falling again.

At Newmarket floodwater reached 11 feet above normal, and Esher and Aldershot in Surrey joined Guildford and East Mosely as floodwaters swept through the towns, flooding all low-lying areas. Out of 3.25 million telephones, nearly 80,000 were out of order according to the General Post Office, and travel continued to be hampered by the enormous scale of the floods. One train leaving Godalming, near Guildford, was only just stopped in time, leaving the station as it headed unknowingly towards a collapsed bridge. This remarkable flooding turned out to be the worst since 1953 in the south-east, the key difference being that almost everywhere away from the coast was affected, whereas the 1953 storms largely impacted areas adjacent to the coast or on tidal river ways. Even Sevenoaks, high up on the Kent Weald, saw terrific flooding, as the North Downs acted as a sponge that soon became saturated. Knowle Park was overrun by torrents of water pouring into small local streams that soon became raging torrents. Nearby towns such as Chipstead, Oxted, Westerham, Seal, Borough Green and Platt were submerged by deep floodwater, causing chaos. Gatwick Airport had to be closed because the runways became submerged; however, with all telexes, telephones and power lines out of service, the lack of any workable communications kept the airport out of action regardless of the state of the runways

The Met Office stated, under scrutiny from MPs early the following week, that 'no existing computer would be able to predict volumes of rainfall to any degree of accuracy' and it would not be until at least 1971 before enough computing power would be in place to undertake the vast number of calculations necessary to do so. Nevertheless, even in the current age of comparatively vast computing power, it is sometimes human intervention combined with data that gives the most accurate forecasts, and some concern at least as to the potential of the situation on Sunday should have arisen from the synoptic situation.

Other factors that worsened the outcome also came into play. As I mentioned earlier, 1968 was one of the worst summers of the 1960s and was consistently wet, so by September the ground was saturated and the water table high. As the clean-up began, it was also apparent just how much rain fell on that fateful Sunday: Bromley (Kent) 129 millimetres; Godstone (Surrey) 124 millimetres; Stifford (Essex) 115 millimetres; Whitstable (Kent) 115 millimetres; Canvey Island (Essex) 110 millimetres. A good deal of further rain fell over and above these one-day totals, but it was the intensity of the rain on the Sunday falling onto saturated ground that tipped the south-east over the edge. Such dramatic floods are rare and were assumed to have a return period at the time of about thirty years. Sure enough, 32 years later, in October 2000, these same areas were visited once again by dramatic and unwelcome flooding.

47

Severe Flooding in Wettest Autumn Ever, 2000

The autumn of 2000 in Britain was a very wet one. So wet, in fact, that not only did this become the wettest autumn since records began (which in the case of England and Wales go back to 1766), but it was the in fact wettest year since 1872, and the third-wettest ever until it was pushed into fourth place by 2012. At the time the floods were firmly linked to global warming, and there was a significant amount of panic – at least at a government and environmental level – that such extremes of rainfall would become a regular event. Luckily, the last fourteen years have only seen two such years: 2007 and 2012. There have also been some very dry years, as well as some average ones in between.

Five wettest years in the EWP (starts 1766)
1. 1872   1,285 mm
2. 1768   1,247 mm
3. 2012   1,244 mm
4. 2000   1,232 mm
5. 1852   1,213 mm

Five driest years in the EWP
1. 1788   612 mm
2. 1921   629 mm

3. 1887   669 mm
4. 1854   672 mm
5. 1780   699 mm

The summer of 2000 was poor, and from mid-June a long period of unsettled and cool weather affected much of western Europe. However, in the UK unusual weather began around 14 September. Low pressure brought heavy persistent rain to the south, with 100 millimetres at Heathrow over a week, while other parts of the south saw even higher totals. Rivers were soon running higher than normal and the ground was saturated. The first week of October saw yet more heavy rain, and flooding began to affect Sussex in particular. At that point the south-east crossed its fingers that the rain would stop, but the worst was yet to come. A huge low-pressure system became slow-moving over Scotland on 9 October, and frontal bands of rain sent pulses of torrential rain across the south. My mother reported being stuck in 2 or 3 feet of floodwater while crossing the A3 at Worcester Park on 10 October. So deep was the flood that waves were being created by moving traffic and the visibility was almost nil due to the torrential rain and spray. According to the Met Office, between 9 and 12 October the following rainfall totals were recorded in Sussex, the worst-affected area during this three-day period:

Station	Rainfall (mm)
Plumpton	156.4
Barcombe Cross	140.8
Uckfield	126.8
Ringmer, Bishops Lane	123.4
Falmer	107.7
Hove, Shirley Road	106.2
Brighton, Lewes Road	102.9

At this point the Medway burst its banks, as did the River Uck at Uckfield and the Ouse at Lewes. Many homes were flooded, and the water rose for some time. One man was swept away by floodwater in Uckfield High Street as he tried to open up a retail store on 9 October but managed to escape the torrent. In fact, at least twenty people had to be rescued by lifeboat from the town that day, and others were airlifted to safety. Canterbury was badly flooded too, just as other parts of Kent and Sussex saw floodwaters rise, swamping hundreds of homes. Less rain fell over the next few days, but many areas remained on high alert as others mopped up with a close eye on the weather forecast.

After a quieter spell, 30 October saw the worst storms since 1990 hit the country. This event brought with it high winds, heavy rain and even heavy snow over the higher elevations to the north. This was a big storm and affected a wide area of the country. Rivers in Somerset and Devon burst their banks, and all the areas affected before, such as Maidstone, Uckfield and Lewes, were again flooded. A tornado touched down at Bognor Regis and tore through a caravan park, leaving a vast trail of destruction, lifting many of the trailers into the air and tossing them asunder. This was one of a series of tornadoes that appeared along the south coast during the lifetime of this storm.

The gales, which were accompanied by torrential rain, left six people dead. Most railway services into London were halted and operators in the south and west were unable to say when they would be running any trains at all. Tens of thousands of people were left without power. Gusts of over 90 mph were recorded from the Mumbles in Wales to Plymouth; trees blew over, lorries were overturned, high tides swamped many towns on the west coast and great floods across the south now reached crisis proportions. Even Eurostar was unable to run due to fallen trees and flooding, while many Channel ferries were unable to come into port for fourteen hours. Overall, England and Wales saw 196 per cent of the average rainfall total for the autumn, amounting to a staggering 503 millimetres. In October alone, Littlehampton in Sussex saw 291 millimetres in total, smashing its previous monthly total for the month, set in 1987.

November saw the flooding move northwards, which threatened to rival the thaw floods of 1947. Luckily, the scale and depth of the flooding waned at times, so did not reach the severity of 1947. However, York saw possibly its worst flooding on record. On 5 November, the Ouse rose to 17.5 feet above normal and the town was seriously flooded. The cost of this flood was immense both for insurers and the local council, who had to part with £1.3 million in costs for flood protection alone, including sandbags. Floods also hit other parts of Yorkshire, notably Leeds and Castleford, where hundreds of homes were swamped in the aftermath of the October gales and subsequent rain.

The soggy autumn of 2000 made this the wettest year since 1872. A government report commissioned under George Fleming to review the causes and effects of this flooding revealed the alarming extent to which residential property has increasingly been built on floodplains, storing up major problems for the future. The report concluded that the changing climate would be responsible for more flooding. It concluded that unusually warm waters off Norway and the North Atlantic were responsible for the elevated levels of cyclonic activity that gave us such endless heavy rain. By linking improved warning systems, flood defences and environmental planning for flood risks, an efficient system to reduce the impact of severe flooding could be developed. However, one final conclusion was reached: the risk of serious flooding was growing, and severe events such as those of 2000 were forecast, in the not-too-distant future, to become commonplace.

48

Record Rainfall: Two Disasters, One Record

Dorset, July 1955

A number of extreme rainfall totals have appeared over the years, often arising from very different regions and synoptic situations. The record for twenty-four-hour rainfall in the UK until 2009 was established on 18 July 1955 in Martinstown near Dorchester in Dorset. On this day, an astounding 279 millimetres of rain fell during a tremendous thunderstorm that caused severe flooding in the town. The storm's effects were relatively local, but flash floods and landslides occurred widely in the affected area and floodwater tore through the streets of Martinstown, also impacting nearby towns such as Weymouth, Dorchester and Bridport. Cars were submerged and wrecked and holiday caravans carried off with tons of debris in waves of mud and boulders. Some people caught up in the torrents were injured, two were killed and much property was badly damaged in an era when residential insurance was not common. Communications and travel were badly disrupted for a time as bridges were swept away and main roads made impassable.

July 1955 was a hot and sunny month. A shallow disturbance moving in from the south and west was prevented from spreading north by the hot, dry air that had built because of the persistent high pressure that had been in situ over the country for some time. As the storm approached in the mid-afternoon it was described as being like night-time, and the torrential rain thundered down, creating a vast inundation, until about 7.30 in the evening, when it suddenly stopped.

The loss of life was not as extensive as that of the Lynmouth disaster three years earlier, largely thanks to the less dramatic topography of the area. This storm was a highly isolated occurrence in a heatwave month during which some locations received no rain at all. The heat quickly returned to Dorset as the great clean-up began. The rainfall record set that day stood untouched for fifty-four years. It seemed unlikely that the wetter mountainous regions of Wales, Scotland and England could deliver the intensity of rainfall to compete with such a violent convective thunderstorm, even with a sustained westerly assault. For years this remained the case; however, all such assumptions were swept aside in November 2009.

Cumbria, November 2009

On the night of 13 November 2009, it looked as if a deep depression would track across Scotland, bringing with it a surprisingly warm, moist south-westerly flow. It hit its target and heavy rain began to fall over much of the north-west of England, but in particular around the Lake District. This area picked up substantially higher rainfall totals than the lower parts to the east and north because of its upland topography.

While this rainfall in itself was not particularly exceptional, in the context of this story it provided the latest in a succession of very wet days that month which, cumulatively, would later become important. The rain fell right through the weekend, beginning to fill rivers and saturate the ground progressively until it looked like flooding would be inevitable. By 17 November, Cumbria at large had received its average monthly rainfall total for November. This may well sound like nothing unusual for the Lake District, perhaps, but it was what happened next that left meteorologists and weather watchers in the UK open-mouthed. The sheer volumes of rain that fell in the following week outdid all previous weeks' rainfall combined, and the effect on the area, its population, infrastructure and economy were both devastating and long lasting.

On Wednesday 18 November, a slow-moving low-pressure system centred just to the south of Iceland became almost stationary. Pressure was high and the air dry and warm to the south east of the UK, creating a particularly warm moist flow for the time of year. The interaction of these air masses meant two key things. Firstly, it fed large amounts of moisture into the system and the warmer the air, the more moisture it can hold. Secondly, the heaviest rain bands were confined to the north-west of England and areas to the south had far less rain.

Rain began from the word go on 18 November, and the Environment Agency, who had feared the worst for some time, warned that the areas most at risk of flooding would be land close to rivers in places such as Appleby, Keswick and Carlisle. The latter had in fact suffered a disastrous flood not that long before, in January 2005, and was only just recovering from its effects. By the end of 18 November the front, which had settled diagonally north-east to south-west across Cumbria, stretched practically to the Azores and trailed slowly across the region as it curled around the centre of the depression. The seemingly endless rain further intensified when the in-flowing moisture rose up on to the mountainous terrain. By the end of November, between 50 millimetres and 70 millimetres of rain had fallen across the area and was still falling.

Overnight the rain kept falling, and Thursday 19 November dawned with most rivers in the area already topping their banks, creating hazards across five of the six districts. Rainfall totals were extraordinary; by 9 a.m., 142 millimetres had fallen at Seathwaite, 152 millimetres at Honister Pass and the 100-millimetre mark was passed widely in the higher elevations of the Lake District. In the twenty-four-hour period between midnight of 19 and 20 November, Seathwaite passed 316 millimetres and broke the previous record of 279 millimetres, which fell on Martinstown in 1955. In the seventy-two hours between 17 and 20 November, a staggering 456 millimetres fell at Seathwaite.

All this water had to go somewhere, and the worst-affected areas were all to the south of the lakes themselves. The River Derwent tore down the valleys from Keswick towards the lower ground at Cockermouth to the confluence with the equally fast-flowing River Cocker. Thursday afternoon saw the town of Cockermouth badly flooded. With the relentless rain falling upriver, as soon as the waters had claimed the town the levels of the flood continued to increase until they almost reached the eaves of houses and shops. By Friday, the town was in need of a full evacuation.

Keswick was also badly affected, and bridges along both rivers began to give way under the relentless pressure. First the Newlands Beck Bridge upriver on the Derwent was swept away, followed by a succession of others. The Lorton Bridge was the first to go on the Cocker, and communications between the towns of Workington and Cockermouth were cut off. Friday saw the flooding in Cockermouth reach over 8 feet in depth, and hundreds of homes were inundated. Some 200 rescues were carried out on that day alone, and a police officer, Bill Barker, who was stopping traffic from crossing the A597 bridge over the Derwent at Workington, lost his life in an instant as the bridge, undermined by the increasingly fierce speed of the water below, gave way and collapsed. Lifeboat crews were powerless to help in any recovery operation because, as one of them said, the sheer force of the water had left them helpless and the currents were of a level of severity that he and his experienced crew had never seen before.

The waters finally stabilised that weekend, but the effects on the area continued. As the extent of the flooding became more apparent, it was clear Cockermouth would effectively be severed from the south as the only road bridge was gone. In fact, sixteen bridges and twenty-five roads were affected, with three major road bridges destroyed, including the key road bridge connecting Workington to the rest of the area. The result of this was that anyone wanting to get across had to complete a 40-mile round trip. Only a month before Christmas, over 80 per cent of businesses were ruined in an area heavily reliant on tourism. In fact, later research identified over 3,000 businesses that were affected and unable to trade across the borough in the aftermath of the flood. Nearly 2,000 residential homes were flooded in total, with the worst-affected district being Allerdale; Cockermouth alone saw over 900 properties affected.

The floods gained national attention but, like all disasters of this kind, faded from public view soon after. Inevitably, the next big story obscures perhaps the most important aspect of any such disaster: the recovery. However, the community fought back hard. Spurred by a fear that visitors would be put off by what they had seen on TV, a series of high-profile advertising campaigns promoting the area and winter breaks across the Lake District were broadcast. These, coupled with cash injections from the flood response fund and the regional development agency, helped with the clear-up. A local 'business hub' was even set up in Cockermouth to temporarily house local businesses that had no premises. By 2010, a remarkable effort had been made towards recovery. However, one major issue remained for some time, and that was the lack of a road bridge, meaning north–south traffic still faced a massive diversion. While a temporary footbridge could carry over 80 tonnes, it was decided that building a new bridge would be too costly. This meant that the Calva Bridge, which had been rendered unusable by the flood, would have to be restructured from its damaged base. To the great delight of both locals and tourists, on 11 February 2011 the bridge finally reopened and by Easter of that year traffic could once more cross the Derwent. From there, bit by bit, normality began to return to the area and to the people that had lived through Britain's worst-ever rainfall event.

49

The Winter Storms Crisis, 2013/14: An Unparalleled Natural Event?

The late autumn of 2013 and the following winter saw some exceptionally cold air over North America in a pattern that pushed the jet stream right over the British Isles. Rather than resetting into a new pattern after a few days or weeks, it became firmly locked into a pattern that lasted months. The result was the wettest and stormiest winter ever recorded in Britain, and a chain of devastating floods and gales that cost the country tens of millions in damage and took many lives.

The summer weather patterns of 2013 were dominated by the widespread impact of a potent north-easterly extension of the Azores high and a long-lasting heatwave that began in early July. August, however, was much wetter. On 24 August, an area to the south and east of London saw over 2 inches of rain falling in just a few hours to the backdrop of intense thunder and lightning. Southend in Essex saw a 52-millimetre deluge and fairly severe local flooding. Kent saw similar rainfall totals, and I recorded 41.6 millimetres at the Sevenoaks weather station that afternoon. This torrential rain delivered the highest single-day rainfall total in the area for some years, but what nobody would ever have predicted was that, soon, this isolated and rather exceptional event was to become an almost daily occurrence.

The first effects of this chillingly destructive spell of weather began in October. The morning of 11 October saw showers push rapidly across London as the sky darkened. Heavy raindrops began to splash onto roads and pavements and, rather like the August deluge, the south and east of England saw persistent heavy rainfall throughout the afternoon. This rain then spread westwards until much of the south was affected by an unusually persistent torrential rain that continued all night. The next morning it was still pelting down, and local flooding became a widespread problem, with some rail services disrupted. It was not until the following night that the rain stopped, but it was not long before a further spell of rain began the next morning. Over three days, many parts of south-east England received around 75 millimetres, equating to a month's rainfall. The north of the country and Scotland escaped this event as pressure had remained high to the north – a reversal of the normal autumn pattern. There then followed several very disturbed days, with bouts of heavy rain and strengthening winds; it began to look like a very wet autumn was on the cards.

By the third week of October, the high pressure had moved further north still and the jet stream dipped south. A series of potent depressions began to form out in the Atlantic, each one of which became progressively more powerful. Around 20 October, the Met Office computers spotted some explosive potential in one of these lows, likely to hit the south of Britain a week later. The models showed the strongest wind field taking a path not unlike that of the 1987 October 'hurricane'. The Met Office began to issue warnings of a potentially destructive storm, and the media began hyping what was quickly dubbed the 'St Jude's Day storm'; for want of a better name, the storm was due to strike on 28 October, the official feast day of St Jude. Being late October, many trees were still in full or partial leaf and, with forecasters concerned that winds could reach 70–80 mph widely across the south of the UK while accompanied by heavy rain, both flooding and structural damage looked possible anywhere across the south of the country.

The forecasts proved lethally accurate. Late on the night of the 27th and into the early hours of the 28th, the wind began to howl. Gusts along the south coast were soon exceeding 80 mph, and 82 mph was recorded on the Solent towards midnight, while at Langdon Bay, just off the coast of Dover, a terrific gust of 86 mph was recorded not long afterwards. These were potentially damaging winds. The water along the English Channel soon began to rise into furious rolling waves covered in a fog of white spray that smashed into the rocks, cliffs and coves of every county and pounded the sea defences at every port to the south and west – all fronted by gargantuan waves. The noise woke me at around 2 a.m. Trees were thrashing around wildly and being bent to uncomfortable angles, with twigs and branches blowing down into the street and garden. It was during these early hours that the southern coasts took their fiercest pounding since the last such severe storm in 2002. The Needles, just off the Isle of Wight, recorded a gust of 99 mph, exceptional for any south coast gale.

Overall, this storm did not come close to the violence of the 1987 'hurricane' and a major gale in 2002 was statistically somewhat more violent. Nevertheless, its consequences were still severe. Four people were killed as a direct result of St Jude; one incident involved a teenage girl killed by a tree falling on to the caravan her family was using during renovation work on their home near Hever. Two were London casualties, a man and a woman. Both were killed in west London after a falling tree opened up a gas main and caused an explosion that wrecked three properties. A further victim, a man in his fifties, was killed when a large tree fell on to his car in Watford, Hertfordshire. Horrified passers-by saw it happen and rushed to help, but no one could shift the large, mature tree and the rescue had to be performed by fire crews. Sadly, it was too late. Another horrendous incident took place on a beach in Newhaven when a teenage boy was swept off the shoreline into the water and drowned. This was not the last incident of its kind during this wild spell of weather, and many people took great risks with waves, floods and the sea – many filmed by passers-by and posted on social media sites or even shown on the evening news as a warning to others. The storm moved east and north and pounded the coastlines of the Netherlands, Germany and Denmark, causing a further eighteen deaths in total, eight of which happened in Germany alone.

Back in southern Britain, there was fairly widespread damage right across the capital; roofs were blown off in some places, and trees came down in many populated districts. But, as is often the case, the main dislocation to transport and services was out of town. Tiles, glass, leaves, branches and other debris littered the streets in many towns and villages. Nearly half a million homes woke up to power cuts on 28 October. In a major effort to minimise the impact of the blackouts, repair crews worked tirelessly in the wet and windy conditions that followed, and within twenty-four hours 300,000 homes had their power restored. However, this left a remaining 160,000 homes still without power and the hard work to get them back on the grid went on for several days. Cranes came crashing down on many exposed building sites, and many rail-side trees, often in full leaf, along with a number of landslides, blocked railway lines, ensuring great numbers of commuters had problems getting to work.

As the country recovered from the storm, October came to a close and so did a very wet month. Over 160 millimetres of rain fell at my station and, at 141 millimetres, it was the south-east's fourteenth-wettest October since 1766. Indeed, on a national level the month also came in at fourteenth, with 157 millimetres of rainfall. Although no record-breaker, it was nevertheless a notably wet month. The first half of November remained wet and unsettled and, as the damage from the gale at the end of October continued to be cleared, water levels rose. On the 12th, another exceptional fall of rain caused local floods in the south.

At this moment, high pressure settled directly over Britain for a full month. During this time it became unusually dry right across Britain, and fog and frost became quite widespread. As an example of the stark contrast between this dry spell and the deluges that surrounded it, in the four weeks from 1 to 31 October I measured 161 millimetres of rain; but in the four weeks from 12 November to 12 December there only 7 millimetres fell. However, after a very wet six weeks of heavy rain, the water table and river levels in the south remained unusually high.

So it was that, by early December, after three weeks of quiet weather, the computer models began to indicate the rain and wind would soon return with a vengeance. On the evening of 5 December, a deep depression loomed large to the north and west. As it drew out into the North Sea, it suddenly changed course and began to sink southwards, rather reminiscent of the 1953 gale that produced a storm surge. Depressions that take this path in autumn and winter tend to be squeezed hard on their eastern flank, forcing the isobars to bunch up into a narrow band that creates a powerful northerly airstream. The resulting wind fields, driven down under deep low pressure, squeeze the sea southwards and displace it outwards, greatly expanding the water level on the periphery and raising it significantly. This hits the land as a storm surge and, when combined with high 'spring tides', usually spells disaster.

When this surge hit the eastern coasts, even some well-protected towns such as Whitby and Great Yarmouth were inundated by surging seawater. Exposed areas of eastern coastal cliffs were undermined by the great tide and surging waves at a number of locations, especially in Norfolk. One such place was Hemsby, where tidal erosion had slowly been eating away at the cliff-top land in the area. This single day, however, saw a massive collapse of the cliff edges that took with it several houses, some still containing the worldly possessions of their owners. Some homeowners had barely time to gather their belongings and get out of their properties safely.

After this storm passed, all indications began to point to a succession of new and equally intense storms following in its path. Very active fronts began to cross the country on the weekend of 13–14 December, and the frequency of torrential rain increased during the following week. I had started a new job in west London, and every day rainfall of tropical intensity would greet me on my commute to and from work. Even central London began to be overwhelmed by surface water that in places merged into sizable floods. This rain sometimes fell as much as an inch per day, these spells separated only by the briefest of dry intervals – some lasting just a few short hours. Then, on the weekend before Christmas, fresh gales arrived.

A fierce and deep low approached the country on 23 December, and it looked again as if it would deliver a direct hit on the south. Meanwhile, far to the north near Iceland, the governing low began to deepen to almost record-breaking levels. As the torrential rain and gales smashed once again into the south, pressure dropped to 934 mb over the north of Scotland (the record low is 925 mb), delivering the lowest air pressure measurement taken in the UK since 1990. Dark skies and thunderous, relentless winds and heavy rain began early in the morning and continued without a break until evening. The next day was a repeat performance, at the end of which over 60 millimetres of rain fell right across the south. In many places this latest deluge proved too much, and many rivers could no longer contain the rising water. From Dorset to Suffolk, severe gales put huge pressure on the country's infrastructure, utilities and rescue services. The River Medway quickly burst its banks, inundating areas around Tonbridge and Maidstone and the villages around Yalding. A large part of the Medway valley, as well as areas along its tributaries, was engulfed by fast-moving floodwater the day before the holiday period was about to start.

Soon 75,000 homes were without power, and by Christmas Eve as many as 130 flood warnings were issued by the Environment Agency across England. In Devon a man was swept away trying to rescue his dog on Christmas Eve morning, and two further drownings occurred, one of them in similar circumstances in South Wales. It was becoming apparent that the flooding was about to badly affect the south-west of England and South Wales as well. Power failed more widely, and soon East Anglia, Somerset and the Isle of Wight joined the thousands in Kent, Surrey and Sussex that had been cut off at perhaps the most critical moment of the year.

Not surprisingly, with some of the most widespread floods in years happening on Christmas Eve, the transport system was also heading for trouble. Attention turned to Gatwick, where the continuing storm cut the power to the North Terminal on 24 December. For the unlucky passengers leaving from that part of the airport, most flights were delayed as they had to be shifted to the South Terminal, causing a vast backlog and severe delays. Many other passengers, however, were even less fortunate and had their flights cancelled altogether. The TV news bulletins that night showed a police officer having to address angry crowds of delayed passengers standing atop an airline desk with a megaphone. A spokesman on the day shared the frustration of the passengers but could only add, 'We remain apologetic and are trying to put things right but it takes the time it takes to get things right.' Network Rail stated that far more damage had been caused by this latest gale than the St Jude's Day storm and one of the many critical rail lines not in operation was the Gatwick service, trapping those delayed passengers that could have gotten home by rail at the airport.

For those on the roads, Christmas Eve saw the severe weather cause disruption and serious traffic issues as many areas became paralysed by rising floodwaters. In Devon alone, thirty cars had to be abandoned as the waters rose and people who set out into dangerous areas, many of them ignoring clearly signposted warnings, found themselves having to be rescued and then under the threat of prosecution. For others, however, the pre-Christmas storms came as a shock as some rivers had risen at an astounding rate, often bursting their banks in a day or so, taking farmers, the authorities and property owners by surprise. The news media reported on a number of people who had to face the prospect of Christmas with either their properties underwater or without power. Some were faced with both issues. Christmas Eve, however, found many riverside restaurants and shops under deep floodwater and facing huge financial losses. It rained heavily for three more days, and everywhere the waters continued to rise, most notably in those areas already stricken by floodwater.

One area that is used to flooding, the Somerset Levels, had by this time become widely inundated. This low-lying stretch of reclaimed land has been the scene of some devastating floods in the past; even during years of normal rainfall, some level of flooding is experienced. However, by 27 December the floodwaters here began to rise very quickly and with unusual vigour. This meant that many of the villages that sit slightly above the usual flood levels, and generally escape the water, began to become submerged. An extremely long and painful journey now began for the communities living and working the land here.

Many of the disasters in this book see a rapid end to the troubles, allowing a clear-up to begin and costs and losses to be counted. Such was the severity and length of this catastrophic series of winter storms, however, that it was a full twelve weeks – in some cases more – before an end came and the clean-up could begin. In the case of the Somerset Levels, even long after the storms ended it was still weeks before the victims could reclaim their property and take stock.

A brief lull in the stormy weather ended on New Year's Day 2014, when yet another fierce gale moved across England and Wales.

During this first week of the year, parts of the south-east saw 90–100 millimetres fall and the floods continue to spread and worsen.

The end of the first week of January saw another severe gale pound the south of Britain from the west and vast waves, some 30 feet high, crashing into the coasts of Wales and the south-western peninsula, creating threatening tidal surges and disastrous inundations with each high tide. As the gales continued through the day, they brought down power lines and felled trees on a wide scale. The south-east of the country fared better on this occasion than the west, and some of the most severe flooding in Kent, Surrey and Sussex slowed for a time and many people were able to rescue at least some of the goods from their homes. The Thames, however, began to rise on a daily basis as the heavy rains further upstream began to filter downstream and millions of cubic tonnes of water began to flow down towards the affluent areas of Windsor, Eton and Henley and on towards Datchet, Chertsey, Egham and Staines. Aberystwyth's seafront received an exceptional barrage as a combination of seawater, rocks and debris smashed on to the promenade, inundating homes and businesses on the seafront, tearing up roads and crushing cars, as well as destroying robust coastal barriers. This was just one single example of life being brought to a virtual halt by the daily onslaught of wind and rain.

By now, 2,000 homes were reported flooded and seven people killed. The menacing violence of the weather, the widespread damage to infrastructure, business and travel and the sheer longevity of the disruption was something not witnessed for generations.

The death toll was certainly testament to this. A further casualty – that of an 18-year-old washed off a Devon beach that day – was to further push up the death toll. The cumulative effects of the rain began to be felt in a number of ways. Landslips on to railway lines became increasingly common, such as one that occurred near Horsham during this first week of January. Soon after, a severe landslide almost destroyed one of the main London lines running up from Hastings and it was four months before the line was fully reopened.

Problems now spread to the north, with the rail line between Carlisle and Workington suspended for a week because of a landslip, and the Thames Barrier was closed for the ninth tide in a row – an unprecedented event. At Newquay in Cornwall, the harbourmaster saw a wreck emerge in the small harbour; this was one that had never been seen before and was previously unknown. On the east coast, numerous Second World War bombs washed up in Essex and had to be dealt with. In Cornwall, the renowned rock and cliff formations of Porthcothan Bay were completely destroyed; and just off Portland in Dorset the famous 'Pom-Pom' rock, which had been an important tourist attraction for generations, was pummelled into oblivion after a sustained spell of ludicrously gigantic waves.

The unfortunate Met Office now began to appear in the media, not for the sterling work they were achieving in forecasting the regular gales and deluges but rather because their rainfall prediction, issued during the autumn for the next three months, was for average to below-average rainfall. Once again, the dangers of long-term forecasting were brought to the headlines by a media now in a voracious mood, looking desperately for human scapegoats in lieu of the wild, uncontrollable forces of nature that were at the heart of the crisis and were answerable to no one. It was equally fascinating to see one newspaper, which had been predicting Ice Age Armageddon scenarios for recent mild winters, turn yet again to forecasts of catastrophic blizzards. It was noted with hilarity on social media, and even in other papers, that among all the scaremongering and headline lunacy this daily conjured up, even their deluded headline writers could not have imagined the sheer scale and severity of scenario that actually occurred.

Meanwhile, across the Atlantic in the USA a very severe winter had begun and unusually deep incursions of arctic air began to become every bit as severe and widespread as the deep Atlantic depressions this severe cold was helping to generate. My youngest brother moved to Boston in September that year and had never experienced anything like it. Temperatures regularly fell below -20 °C and the winter brought with it more severe winter storms than usual.

The pronounced dip in the jet over the north-east of the USA also caused pressure to remain stubbornly high over the far west and south-western states. California saw a disappointing winter in terms of rainfall. San Francisco often sees day after day of rain and drizzle, feeding the redwoods and turning the landscape green. However, winter 2014 saw these rains widely fail to appear across the south of the state, and Los Angeles saw just 2 millimetres of rain during the whole of January against an average nearly 80 millimetres, while San Francisco received even less; only 0.25 millimetres against an average of 110 millimetres.

Back in Britain, a major debate broke out concerning the Somerset Levels. This land, reclaimed from the sea in the thirteenth century, has always acted to some degree as the floodplain for the Bristol Channel. It was here, in the seventeenth century, that one of the worst storm surges ever recorded in the British Isles took place, and it remains vulnerable. Nevertheless, over recent years the Environment Agency, which manages the waterways in the area, had cut back on the level of maintenance they undertook locally. Many locals had long been angry at this change because they feared it would increase the risk of flooding, but the Environment Agency didn't feel that such maintenance, particularly dredging, would necessarily be beneficial. Whatever the answer, the rain just continued. As January progressed, the floods continued to rise. By the time the next violent storm struck, on 24 January, the Levels had been underwater for five weeks. The villages of Moorland and Muchelney, which had so far escaped the floods, began to be slowly submerged. The Environment Minister, Chris Paterson, made a rather late and possibly ill-advised visit to the area and was met with fury from the locals, who blamed the government and the Environment Agency for the floods pretty much in their entirety; the 450 millimetres of rain that had fallen since 28 October wasn't mentioned. Shortly afterwards, the government brought in the Army to assist with the evacuation and protection of the local populace.

January broke the England and Wales Precipitation (EWP) record for rainfall, giving over 185 millimetres of rain when averaged out across the country. In the south-east of the country January was also the wettest ever, with 182 millimetres, as it was in the south-west, where a staggering 236 millimetres was measured over the month.

At Sevenoaks I measured 202 millimetres, more than in any other previous month. Amid a series of violent storms, on 17 January our street awoke to an almighty flash and bang at 6 a.m. A bolt of lightning hit our house and blew out the power, internet and telephone, leading to many days of disruption. And yet, despite the endless gales, lightning strikes, torrential rain and floods, it was the following Saturday evening that saw some of us experience one of the most bizarre events of this epic spell. This event affected much of the south-west, the Midlands, East Anglia, Greater London, Surrey, Kent and Sussex.

On Saturday 25 January, a narrow band of thunderstorms appeared on the radar travelling north-west to south-east, reaching the Bristol Channel early in the afternoon. As the band moved east, it suddenly began to intensify over central southern England and extended north across parts of the Midlands. As the squall approached the east, it narrowed and became increasingly intense. Sometime before the storm arrived, from our house thunder could be heard to the west and a moderate rain began to fall. Then a great black squall line appeared on the horizon and the sky turned from daylight to complete darkness in the space of four of five minutes. Suddenly, a loud rushing noise was heard from the west and the sky erupted into mayhem. Violent winds bent trees double, several coming crashing down in our vicinity within seconds. The road became white with large hailstones and blinding blue flashes of lightning mixed with roaring thunder; visibility was reduced almost to zero. The noise was tremendous and the power that had gone out during the earlier random lightning strike failed again, and the Sky dish was unable to communicate with the heavens. After about five minutes the most extreme phase was over, and after a quarter of an hour the rain suddenly eased and the sky began to lighten somewhat, although, being winter, darkness was to follow soon after. Hail was piled in white drifts for many hours afterwards by the sides of the road.

On our way to Canterbury that night to have dinner with my parents-in-law, we came across the fire service attending to the scene of what looked like a tornado's aftermath in the Wildernesse area of Sevenoaks. Torn and twisted branches and fallen trees littered the flooded roads along with much debris, and the roofs of several houses looked badly damaged. Many people posted on my weather station's Twitter account that night that it looked as though tornadic activity had occurred in many places during this squall; however, in the darkness and chaos of the squall it would not have been easy to see what was going on.

After further severe gales and heavy rain on 27–30 January, very few places were spared flooding. The Mole burst its banks, and one could see from the M25 that raging torrents of water had spilled out into the surrounding fields, submerging a wide area. That weekend we went on a trip to the old Roman town of Silchester, just north of Basingstoke. Nowhere on the site was accessible without wellies as floods 2 to 4 feet deep swamped every field. Ducks, seagulls and geese swam on these vast lakes formed not by overflowing rivers but by the incredible rainfall, now approaching 450 millimetres in less than twelve weeks.

Next it was the turn of the Thames to make the headlines, and the river began to overflow across many of the lower reaches that had so far been spared. As the next violent storm barrelled towards southern Britain on 4 February, the country now braced itself for the very worst. The storm that hit the country on 4 February was probably the worst of the winter and became notorious for the destruction of a large section of the famous Dawlish Railway that had been constructed by Brunel in the nineteenth century. This stretch of railway had withstood the elements since its construction in 1846 as the South Devon Railway, becoming the single most important rail connection between the south-western peninsula and the rest of Britain.

On the night of 4 February, winds reaching 92 mph at the Scilly Isles began to batter the south-west of the country and torrential rain once again began to pound down on to the streets and houses of the south. By now each storm that came in was covered live on TV as 'Breaking News', in much the same way as all the most serious events we now experience are. For those living above the railway line on the coast at Dawlish the night brought real terror. The sea was so fierce that it smashed through the thick sea wall and immediately went to work breaking up and washing out the supporting ballast under the railway. In a few short hours, a 30-metre stretch of the railway was hanging suspended over the wild sea, the area was flooded and nearby houses began to collapse as their windows were smashed by debris flying off the collapsing rail line. Residents described the awful sound as each succession of waves broke down the sea walls and then began to thud into the railway, shaking their houses to their foundations. As the sea smashed up the ballast and supporting infrastructure of the railway line, great groaning and rumbling sounds bore testament to the destruction of 170 years of historical engineering. Afterwards, Network Rail assessed that it had at least six weeks' work before it in order to rebuild the line and make it safe. By morning, 44,000 homes in the south-west were without power. The sea broke over the defences at Looe and extraordinary footage of giant waves breaking right over Chesil Beach in Dorset provided fresh evidence that the power of these storms was exceptional. A further life was lost in Wiltshire as trees brought down power cables, electrocuting a passer-by, while in Birmingham a woman was seriously injured when a tree fell on her car. The M25, M40, M20 and many local roads were flooded and rail disruption became so widespread that it would be impossible to recount all the local disasters that occurred throughout the day and following night.

The government was now concerned as to the extent of the floods and the length of the crisis. Although they pledged £100 million to help those affected by the floods, many people were commenting on Twitter that if forecasts proved correct and such storms would become more common in the future, even modest rises in sea levels would cause major damage without the improvement of coastal and river defences. The government was in an awkward position; construction in floodplains has continued unchallenged in the UK in recent years, and surely builders and those who buy properties in vulnerable areas cannot expect the taxpayer to support an increasingly risky investment. On the other hand, with space at a premium in the crowded south-east, could any government in the UK afford to limit such developments? After some very negative television coverage from the local communities in the Somerset Levels, the government quickly withdrew their support for the Environmental Agency's view on dredging and announced that by March the activity would begin once again.

The torrential rain and high winds continued up until at least 6 February, and the Thames rose further. Residents from towns such as Datchet, Egham, Staines and Chertsey to those upriver at Eton and Windsor were swamped. Even princes William and Harry were filmed helping locals to sandbag their homes. On 7 February, I took a flight from Heathrow to Sweden. As we rose above the ground, within a few metres of the runway were the first floods. As we turned towards the east and south, I could see the entire extent of the flooding, probably at its worst. Water stretched as far as the eye could see, and the area was really just a series of lakes.

The next storm arrived about a week later, and this relatively long lull allowed some time for the country to clear up from the previous week. It therefore caused great alarm when the storm forecast to hit the country on 13 February was given a red warning from the Met Office, denoting a direct danger to life. On this occasion, Wales, Ireland and the north-west were worst hit. A gust of 112 mph was recorded at Great Dun Fell in the Pennines, while the Mumbles near Swansea saw a gust of 92 mph and off the Isle of Wight the Needles saw a staggering gust of 96 mph that day. Another inch of rain fell over the east, with closer to 2 inches in the west, and flooding everywhere got worse. In Somerset, the Levels, which were now in the eighth week of a deep crisis, now saw the flooding reach its peak. As the rain continued, evacuations were necessary in many towns such as Egham and Maidenhead, where the Thames continued to creep ever higher. Worcester now found itself the latest victim of the heavy rains, with the river there creeping to a record level of 5.65 metres, and the surrounding areas of Worcester and adjacent parts of Herefordshire braced themselves for severe flooding.

At this moment, the weather models showed that the conveyor belt of storms may have run out of steam. The next disturbances brought lighter rain and showers to the areas most affected, and between 16 and 28 February there were no heavy rains or gales across the south. The first week of March saw one final burst of heavy rain affect the south, but even this did not come with the gales and destruction to which the country had become accustomed. Nevertheless, nearly an inch of rain fell across a wide area. The floods on the Thames had begun to ease soon after, and this final burst of rain had a temporary effect on the river's levels, raising them once more but not to the levels they had reached in February. This was the end of the crisis. March now saw a major reversal in the meteorological fortunes of the British Isles. No rain fell at all between 5 and 19 March, and the weather became clear and unseasonably warm, reaching 20 °C or more in the London area

So what of the cost of the storms? Eric Pickles, the Home Office Minister, used an assessment by accountants PwC to gauge the impact. According to the report, since October the winter storms had cost the country £630 million. This included not only damage to property but also the costs of lost business and the repair of a greatly damaged infrastructure, not to mention the cost of overtime for the overstretched emergency services. It took until April for the Somerset Levels to drain completely, and dredging began in earnest in March, but it was not long before the *Guardian* published a figure, also calculated by PwC, of £500 million. This was the estimated cost of insurance claims stemming from the winter storms crisis, bringing the total impact to well over £1 billion. In terms of human life, the cost was also heavy. At least twelve people lost their lives as a direct result of the storms and many more were injured, several very seriously.

The rainfall statistics for the winter provided sobering reading. Despite the dry period at the start of December, England as a whole saw the wettest meteorological winter (the period December to February) in a record going back to 1766. January was the wettest ever, and February the second-wettest ever. This same ranking sequence was also true regionally across the south of the country.

The five wettest winters in England and Wales since 1766
1. 2014   456 mm
2. 1915   423 mm
3. 1990   420 mm
4. 1877   418 mm
5. 1995   415 mm

The five wettest winters in the south-east since 1766
1. 2014   451 mm
2. 1915   390 mm
3. 1990   364 mm
4. 1877   356 mm
5. 1995   335 mm

The five wettest winters in the south-west since 1766
1. 2014   609 mm
2. 1990   540 mm
3. 1995   531 mm
4. 1994   508 mm
5. 1915   496 mm

The five driest winters in England and Wales since 1766
1. 1964   88 mm
2. 1858   92 mm
3. 1891   105 mm
4. 1814   114 mm
5. 1934   118 mm

The five driest winters in south-east England since 1766
1. 1964   63 mm
2. 1934   71 mm
3. 1992   72 mm

4. 1976 76 mm
5. 1891 77 mm

This was also an extremely mild winter. For the first time since 2007 there was no lying snow at my weather station at any time from November to March. That contrasts strongly with the previous year, when the total over the same period was forty days.

Across central England, only eleven winters have been warmer since 1659, putting 2014 in the very highest percentile range with a mean average of 6.07 °C. The warmest-ever winter, 1869, had a mean average of 6.77 °C but was delivered in calm and sunny weather dominated by high pressure and following one of the hottest summers of the nineteenth century. So did the wild and stormy winter of 2014 really present what the government described as 'an unprecedented natural crisis'? In terms of rainfall, it was indeed unprecedented. However, rainfall records only go back to 1766. One of the stormiest recorded winters ever, and one that appears to have been so stormy and wet that it may well have been a true a challenger to 2013, was 1686. Although no rainfall records exist for that year, the UK was battered by endless gales and rain that took a significant toll on shipping, and this year stands out as remarkable not only for its storminess but also for its warmth. Coming during the zenith of the Little Ice Age (1683/84 was the coldest winter ever), at 6.33 °C it held the record for the highest mean temperature for any winter for 289 years – right up until 1975.

Interestingly, this wild winter both highlighted and confirmed several new and existing theories that the Met Office, and its professional physicists and meteorologists, suspected combined to deliver not just this prolonged mild, stormy spell but also many of the cold winters and hot summers in the last fifteen years. The first part of the theory, broadcast by the BBC in 2014, focussed on the Quasi Biennial Oscillation (QBO), winds that blow across the tropics in a sustained direction over a prolonged period. Occasionally, these equatorial winds reverse direction and disrupt the normal climatic patterns, causing a 'knock-on' effect on weather patterns across the globe. Such a reversal occurred in 2013, and this disruption caused tremendous flooding in Indonesia. Researchers found that this disruption in Indonesia was very significant for the northern hemisphere. The changed Indonesian weather patterns caused an unusual wave effect in the jet stream, resulting in highly pronounced buckles. The jet was pushed north of California in the winter, causing drought conditions in the western USA. As the next wave pushed down far to the south, so bitter weather covered all of eastern North America. The next wave then pushed the jet stream into the heart of north-western Europe, bringing a very mild winter. It was now that the final factor to cause the record storminess came into play. The arctic and the far north of Europe have seen increasingly amplified warming in recent years. This is accelerating because sea ice is shrinking so fast that less heat is reflected back into space from these regions, warming them exponentially. The impact of these changing climatic conditions is now hugely evident. However, as it warms to the north, the difference in temperature that drives the jet stream and our Atlantic weather is reducing. This in turn has slowed down the jet stream and its movements, the effect being that it is getting flatter, and therefore stuck for far longer in a single pattern. This has led to prolonged and more extreme spells of one type of weather, sometimes lasting months instead of days.

The evidence here shows beyond doubt that changes in the climate we are seeing are highly complex and are having unexpected consequences on a global scale. More extreme weather means different things in different places, and for Britain flooding will certainly become an expensive and unwelcome part of our future climate.

PART VII
MILD WINTERS

50

A History of Mild Winters

Contrary to what terms such as the Little Ice Age might conjure up in people's minds, mild winters are the default winter weather pattern in Britain, and even the Little Ice Age was no exception to this rule. Mild winters are, of course, somewhat difficult to identify outside of the instrumental record because they normally have little negative impact. Nevertheless, records of warm dry winters go back a long way. The first reference that I can find for a specifically warm winter was that of 1240.[1] This winter was both warm and dry, and the following spring saw a significant drought, certainly in the south of England. This came about during a spell of very warm, dry years (see chapter 18) and can be likened to the extremely warm, sunny winter and spring seasons of 1989 and 1990.

One of the key issues with identifying particularly mild winters in the historical record is that they are largely benign, insofar as when it is mild and bright in winter there is not a great deal to write about. Nevertheless, from medieval times it was noticed that the recurring diseases that occurred most frequently in summer, such as the plague, the ague (malaria) and the 'sweating sickness', almost died out in cold weather. Cold winters were therefore often welcomed, despite other hardships they might entail.

It is likely that the winter of 1540/41 would have been extremely mild and dry, as these years brought spectacular warmth to the whole of Europe and drought continued through the winter and spring, with a second hot spring and summer following the extreme heat of 1540.[2] This episode is mentioned widely throughout the Continent and saw the Seine dry up in Paris and the Thames in London become dominated by saltwater as the river flow waned. The winter of 1653/54 is also mentioned as a very dry and warm 'winter half', and this came in a period of increased drought in the seventeenth century when Britain's climate was more Continental than it is today. It is important to note that dry (especially then) did not necessarily mean warm, and some of the most bitterly cold weather often brought a dearth of rainfall, much as it can do today.

However, it is from 1659 that our temperature record, albeit basic in the early years, begins, and this coincides with Samuel Pepys' description of the 'dry, dusty' winter of 1660/61.[3] He described how some flowers had begun to bloom in January and that he has never known such a warm and sunny winter. As there are reports of stormy Atlantic weather to the north, one can assume that this was not general across Britain and that pressure must have been high to the south and south-east of the country with warm, dry continental air flowing across the south. The next winter was also very mild indeed, but it was certainly a far wetter affair, with copious rainfall and some severe gales as well. Nevertheless, when compared with other mild winters these two are not terribly high up on the list, at least in instrumental terms.

When comparing colder winters, what is very clear is that the sixteenth to nineteenth centuries all dominate the cold winter month and season rankings. No real surprise there. However, no similar grouping can be applied when looking at the mildest winter months and seasons. These seem far more evenly spread out. In fact, from a data perspective, 40 per cent of all the mildest winters happened in the nineteenth century. Interestingly, 40 per cent is also the value for representatives from the twentieth century. For the eighteenth century the figure drops down to 15 per cent, and the seventeenth century provides to 5 per cent. The current century is in its infancy but has so far produced two: 2007, the culmination of an extremely warm winter period; and the stormy winter of 2013. What is also intriguing is that the last decade of the twentieth century is vastly overrepresented. It is clear that there has been a change of scenario since 2008 in terms of winter weather. It is impossible to say why this is, or for how long it will last, as we should really have seen a continuing trend to milder winters; but that has just not materialised. The 1970s, for example, saw some very mild winters, but the next decade saw some very cold winter months and spells, with the mildness only returning at the end of the decade.

Back to the actual record, at the head of the bunch is 1869 (see below). This is not a surprise; the summer of 1868 was one of the hottest in the nineteenth century, and the heat rolled on into the winter and was exceptional. However, there was a blip. November 1868 was actually extremely cold, with fog and frost regular visitors. However, from the December it turned out to be one of the top-ten warmest, and its February was the second-warmest February in the entire CET series. Another nineteenth-century winter, 1834, was also extremely mild and ranks second at 6.53 °C overall. In fact, it would have taken the number-one spot had February not been a good deal less warm than January, with a startling mean average of 7.1 °C. The next three are all from the more recent past but all just as exceptional. February 1989 was very much a spring month. Daytime temperatures were in double figures, there was no frost and the sun shone day after day. It was far more akin to winter in the Spanish Costas than Britain. This weather was also widespread. Scottish ski resorts received very little snow. The exact same pattern was established in 1990, albeit after a stormy January. February was exceptional. I remember sitting out with colleagues in Russell Square that month with people sunbathing and all the Australians in London wondering why they had been warned about the misery of the British winter. Nevertheless, the exceptions are clear. Between 1989 and 1990 sits 1686, the sixth-warmest winter on record. By all accounts, this was not a month of calm winds and sunshine but was wet and stormy, which brings me to my final point on mild winter weather. There are two clear categories of mild winter. One is the warm, wet and windy variety; the other calm, sunny and mild, with spring-like characteristics. As is often the case when an exceptional period of weather happens now, the headlines will refer to the 'jet stream' being responsible. Indeed, the direction and pattern of the jet stream is critical to the character of the weather as it will control the types of air mass that we experience.

Nevertheless, the important thing in my view is to question what drives the jet stream into specific patterns. It is well known that, in winter, the differences in pressure in the North Atlantic against average are significant when placed into an index; this is the North Atlantic Oscillation (NAO). When this falls strongly negative in winter, we are likely to see blocked patterns of weather in the region; this will most likely mean cold weather. The Arctic also has an index based on the same principles and, in general, when it is low it will indicate colder patterns. The key factor in driving these indexes appears to be ocean currents and the mean sea temperatures (SSTs). These factors are connected to the global engine discussed earlier that drives our weather and is closely linked to the tropical winds that appear to be a major downstream influence and are reflected in the NAO at any given time. This in turn drives the strength of the jet stream as a manifestation of the patterns at play. This is not an exact science by any means; the correlations need interpretation, and other factors obviously have an impact. Broadly speaking, long-term forecasts that assess the factors driving a negative NAO may well be able to identify blocked weather patterns or conclude whether an active Atlantic will bring a mild winter.

Top 20 mildest winter rankings in central England since 1659

Year	Dec., Jan., Feb. average
1869	6.77
1834	6.53
1989	6.50
2007	6.43
1975	6.43
1686	6.33
1990	6.23
1796	6.20
1935	6.13
1998	6.10
1734	6.10
2014	6.07
1995	5.90
1943	5.90
1877	5.90
1822	5.80
1925	5.77
1899	5.77
1846	5.77
1761	5.77

51

A Seasonal Reversal, 1974/75

The 1940s and the 1960s are well known for their propensity towards more blocked weather patterns. During the 1940s this resulted in some hot summers, but during the 1960s this was not the case; no summer from that decade falls into the category of very warm or hot. The 1970s saw a shift in this pattern to a more mobile, westerly one, and after 1971 there were no distinctly cold winters at all until 1978/79. It was in this period that the warmest winter in Britain since 1869 came to pass. At the time, this season turned out to be one of the three mildest winters ever measured in the instrumental record, with only 1834 sitting between it and 1869.

Across most of north-western Europe, 1974 was a wet year. Continuous rain and thunderstorms became a running joke for my dad, who would always refer to Brussels, where we had just moved, as the rainiest city in the world. In Britain the summer was equally dismal, and September was also very wet indeed. In London the highest temperature of the entire year was only 25 °C. The wet September and November caused serious flooding in Belgium, and floods affected much of the south of the UK in the autumn. I remember the first serious floods I ever saw were in November 1974, driving to Ostend to catch the ferry to Dover. The flat fields of Flanders were submerged as far as the eye could see. A consequence of this was a critical shortage of sugar in Belgium. My mum witnessed two smart, blue-rinsed elderly ladies come to blows over a bag of sugar at Rob in Brussels, Belgium's most upmarket supermarket. They apparently drew a significant crowd, and it was only when the store manager waded in that they were pulled apart.

The autumn was a cold one and ranks fiftieth in the all-time coldest seasonal rankings, with a monthly average of 8.9 °C. This poor summer and cold autumn led many, both in the media and among meteorological communities, to speculate that a cold and wet winter might follow.

This was not to be. Temperatures in November were generally in the mild 10–15 °C category, but not only did they fail to drop in

December, it in fact got progressively warmer. December saw no frosts recorded in London at all, and the month was almost a whole degree warmer than November. The maximum temperature exceeded 10 °C on twenty-two days, and the period between Christmas and New Year was exceptionally mild for the time of year, with readings of 13 °C on most days and 15 °C recorded on 28 December. Christmas that year was a wet one in London and Brussels, and the unusual warmth was drawing a lot of comment across northern Europe. The New Year brought no let-up in the very mild weather, and, after a short spell of temperatures under 10 °C during the middle of January, a spell of temperatures between 10–15 °C set in once again, with 15 °C reached on 15 January.

This extraordinarily prolonged winter warmth brought notes of early spring right across the UK; daffodils actually came to flower in central London and across many western and southern districts in February. Unlike many other phenomena, warm winters produce few obvious detrimental effects. Nevertheless, it is not everybody's cup of tea. A warm winter perhaps draws concerns from farmers who are worried about insect infestations; however, certain crops may actually benefit from the warm weather.

As the 1975 winter drew to a close, the media and public in the UK were talking about a hot summer. However, one old adage that still rings true across the ages is 'ne'er cast a clout 'til May is out' and, in 1975 at least, this proved remarkably propitious. In a direct reversal of the winter trend of progressively warmer temperatures though the season, as spring came so the temperatures dropped and from mid-March winter began. Snow fell on ten March days after the 15th, and air frosts were recorded on twelve days in the month at Gatwick. On 27 March, in heavy, driving snow, the temperature only just climbed above freezing in central London. There had already been heavy snow showers in Brussels just before then, and the nights were producing hard frosts. Over the Easter period that followed, daytime temperatures in southern England would creep up in any sunshine. However, when showers fell they were invariably of hail or snow, and temperatures dropped fast when they began.

On 27 March we were delighted to wake up to several inches of snow in Kent. We were able to toboggan, throw snowballs and play outside for hours. My birthday was two days later and snow fell again that evening. It was a great birthday; Easter eggs, birthday presents and snow. It did not happen again for twenty-one years. In fact, that day saw Heathrow closed for several hours as snow was cleared from the runway. Every county in the country reported snow that morning.

This unusually cold Easter weekend in Scotland saw so much snow build up, despite the mild winter, that a series of avalanches injured six people, two seriously, and the London Easter Parade took place in 'showers of snow, sleet and icy rain'.

The next day we went into to London to go around the Tower of London and see the Crown jewels for the first time, and it was raining. However, on returning to the countryside everything was again covered in thick snow that lasted several days. Thereafter the cold eased off and temperatures crept up.

Winter gave itself one last, very tardy appearance in the oddly reversed 1975 winter and spring seasons. On 1 June, pressure rose sharply to the north-west of the UK and a depression moved east over Scandinavia. In its wake, tightly packed isobars drew down a strong northerly airstream over the UK that dived southwards and by 2 June covered all of Britain. The result was snow falling as far south as the high ground of south-east England, south of London, and sleet along the south coast. Scotland had falls of several inches on high ground, settling down even to lower levels by morning. Buxton in Derbyshire and Bradford in Yorkshire both had county cricket fixtures that had to be abandoned because at least 2 inches of wet snow accumulated, and snow fell for much of the day here as showers and thunderstorms swept south.

Both this event and the cold and snowy spring deeply confused several leading climatologists and, coupled with the two big lulls in the Gulf Stream's influence over the last forty years, they saw this as potentially signalling a return to a 'mini ice age'. Discussion, not in the tabloids but in the leading quality papers, showed how climatologists were increasingly concerned that a reduction in the long-term number of westerly days was enabling the ice sheets at the poles to increase in size during winter and reflect back enough sunlight to start a rapid climatic downturn. Indeed, over the previous few years, satellite photos had shown that this was actually happening. This kind of debate seems to have begun in 1963 and rumbled on during the 1970s until the discovery of a hole in the ozone layer in the mid-1980s led scientists to research that indicated the Earth had actually began to warm rapidly. So much more is understood now about past climate thanks to dendrochronology, ice-core research and other techniques that have shown the often inexplicably complex shifts of the Earth's weather since 1975. As it happened, rumours of summer's demise were greatly exaggerated and the high pressure to the north sank rapidly south. In just over four days, the maxima were over 25 °C across much of England and Wales, with 28 °C reached after a week. A superb, memorable summer followed and talk of an ice age was soon to be replaced by that of drought.

PART VIII

MIST, FOG AND SMOG

52

Mist, Fog and Deadly London Smog

It must be very strange in today's world for young people to watch old movies that always show London shrouded in fog. When I was growing up, I took for granted the constant fog that dominated every Sherlock Holmes or Hammer Horror film I saw. I imagined that this was perhaps an attempt at creating a spooky atmosphere in these movies, but I was unaware that fog was far more common only twenty years before, and was a fact of life before 1950.

The Clean Air Act, passed by the government in 1956, was largely implemented because medical evidence and public pressure to reduce the terrible levels of industrial and domestic pollution in built-up areas had become overwhelming. Regular smogs were responsible for the deaths of thousands of people with breathing difficulties caused by these extraordinary dense fogs that could reduce visibility to zero. Most people used coal fires at that time, but the Act made it an offence to burn coal in certain residential districts designated 'smokeless zones'. The aim was to push people into using smokeless forms of heating, such as electricity and gas, to prevent a repetition of the Great Smog of 1952. In the event, London did see one last smog event take place in December 1962. However, this legislation paved the way for a great change in air quality during the 1960s. As the benefits of the Act became clear to all, the air quality and visibility radically improved, and a further expansion of the scope of the Act took place in 1968.

During the Victorian era, and in particular around the turn of the century, urban pollution was so intense in Britain's cities that no such thing as a clear day existed. Visibility beyond a certain point became a thing of the past, and instances of TB, bronchitis and pneumonia became a menace to society where once cholera and plague had been its scourge. The sun was blotted out by smoke on many days in any given month, and the dense particulate matter would frequently combine with moisture in the atmosphere to produce foul-smelling smogs.

Following the Clean Air Act, the air quality in our cities improved dramatically. Measurements taken from 1980–92 compared to those of 1960–74 show the difference. At Manchester, days of 'good visibility' (i.e. over 40 kilometres) rose from 27 per annum to 103; at Birmingham the figures show a rise from 51 to 116 and at Heathrow from 77 to 147. The number of foggy mornings halved at all these locations. Earlier figures would have shown far more fog, and visibility above 40 kilometres would have been very rare before 1939 in most British cities.

Outside of man-made pollution and smog, fog itself is of course a natural phenomenon. In rural areas, the above figures are not really relevant as the statistics have hardly changed at all over the years. Fog takes a number of forms, all of which most people are familiar with. Fog is defined as a visibility of 1 kilometre or 1,000 metres or less at any given point. When fog appears but enables visibility greater than 1,000 metres, it is described as mist.

There are three main types of fog: radiation, advection (that includes sea and thaw fog) and hill fog. As a rule, fog is formed by the presence of small droplets of water being present in the air. The humidity needs to be at, or around, 100 per cent for fog to form, although in areas of high pollution this can be lower. This is basically the same principle as that governing the formation of clouds, except fog sits along a shallow layer along the ground. The smaller the water droplets that are suspended, the thicker the fog. If the temperature is below freezing, the fog can deposit frost in the form of hoar or rime deposits that can sometimes cling to trees and exposed surfaces. However, this freezing fog also causes hazards for traffic that are hard to spot, such as black ice and frost.

During the autumn and winter, radiation fog is common in Britain. In this case there will most likely be an anticyclone in control of the weather, with light or calm winds. The afternoon sky may well be clear, especially in the autumn and spring months, but as the air cools during the night the residual water vapour in the air will begin to condense and with sufficient humidity will form into fog. Radiation fog is particularly dangerous for traffic, as it can be dense but forms in patches. Road accidents in these conditions have caused great loss of life. Smog can in fact be added to this type of fog (see chapter 5), this being fog with industrial particulate matter trapped within it. This happens at ground level because heavier, cold air is trapped under the fog as the sun creates a layer of warmer, lighter air above. In London, these episodes were widely known as 'London particulars'.

Perhaps the worst of these in the last century happened ten years before the final occurrence in 1962. This was the great London smog of December 1952. To say that visibility in these smogs was reduced to nil is no exaggeration. The thick, toxic industrial particulate matter from industry combined with coal fire emissions, making it virtually impossible to see anything. Even at walking pace, using any form of transport would be a risky endeavour and many accidents took place. In 1952, 'fogmen' were employed to precede public transport with lit flares. They also led processions of cars along streets and were responsible for the safe running of trains. Nevertheless, men died on the railways on the second day of the smog, killed as they worked on the line as a train driver proceeded past a signal he could not see.

One alarming phenomenon that was reported in all the papers was an explosion in opportunist thefts and robberies. One jeweller from Edgware was almost killed by baton-wielding thieves, but the most common crime was mugging. Clearly there was neither a chance to see your attacker or see where they fled. The fog began on a Saturday, 6 December. Over the weekend it caused few problems beyond a disrupted sports schedule. However, by Monday, major disruptions occurred as the nation tried to get in to work, with trains in and out of town few and far between, and no realistic chance of movement by bus or road.[1] A taxi driver operating around Euston said that he managed one fare on Monday but only reached his destination because the passenger had walked alongside the cab most of the way. One result of such a polluted atmosphere was the onset of respiratory tract infections and complications, and episodes of bronchitis flared up as a direct result of the fog. This affected largely the very old and the very young, often those with pre-existing conditions; nevertheless, it was reported that at least 4,000 people died as a result of this smog in the four days that the smog lasted, or shortly thereafter. On Tuesday 9 December the fog began to lift, but the effect was to be profound, resulting in the banning of major industrial pollutants and coal fire emissions in urban areas four years later.

Moving on to our next type of fog, we come to the familiar hill fog, known to almost all of us in Britain. This is essentially low cloud and is most common during the passing of a warm front and a section of mild air at the front of a disturbance, often with a subtropical origin. The cloud base often trails down very low during this type of weather, and many people will have seen hill fog even on quite modest hills in these conditions, during which time even low-lying coastal areas can see reduced visibility as the very high moisture content will bring the fog down to quite low levels. These conditions may last for some time, especially in autumn and winter when there is notable warmth of subtropical origin being dragged up from the Atlantic. You may also notice that when a warm front is slow moving nearby, conditions become misty even at ground level; this means the cloud level has dropped almost to the surface because of the damp air mass around you. When a cold front finally passes, the air will become cooler and the moisture will then decrease; the fog will then lift and clearer, often showery weather will follow.

The final type of fog to consider is what is known as advection fog. In essence, this forms when there is a significant difference between the air mass overhead and the temperature of either a colder body of water or moisture-laden landmass below. For Britain, this generally refers to two common weather phenomenon most of us will have seen. Firstly there is thaw fog. When snow has been on the ground, and most likely frozen hard after a few nights frost, the ground temperature will stay below freezing. However, quite often a thaw is brought by milder air that has high moisture content; often this will mean cloud and drizzle or rain. It is possible, but unlikely, that it will remain dry during this time. Nevertheless, higher temperatures in the air than on the ground, coupled with an almost 100 per cent humidity level, mean that the moisture layer at the ground condenses into droplets and will form a mist or fog.

A further manifestation we often see, mainly in spring and summer, is haar, sometimes called sea fog or sea fret. This will be familiar to many east coast inhabitants, as the cold sea meets a warming air mass in spring, causing dull cold conditions at the coast. Temperatures will be pegged back, sometimes 10° or so lower than further inland. However, hot summer weather can also cause this phenomenon almost anywhere. Brighton, for example, sometimes sees sea fogs hanging over the beach when hot, clear summer weather comes to the region, giving a humid and rather uncomfortable feel to the air and lowering the temperature by several degrees. When the south of England was basking in temperatures of 38 °C in August 2003, the temperature at the shoreline in Brighton only reached the mid-twenties as a sea fret rolled across the beach, obscuring the strong August sun.

PART IX
UNUSUAL NATURAL EVENTS

53

The Laki Eruption and Sulphur Cloud, 1783

The second most violent volcanic eruption in modern times caused tragedy and suffering in Europe on a vast scale, and the majority of those affected outside of Iceland remained unaware of its cause. The eruption caused severe hardship in Iceland, with darkness and toxic fumes poisoning cattle and human beings alike, and led to mass starvation as most crops failed. One quarter of the population was wiped out in a country that had only been inhabited for a millennium. The eruption coincided with an extremely hot summer in northern Europe, but the sulphur dioxide in the atmosphere then contributed to a cooling process that caused a long and severe winter, killing even more of Europe's population.

On 8 June 1783, an unusual type of volcanic eruption began in southern Iceland. A series of ground fissures appeared and began to spew out vast amounts of lava and gas in a long line, rather than from a conical volcanic crater on a mountaintop in the more traditional eruptions. As many as 130 craters appeared in the ground, all of them actively spewing out lava, gas and ash.[1]

The consequences of this eruption were severe and relatively swift. The lava spilled out into groundwater and, given on an enormous scale, produced vast clouds of sulphur dioxide that spread across much of Iceland. Local reverends saw this apocalyptic event as a punishment, offering divine retribution for the sins of the Icelanders. However, the reality was that most of those relying on farming and cattle to sustain themselves were in deep trouble, regardless of their moral state. Crops were quickly poisoned by the sulphur dioxide concentrations in the air, and the grass, used to make hay, was spoiled beyond repair. Cattle died out in vast numbers; within a few months, without crops or meat, so did many thousands of Icelanders. Those on the coasts, who made a living from the sea, fared rather better. Iceland was then ruled by Denmark, several weeks away by ship, and no strategy was put in place to feed the starving using the fish and produce from the less affected parts of the country; instead, much of the country's food surplus continued to be exported, leading to catastrophe.

In England, the cloud of noxious sulphur dioxide came suddenly and without warning on a north to north-easterly airflow around a high pressure that was to affect the islands for much of the summer. On 23 June, a smelly haze filtered across the whole country. Over 120 teragrams of sulphur dioxide (SO2)[2] was pumped into the atmosphere, and Britain was close enough to feel its effects more than most other countries. The sun was dimmed from that morning onwards and would appear 'blood red' in the daytime, as if it were sunset or sunrise. It is hypothesised that a greenhouse effect caused an existing high-pressure system to trap the hideous fog the sulphur dioxide caused. This lasted without a break until 20 July, when the air once again cleared. Nevertheless, it then reappeared on occasion throughout the summer. Trees, plants and crops appeared black and burnt and often died without obvious cause, baffling farmers and causing widespread hardship.

The sulphur cloud spread widely across North America and Benjamin Franklin, who observed the phenomenon from Paris while there on diplomatic service, was also aware of dramatic cooling across New England through correspondence and was one of the few scientists who figured out the origin of the problem. Having seen written reports on the plight of Iceland, he made the connection between the eruption and the effects on Europe and the USA. However, Franklin would not have been able to identify the specific cause of the widespread crop damage and suffocation of livestock and humans as sulphur poisoning.

There is no question that the eruption affected weather systems in Europe, but it is also thought to have weakened the summer monsoon across the Indian subcontinent in 1783 by interfering with the normal patterns of air mass and circulation that cause the monsoon rains. This caused widespread famine in India over the next twelve months.

Not only did the poisoned atmosphere bring destruction to plant life, it also began to kill people outright by causing severe breathing difficulties and complications. The sulphur inflamed the lungs and trachea of vulnerable people, causing infections and suffocation. Up to 20,000 people are thought to have died across the UK as a direct result of this pollution. Hardship attributable to Laki was also apparent across Scandinavia, France, the Low Countries and Germany.

After a very hot summer driven by high pressure, the ash began to produce a cooling effect that began in the autumn with below-average temperatures, leading to a weak sun that was often red and dim and failed to produce its normal warmth. In fact, January 1784 was exceptionally cold and had a CET of -0.6 °C. This only exacerbated the impact of the previous summer's crop failures, and the price of grain and other commodities rose while wages fell; many people in Britain died of starvation that winter. It is possible that as many as 6 million people died globally from one or other of the impacts of the Laki eruption. In modern times, most Britons – and, indeed, peoples in the rest of Europe –regarded the threat of Icelandic volcanoes as a distant one, if they regarded it at all. That was until an eruption from the crater of Eyjafjallajökull brought the entire European air industry to a complete standstill in April and May 2010. In this case, the lava and gas burst out into a deep layer of snow and ice on the mountain, causing a particularly fine ash cloud that was dangerous for aircraft jet engines. The huge cloud of ash then drifted southwards across Europe on a northerly airstream, grounding flights in most European capitals for more than a week. It has since been postulated that increased activity in this area preceded previously larger eruptions at other nearby volcanoes, and a new 'fissure eruption', most likely from the fissure volcano at Katla in Iceland, could not be ruled out. As it happens, a fissure eruption has since occurred at Bardarbunga in Iceland, but the lava flows have not caused sulphur clouds on anything like the scale of Laki, which produced more lava than any other recorded volcanic event. Nor was there ice present, nor much ash, so Europe was spared the chaos of a recurrence of the 2010 ash cloud's disruption to air travel.

54

The Lewes Avalanche, December 1836

An event unlike any other recorded in lowland Britain before or since took place just after Christmas in 1836. On 27 December, a deadly avalanche hit the town of Lewes in Sussex, killing several inhabitants and trapping many alive in the rubble. This seems to be the only recorded occasion of an avalanche causing death and serious damage in lowland Britain, although there have been many fatal avalanches in highland regions in the past.

The winter of 1836/37 was an odd one. In Victorian times, this winter was often referred to as Murphy's Winter after an Irishman by that name who had successfully predicted in an almanac that it was going to be cold.

The cold began in earnest in October; snowfalls on the 28th and 29th were widespread across Britain and as deep as many winter falls in places. In Edinburgh 4 to 5 inches were reported on the 28th, and 2 inches fell even in central London. At Cobham in Surrey the snow, up to 4 inches deep, lay on the ground for five days. However, while December and January were quite cold, February was mild; the cold spring that followed was the most severe part of the winter. In fact, this is the coldest spring in the entire CET. March was extremely cold and snowy, with a mean average of 2.3 °C, ranking ninth-coldest in the CET. However, April was even more dreadful in terms of a spring month – at 4.7 °C it ranks as the fourth-coldest ever, containing long spells of snow and cold, especially in Scotland. March, April and May were so below the long-term average that they led to the record low mean average of 5.63 °C for spring. Compare this with the 2011 spring seasonal mean of 10.23 °C, which is the highest ever.

December 1836 began and continued mild and wet in England. As late as the 22nd, 10 °C was recorded in Manchester on a south-westerly wind. The next day, however, high pressure began to exert its influence and maxima of only 4 °C on the 23rd ushered in a cold spell. In fact, the temperature did not rise above freezing for several days from Christmas Eve and a thaw only began on 6 January, when temperatures lifted to 6 °C or above and rain fell widely in lowland counties.

On the afternoon of Saturday 24 December, a channel low pushed snow across most of southern England, badly affecting counties as far north as Leicestershire and Northamptonshire. However, the strongest winds and heaviest snow fell in the south, and the east and south of England bore the brunt of an easterly gale. According to one report, a resident of Lewes named Mr Thomson, who had been in London, left the capital for Lewes by carriage on the 24th at eleven in the morning. Snow began to fall as he left and had soon become intense; combined with strong winds, it was soon impeding his travel. The horses struggled in the deep, blowing snow and he did not reach home for twelve hours. Lewes was covered in deep, drifting snow.

The *London Globe* reported on 28 December that the snow had remained deep in the capital throughout Christmas Day and that further falls had occurred since. In an age when the mail coaches – transporting letters, funds, local newspapers and people – were critical to all business and communications, the cessation of all mail activity during this week of blizzards had an immediate impact. After the Christmas celebrations were over, life should have been returning to normal. The *Globe* reported that the snow had spread across most of the country and that 'business has consequently been almost at a standstill in the city and the effects of non-intercourse begins to be severely felt among commercial men. We believe that never before within the living memory of the oldest persons has there been so great a stoppage of the mails in the neighbourhood of London, as at this moment.' Only two mail coaches due that day, those from Portsmouth and Poole, had made it in to London. Every other mail coach due that day (or earlier) failed to arrive, including those from Brighton, Dover, Chester, Edinburgh, Hastings, Liverpool and Manchester. A mail coach that set out for Brighton on Monday only reached Crawley before having to turn back and return to London.

In Lewes, a high, steep cliff that hangs over the outskirts of the town, Cliffe Hill, was deeply covered with huge drifts. The strong winds are reported to have driven the snow into a sharp cornice that developed along the edge and grew in the protracted period of snow that lasted into Christmas Day before abating. The cornice held in the cold days and nights that followed, towering over a row of 'poor houses' 100 metres below, hanging precariously and threatening the tiny and poorly built cottages below. Few local people would have known about, or predicted, the behaviour and dangers posed by snow in such circumstances.

Over the next two days, members of the local authority, along with the general public, saw the overhanging tonnes of snow but did not consider there to be a danger. Most snow in lowland Britain melts away into slush in the rain or slowly in the sun over time. However, a build-up of snow like this presented certain danger because the structure would have to give way as soon as any warmth arose.

Boxing Day saw the weather improve after a cold night. In a clear precursor of what was to come, part of the overhanging cornice came crashing down that evening, badly damaging a timber yard below, and a further fall of snow spilled into the nearby River Ouse, hampering its flow.

Tuesday 27 December dawned bright and sunny, and the temperature, which reached 1 °C in London that day, began to rise slowly in the sun. Almost immediately, large cracks and fissures in the snow cornice appeared. A man walking along the edge above the town clearly saw the danger, as did a young man who, when realising the imminent likelihood of collapse, shouted in the alley alongside the cottages, known as Boulder Row, imploring the residents to leave. The tightly crammed cottages were full of mothers and children and, with the weather so bitter, the families said that there was nowhere for them to go. The man in question then fled. The cornice collapsed almost immediately, and tonnes of snow crashed down into Boulder Row. Eyewitnesses described how the avalanche first powered into the foundations, collapsing the walls before it spilled over the tops, burying them completely and leaving a great 'mass of white'. According to the *Brighton Guardian* of the following day, one of the women – Mrs Robinson – had heeded an earlier warning and escaped her cottage with her baby. However, as reported in the local paper that week, 'rendered desperate by the strong affection of a mother, she rushed back into the house to save her remaining children, when, shocking to relate, the avalanche poured down upon the whole family and buried them alive'. Mrs Robinson was dug out, dead, still clutching her baby; sadly, the other children also died. The violent compression of the fast-moving snow had actually pushed several houses bodily and tossed them right across the road, with rubble and snow sitting against a high flint wall overlooking the river bank.

The aforementioned Mr Thomson organised the rescue bid and very soon had equipped a team of rescuers who were desperately digging against the clock to find survivors. A Mrs Taylor was brought out 'barely alive', and her five children were saved. They dug through the afternoon as shocked and horrified locals looked on. The gravity of the situation was clearly apparent, and the rescue effort progressed without a break until fourteen of the fifteen trapped residents had been extricated from the wet and icy mass that had so recently been their homes. By 4 p.m. there was only one victim – a young boy – still buried, and the rescuers could hear him making shallow groans. Shortly before they reached him, the call was raised that another fall of snow was imminently going to come down, and sure enough it soon crashed down on to the site; as soon as it settled the final victim was brought out, alive but injured.

Sadly, a total of eight of the victims buried in the aftermath were killed. All of them are buried at the nearby South Malling church, where a memorial to them and to this unusual tragedy was raised by the local parish. Almost certainly, a better knowledge of the dangers an avalanche poses would have saved lives here – but snow for most British people is generally a benign material, beyond causing inconvenience to travellers. On the site of this event, a pub stands near to where the houses were; its name is the Snowdrop Inn. While many people think this refers to the tiny flower, others are well aware this was a snow drop of a very different kind.

55

The Folkestone Earthquake, April 2007

It was a beautiful sunny Saturday morning in April. I was lying in bed at our flat in Folkestone watching the sun flicker through the blinds as I slowly woke up and contemplated making a cup of tea. I got up to go to the bathroom next door and put on the light. I was about to turn on the shower when a sudden and violent jolt seemed to move the whole building; immediately the electricity cut off. A second, far more violent, jolt accompanied by much shaking had me on the ground in the dark and lasted for several seconds before stopping altogether. The sounds of clattering and banging around the flat accompanied the whole event, which was over in under half a minute. Outside, a number of car alarms were going off; otherwise it was quiet. It was 8.18 a.m. on 28 April 2007.

Earthquakes are not a familiar or expected part of British life. My very first thought was that a lorry had run into the building. Opening the bathroom door, the first thing I noticed was that a large crack had appeared on the wall of the living room, from the front right through to the back of the room. This crack actually went all the way through the flat to the back bedroom. The street was full of people, many in their nightclothes, milling around looking startled. Across the road some slates were lying smashed across the pavement and the road surface. I knew then that there must have been an earthquake.

My experience of earthquakes before then was limited to one in San Francisco in the late 1990s, and a 5.3 that struck Brussels in April 1993. The Californian affair also happened while I was in bed. The flat shook and grumbled for what seemed like a minute, but there was no damage that I could see. The TV and media, though, reacted as if it were the big one. The Brussels earthquake stemmed from a known fault that runs through the Netherlands at Roermond to Liege in Belgium. This shook a very wide area, taking in Cologne, much of Belgium and the western and southern Netherlands, and was even felt in Lille. That one happened in the middle of the night and woke the entire city. Most of the damage was closer to the epicentre in the Netherlands and down into Germany, where the bells of Cologne Cathedral pealed out unexpectedly across the city as the earth shook.

What made the Folkestone earthquake so different was that it caused a relatively significant amount of damage for its size. Local Kent radio initially reported that a bomb or explosion, possibly emanating from the Channel Tunnel, was the cause. However, official confirmation from the British Geological Survey (BGS) emerged after only a few minutes that a 4–5 Richter-level earthquake had hit the area.

The epicentre of the quake was just 1 kilometre north of the centre of Folkestone, just out to sea, and had been remarkably shallow; only 5.3 kilometres under the surface. It was concluded later that this shallow level, along with the rare occurrence of tremors in the area making the ground very brittle and compact, intensified the impact on the town and caused the widespread damage. The BGS also gave the quake a 6 on the European Macroseismic Scale (EMS), which is quite high and is described as 'slightly damaging'. The scale runs to 12, with an unpleasant 'all structures destroyed and ground changes' description attributed to the top of the scale. Again, although not a powerful quake on the Richter scale, it was felt very widely across much of Kent, East Sussex, Essex, Suffolk, across the channel in Calais and even in Brussels.

In the streets of Folkestone, some roads saw almost every house suffer some damage. Tiles and whole chimneys had been shaken down; some fell directly into the houses themselves, causing internal damage and covering rooms in soot. Others collapsed into the streets below. In some places cars were entirely crushed, and several roads in the area were shut off as loose bricks, masonry and chimneys threatened to fall. Many people had been asleep or just getting up when it happened and were truly shocked by the force of the tremor, which came out of the blue.

However, this area has actually suffered earthquakes before. In 1950, a 4.4 quake centred off the coast near Calais affected a similar area but caused little damage in Kent. However, two very significant earthquakes, both measuring 5.8 on the Richter scale, originated in this part of the channel, one in 1580 and the other in 1382 – both causing widespread damage and fatalities.

The earlier quake is somewhat less attested to than the Tudor tremor. Nevertheless, we do have a reasonable picture of what happened. It struck on 21 May 1382 (notice how earthquake activity tends to happen in spring), during the reign of Richard II. The quake interrupted the famous trial of the Lollard heretic John Wycliffe at Blackfriars in London. This 'synod' was seen as critical in stopping the Lollard movement. This group believed the Catholic Church was fundamentally corrupt and sought reform. John Wycliffe was their leader and was on trial for his beliefs. For this reason, at the time, it became known as the 'earthquake of the synod'. Canterbury Cathedral was badly damaged and the entire campanile, or bell tower, collapsed, while much of the cloister wall was wrecked. To the west, at Hollingbourne, the church there sustained 'grave ruin' and reports from Flanders talk of great numbers of chimneys being destroyed.

The earthquake of 1580 was more extensively reported. It began at 6 p.m. on 6 April. In London, where there was widespread damage, two child apprentices were killed as masonry and bricks dislodged from the roof and crashed down onto them at Christ's Church Hospital. Numerous chimney stacks were brought down, as was the pinnacle on top of Westminster Cathedral. In Dover, part of one of the white cliffs collapsed, as did sections of the castle walls. Numerous churches were damaged, with chimneys, tiling and masonry collapsing across the town. Saltwood Castle was rendered uninhabitable until restoration work 300 years later. The church at St Peter's in Broadstairs still attests to the quake, with a large crack caused by the tremor visible there.

Across the Channel at Calais, the tremors were felt for up to fifteen minutes. Part of the town wall collapsed, as did the watchtower. A tsunami, several feet high, engulfed the town shortly afterwards, killing several people and drowning large numbers of livestock. As the waves rose in the Channel, numerous vessels were damaged or overcome by the swell and as many as twenty-five lost. The waves also hit Dover and the south coast of England, causing much damage and a number of deaths, whilst Boulogne and Mont St Michel, some distance apart, were hit by the tsunami as well. The damage spread far beyond the coastal areas. Churches and buildings were damaged and scores of people killed in Saint-Amand-les-Eaux in Picardy. Both Mons and Lille both suffered substantial damage, and in Belgium damage was sustained in Gent, Oudenaarde and Antwerp. People working the fields in Flanders reported a loud rumbling noise and saw the fields rolling and oscillating around them. In England, the quake was felt as far inland as Cambridge and Ely, where stones and bricks dropped off the cathedral and churches sustained slight damage. In Essex, part of Stratford Castle collapsed, such was the duration of the shaking. Another Dover Strait quake was felt in 1776 and has prompted the theory that a subduction fault lies across the channel, which has been labelled the Kent–Artois shear zone.

Of course, the Channel itself is not the only originator of tremors in the UK. A significant earthquake caused widespread damage in East Anglia in April 1884, and badly affected Colchester and many parts of Norfolk and Suffolk. The earthquake was also felt in London, where some damage was reported. In 1931, an earthquake centred in the North Sea at Dogger Bank registered 6.1 on the Richter scale, the most powerful ever measured in the UK. This happened at 1 a.m. on 7 June and was felt across all of the UK, and in parts of Belgium, the Netherlands and France. Luckily its position, far out to sea, meant that what damage did occur was fairly limited and no one was injured.

For Folkestone, the impact was quite different. In the town alone, a total of 474 homes were damaged. Of these, 307 suffered minor damage, 94 were seriously damaged and 73 were rendered uninhabitable. A total of 200 emergency calls were received by the services, and teams of forty firemen assisted at the aftermath alongside numerous police officers. Amazingly, no one was killed and only one person was injured by falling debris and hospitalised. It seems likely that casualties were avoided because most people were at home, many in bed, not out and about. Had this been a weekday, the town would have been much busier and the outcome perhaps not so favourable.

As the insurers began to make their assessments, fire crews shored up homes and the homeless were found shelter. The final bill was estimated at £20 million, and an appeal was launched locally and across social media to raise money for those affected.

Most people in the UK are unlikely ever to be affected by an earthquake and, rather like tornadoes, their rarity means they are quite rightly not perceived as a realistic threat. However, they can and do occur, and while it is impossible to predict where or when they may strike, as this tremor proved, they can be surprisingly destructive.

56

The Great Fire of London, September 1666

A sweltering summer drought left London tinder dry by September 1666. Persistent easterly winds, which had dominated the season, strengthened markedly on the weekend of 2 September, fanning a domestic fire that had started in the streets of Cheapside. By the end of that day, strong to gale-force winds had driven the conflagration into a gigantic firestorm that destroyed the homes of 87 per cent of those living within the old city walls and making tens of thousands homeless, as well as reducing some of the city's great religious and secular landmarks to smouldering rubble.

June and the first half of July 1666 were dry, warm and sunny in London. However, there was a break in the weather during July, with some rain and thunderstorms. In August, however, the high pressure reasserted itself and conditions became dry and hot again, with the hot spell lasting throughout the month. The drought was exacerbated by an unusually dry and cold autumn in 1665, and an equally dry winter.

The shortage of water, however, became particularly pronounced during the end of the summer. By September there had been very little rain since the end of July, and the heat had made the wood and thatch houses, tightly packed in narrow streets, a severe fire hazard.

To provide some further context, it is fair to say that London in the 1660s was a large, unplanned sprawl of often flimsy wooden tenements and houses; there were few residential houses made of brick. The renowned diarist Samuel Pepys has provided a compelling eyewitness account of the fire; Pepys lived to the east of Pudding Lane, where the fire started, so his household just managed to escape the worst of the flames even though they came quite close to where he lived. Pepys' account of the fire is a fascinating description of an early urban disaster unravelling in front of an eyewitness whose thoughts, and those of others at the time, give us invaluable contemporary insight. The world was turned upside down for Pepys and his household, much as it was for tens of thousands of other Londoners, as the landscape they had always known was swallowed up by the flames and changed beyond recognition.

It began early on Sunday morning at an unattended oven at Thomas Faryner's bakery in Pudding Lane. Today this spot is marked by the great monument to the fire built at the end of the seventeenth century. A serious fire soon engulfed the house, and the Faryners were forced to escape from the burning building through the upstairs into a neighbour's window. One of their maids feared the drop and would not climb across – this poor girl became the fire's first victim.

The fire brigade arrived and, seeing the seriousness of the flames, decided the neighbouring buildings needed to be destroyed to inhibit the spread of the fire in each direction. This was standard practice at the time and often the only way of preventing the spread of a house fire because of the use of wood in construction and the proximity of other houses. However, the Lord Mayor of London, the oddly named Lord Bloodworth, was responsible for making the decision and apparently refused, famously claiming that 'a girl could piss it out'. Shortly after, those very houses were themselves aflame – and Bloodworth was nowhere to be found.

It was from around this time on Sunday morning that the easterly wind picked up from a nagging breeze to a freshening wind that strengthened further through the morning. As it increased, so the flames grew quickly out of control and panic began to spread. The lighters, who operated small boats (or 'lights') up and down the river, were soon charging the modern-day equivalent of hundreds and then thousands of pounds to move people's belongings.

The streets became rammed with many thousands of local people, traders and gentry alike, all fleeing the flames. Churches and stone-built buildings not directly in the path of the flames – and viewed as less likely to succumb to them – soon filled with people's belongings, particularly St Paul's Cathedral. Samuel Pepys went down and stood on the embankment at the Tower. Pepys, who had lived and worked in London most of his life, looked on in disbelief as his beloved city was consumed by the flames. That night, sitting in an alehouse across the river on the south bank, Pepys and his friends watched what he describes as 'one solid arc of flame' reaching across the northern bank of the Thames and beyond, and the fire showed no signs of moderation. Earlier Pepys had found Bloodworth, who had vainly turned down the king's offer of soldiers to help bring down houses and contain the conflagration, 'crying out like a fainting woman'.

The next day, he fled. The gusty east wind veered south-easterly, and the flames now pushed both north and west rather than just west. King Charles, maddened by the mayoral and civic authorities' failure to act, took the situation into his own hands, looking to his brother James, Duke of York, a clearly experienced military man, to fight the fire head-on. He began by dividing the affected areas up into command post sectors while his forces shut the wall gates and pressganged the remaining able-bodied population into fighting the flames.

Tuesday dawned, and the people of London were still fighting a losing battle. London Bridge and its famous houses were gone, St Paul's was aflame and the wild conflagration had spread as far west as the Temple Bar. As if things could get no worse, the flames now began to spread back eastwards, threatening Pepys' house as well as the few areas in the centre of town that had so far escaped. Rumours of foreign terrorists and papist plots abounded, and eyewitnesses provide harrowing evidence of how mobs lynched and murdered perfectly innocent people in one of London's darkest hours.

On Tuesday evening, after three full days of wanton destruction, the wind dropped. From that point on, the Duke of York's men began to gain control of the fire. By Wednesday the worst was over, and the fire was out by Thursday.

However, in its wake lay a smouldering, devastated ruin that was once one of the world's most vibrant cities. In all, 13,200 houses were burnt down and the fire ravaged a total area of 373 acres. Furthermore, eighty-four churches and forty-four company offices fell victim to the flames. It was said that ten people died during the fire but almost all sources, current and contemporary, have challenged this figure. The fire burnt with such fierce heat that many victims may have left no trace of a body behind.

When the parliamentary commission set up to establish the cause of the disaster finally published its report, in 1667, it confirmed that the fire was an act of nature, caused namely by 'the hand of God with no conspirators lighting the flames; only the great wynd and the season so very dry'. This rendered the mob lynchings and executions of foreigners as pointless murders driven by deep-seated mistrust of outsiders and the religious prejudice that became so dominant during the Reformation. Such prejudices were highlighted by a court's hasty decision, even after the real causes of the fire were broadly established, that a Frenchman, described as 'simple', was convicted and hanged based on a confession. When his travel documents were produced they clearly showed he had only arrived in London several days after the fire began.

Every great disaster, however, offers great lessons to those willing to learn them. As London had grown unplanned and haphazard since the Roman city crumbled away, an opportunity to bring back order, control and civic planning arose. Many jumped at the king's call to submit new designs, and great ideas flooded in.

To some degree, the real opportunity was missed; many of the schemes proved too complex and costly to implement. While the commission to rebuild St Paul's Cathedral was given to Sir Christopher Wren in 1669, it took until 1711 to be completed. King Charles encouraged the homeless of London with 'a skill' to migrate away to towns and villages across the country and made it clear that the state expected that they were to be taken under the wing of these new communities. Nevertheless, after the legal wrangling and site clearance was over, the rebuilding gathered pace and new streets, better dockyards and far superior housing all combined to leave a more manageable city, but not the Renaissance marvel it could have been.

The fire also killed vast numbers of vermin contaminated by

plague. The year before the fire, 1665, saw a horrific resurgence of bubonic plague through the summer, and Pepys reports regularly in his diary of the houses 'shut up', where victims lay dying of this awful and untreatable illness. It is estimated that as many as 80,000 people died in the city during this outbreak. In the year following the fire, the bubonic plague did not reappear in London for the first time in many years. From then on, the illness no longer played a role in the city of any great significance; cholera was soon to become the next great killer.

Regarding the weather, if there had been light winds and a wet season would the fire not have happened? While one cannot say for certain, there can be little doubt that the outcome would not have been the same had the weather been different. On the Monday following the fire, 9 September on the contemporary calendar, cloud, rain and strong winds moved in from the North Sea and weeks of wet, cold weather soon meant that the great drought was over.

Notes

Introduction
1. Lamb, H. H., *Climate History in the Modern World* (2nd ed.; Routledge, 1995).
2. *Ibid.*
3. Oppenheimer, C., *Eruptions that Shook the World* (Cambridge University Press, 2011).
4. Lamb.
5. IPCC Fifth Assessment Report (2013).

Part I
1. Currie, I., Davison, M. and B. Ogley, *The Kent Weather Book* (Froglets, 2007).
2. Reported in a number of contemporary newspapers.
3. *Ibid.*
4. *Manchester Guardian*, January 1891.
5. *Ibid.*
6. This reading was equalled at the same location in January 1982.
7. BBC analysis in *Winterwatch: The Big Freeze* (1963).
8. *Ibid.*
9. *Ibid.*
10. Barrow, E. and M. Hulme, *Climates of the British Isles: Past, Present and Future* (Routledge, 1997).
11. Lamb, H. H., *Climate History in the Modern World* (2nd ed.; Routledge, 1995).
12. *Ibid.*
13. Fagan, B. M., *The Little Ice Age* (Basic Books, 2001).
14. Barrow and Hulme.

15. Lamb.
16. Fagan.

Part II
1. Lamb, H. H., *Climate History in the Modern World* (2nd ed.; Routledge, 1995).
2. Miles, D., *The Tribes of Britain* (Phoenix, 2005).
3. Lamb.
4. Salway, P., *A History of Roman Britain* (Oxford University Press, 1993).
5. *Ibid.*
6. *Ibid.*
7. *Ibid.*
8. Kingston, J., *Climate and Weather* (Harper Collins, 2003).
9. Salway.
10. Kingston.
11. Lamb.
12. Kingston.
13. Lamb.
14. Lamb; Kingston.
15. Oppenheimer, C., *Eruptions that Shook the World* (Cambridge University Press, 2011).
16. Barrow, E. and M. Hulme, *Climates of the British Isles: Past, Present and Future* (Routledge, 1997).
17. The European Economic Community (EEC) is now the European Union after the Maastricht Treaty of 1992.
18. Kingston.
19. Met Office data.
20. Met Office official record.
21. Météo France.

Part III
1. Holford, I., *British Weather Disasters* (David and Charles, 1976)
2. Currie, I., Davison, M. and B. Ogley, *The Kent Weather Book* (Froglets, 2007).
3. KNMI, 'Watersnoodramp 1953' (Online: http://www.knmi.nl/cms/content/19003/watersnoodramp_1953).
4. Holford.
5. *Ibid.*

6. Stirling, R., *The Weather of Britain* (Giles de la Mare, 1997).
7. Météo France.
8. Contemporary media reports.
9. BBC report, 2007.
10. Kingston, J., *Climate and Weather* (Harper Collins, 2003).
11. Stirling.

Part IV
1. Meteorological Society report.
2. *Manchester Guardian*, October 1913.
3. *Ibid.*
4. Holford, I., *British Weather Disasters* (David and Charles, 1976).

Part V
1. http://www.metoffice.gov.uk.
2. Currie, I., Davison, M. and B. Ogley, *The Surrey Weather Book* (Froglets, 1993).
3. *The Times*, June 1911.
4. *The Times*, June 1914.
5. Holford, I., *British Weather Disasters* (David and Charles, 1976).
6. Holford.
7. *Manchester Guardian*, May 1920.
8. Holford.
9. *The Daily Express*.
10. *The Times*, July 1923.
11. *Manchester Guardian*, July 1923.
12. Holford.
13. Numerous contemporary reports.
14. Holford.
15. Contemporary eyewitness reports.
16. Stirling, R., *The Weather of Britain* (Giles de la Mare, 1997).
17. *Ibid.*
18. Currie, Davison and Ogley.
19. Contemporary news reports.
20. The Haycock Report (2011).
21. *Ibid.*
22. Stirling.
23. Haycock.

Part VI
1. Stirling, R., *The Weather of Britain* (Giles de la Mare, 1997).
2. Currie, I., Davison, M. and B. Ogley, *The Kent Weather Book* (Froglets, 2007).

Part VII
1. Kingston, J., *Climate and Weather* (Harper Collins, 2003).
2. Lamb, H. H., *Climate History in the Modern World* (2nd ed.; Routledge, 1995).
3. Pepys, S., *The Shorter Pepys* (Penguin Classics, 1993).

Part VIII
1. Stirling, R., *The Weather of Britain* (Giles de la Mare, 1997).

Part IX
1. Scarth, A., *Vulcan's Fury* (Yale University Press, 1999).
2. Oppenheimer, C., *Eruptions that Shook the World* (Cambridge University Press, 2011).

Bibliography

'The Hadley Centre Central England Temperature (HadCET) dataset' (Online: http://www.metoffice.gov.uk/hadobs/hadcet/, accessed 28/10/2014)

Barrow, E. and M. Hulme, *Climates of the British Isles: Past, Present and Future* (Routledge, 1997)

Cole, W. A. and P. Deane, *British Economic Growth, 1688–1959* (EH.net, 2001)

Currie, I., Davison, M. and B. Ogley, *The Norfolk and Suffolk Weather Book* (Froglets, 1993)

Currie, I., Davison, M. and B. Ogley, *The Surrey Weather Book* (Froglets, 1993)

Currie, I., Davison, M. and B. Ogley, *The Sussex Weather Book* (Froglets, 1995)

Currie, I., Davison, M. and B. Ogley, *The Kent Weather Book* (Froglets, 2007)

Defoe, D., *The Storm* (Penguin Classics, 2003)

Eden, P., *A Change in the Weather* (Continuum, 2005)

Fagan, B. M., *The Little Ice Age* (Basic Books, 2001)

Fisher, R. V., Heiken, G. and J. B. Hulen, *Volcanoes: Crucibles of Change* (Princeton, 1985)

Holford, I., *British Weather Disasters* (David and Charles, 1976)

Hudson, P., *That's the Forecast: The Best and Worst of Yorkshire Weather* (Great Northern, 2005)

Hurley, J., *Snow and Storm on Exmoor* (Exmoor Press, 1978)

Kingston, J., *Climate and Weather* (Harper Collins, 2003)

Lamb, H. H., *Climate History in the Modern World* (2nd ed.; Routledge, 1995)

Mays, J. and D. Wheeler, *Regional Climates of the British Isles* (Routledge, 1997)

Miles, D., *The Tribes of Britain* (Phoenix, 2005)

Oppenheimer, C., *Eruptions that Shook the World* (Cambridge University Press, 2011)

Pepys, S., *The Shorter Pepys* (Penguin Classics, 1993)

Rothery, D., *Earthquakes and Tsunamis* (Bookpoint, 2010)

Salway, P., *A History of Roman Britain* (Oxford University Press, 1993)

Scarth, A., *Vulcan's Fury* (Yale University Press, 1999)

Stirling, R., *The Weather of Britain* (Giles de la Mare, 1997)

Acknowledgements

My sincere thanks to the following: Ian Mansfield, Amberley's Christian Duck and Alex Bennett, Eric G. Heath, Martin Ystenes, Sam Moore www.sussexscenes.co.uk, David R. Ward, Mike Harris, Steve Garrington, Alan Edwards, Norwich Millennium Library, Maurice V. Atkinson, Andrew Popkin at alamy, Colin Pickett, Topfoto, the *Grimsby Times*, the Press Association, Barry Ferguson, Stuart Pearce, Andy Veitch, Royan Fettes, John Bentley, Richard Saunders, David Kitching, The Marlipins Museum, Wootton Bridge Historical, Rob Wilcox at bude-past-and-present.org.uk, Ray Boyd, Lori Newman, Linda and Barry Mansfield and the entire Nobbs family.